THE MALAYAN EMERGENCY 1948-60
The Domino That Stood

Also from Brassey's:

WILLIAMS
Redcoats Along the Hudson: The Struggle for North America 1754-63

BEESTON
Looking for Trouble: The Life and Times of a Foreign Correspondent

SHEFFIELD EL AL
Leadership & Command: The Anglo-American Military Experience Since 1861

THE MALAYAN EMERGENCY 1948-60

The Domino that Stood

Donald Mackay

BRASSEY'S

London * Washington

Copyright © 1997 Brassey's (UK) Ltd.
All Rights Reserved. No part of this publication may be reproduced, stored in a retrieval system or transmitted in any form or by any means; electronic, electrostatic, magnetic tape, mechanical, photocopying, recording or otherwise, without permission in writing from the publishers.

First English Edition 1997

UK editorial offices: Brassey's, 33 John Street, London WC1N 2AT
UK orders: Marston Book Services, PO Box 269, Abingdon, OX14 4SD

North American orders: Brassey's Inc., PO Box 960, Herndon, VA 22070, USA

Donald Mackay had asserted his moral right to be identified as the author of this work.

Library of Congress Cataloging in Publication Data
available

British Library Cataloguing in Publication Data
A catalogue record for this book is available from the British Library

ISBN 1 85753 118 3 Hardcover

Typeset by Harold, Martin and Redman Ltd
Printed in Great Britain by Redwood Books, Trowbridge, Wiltshire

For Ginny

CONTENTS

List of Illustrations   *viii*
Foreword by John Erickson   *ix*
Acknowledgements   *xiii*
Glossary   *xiv*

1	*Violence, Disruption and Bloody Mayhem*	*1*
2	*The Battlefield Mapped Out*	*3*
3	*The First Steps to Chaos - The Collapse of a Myth*	*11*
4	*A History of Subversion*	*18*
5	*'One may smile and smile and be a villain'*	*23*
6	*The Impulse to Armed Struggle*	*26*
7	*Strengths, Weaknesses, Opportunities and Threats*	*35*
8	*'All over bar the shouting'*	*42*
9	*Thinking Again*	*48*
10	*A White Knight Rides In*	*54*
11	*The Descent into Terrorism*	*63*
12	*Learning How to Win*	*71*
13	*Trying Hard to Lose*	*79*
14	*Briggs - The New White Knight*	*86*
15	*The Worst Is Yet to Come*	*93*
16	*Dissent, Deceit and Defection*	*101*
17	*The Unkindest Cut of All - Gurney's Death*	*111*
18	*Two Manifestos of Failure*	*115*
19	*A Very Necessary Purgative*	*122*
20	*Breaking the Circle - The Subalterns' War*	*133*
21	*The Birth Pangs of a New Nation*	*141*
22	*Learning the Lessons*	*149*

Bibliography   *155*
Notes   *157*
Index   *171*

LIST OF ILLUSTRATIONS

MAPS

Federation of Malaya, 1948   xvii
Federation of Malaya, 1948: Principal Areas of Production.   xviii

PLATES

1   War and Peace. An armoured car of 15th/19th Hussars takes post beside a Chinese temple. (Soldier Magazine)
2   Searching an abandoned squatter *kongsi* on the edge of some rather scruffy rubber. (IWM)
3   Planter at work, complete with police escort and assorted guns and dogs. (The author, Sungei Kahang, Johore, 1953)
4   Derailed trains were easy to arrange. (IWM)
5   Burnt buses were a most gratifying contribution to meeting quotas. (IWM)
6   Templer gets results - the road into Tanjong Malim, resplendent with guard post and barbed wire. (IWM)
7   Ambush country. With *belukar* as close to the track as this, ambushes could be set within a few feet of the target. (IWM)
8   A resettlement village under construction - no barbed wire yet! (IWM)
9   A soldier of 1st Bn Suffolk Regiment inspecting a Chinese tapper's ID Card - just the sort of police work the troops hated doing.
10 Identity Card. By some sleight of hand Chinese village photographers made all their sitters look Chinese, whatever their ethnic origins.
11 Air drops often prejudiced operations, however expertly they were carried out. (Wilmot)
12 Bandit camp, 1955/56. Earlier camps could be much bigger and more sophisticated. (Wilmot)
13 Bandit camps were always burnt after being cleared. (Wilmot)
14 Straight rows of crops in jungle *ladangs* were easily identifiable from the air. (Wilmot)
15 Higgedly-piggedly planting was much harder to see clearly. (Wilmot)

CREDITS

Nos. 2,4,5,6,7,8,9 with the permission of the Trustees of the Imperial War Museum, London.
Nos. 11,12,13,14,15 by courtesy of Major Gordon Wilmot.

FOREWORD

With the passage of almost half a century since its beginnings in 1948, the Malayan campaign has tended to slip into history, half remembered if remembered at all. It is probably fair to say that mention of Communist insurgency in the years of the Cold War immediately recalls Vietnam, that protracted struggle which in spite of the commitment of huge American resources ended in a defeat whose sting hurts to this day in many quarters. The preoccupation with insurrection and guerrilla warfare produced a huge literature which ranged over the entire globe, from Greece to the Philippines, from Algeria to Cuba and a complex set of writings on the theory and practice of counterinsurgency warfare.

In general terms the regular military forces of Western industrialised states came off badly when committed against 'Communist guerillas', though there was more than a trace of irony in the fact that many of these guerrilla forces and organisations in South-East Asia owed their early training in tactics, subversion and sabotage to those same Western armies, enlisting them in the struggle against the Japanese. The Malayan Communist Party, founded in 1931, was no exception. Though an illegal organisation, its members liable to arrest, once the Japanese invaded Malaya in 1941, the British authorities conveniently ignored 'illegality' and accepted Loi Tak's offer of assistance. Prior to the surrender of Singapore in February 1942 some 200 men had received some training in weapons and demolition as well as jungle survival. This was the nucleus of what became the Malayan Peoples Anti-Japanese Army, the MPAJPA, ending the war some 7,000 strong and well-stocked with arms. It was, as one American analyst observed wryly, a wartime policy which eventually generated serious post-war problems, a situation by no means confined to Malaya.

The title of Donald Mackay's book is also a reminder that these were the days when 'world Communism' was seen as an inexorable march towards predestined victory as bastions fell one by one, the 'domino effect' brought about by support for subversion and guerilla warfare on the part of the Soviet Union and Mao Tse-tung's Red China. If it had been as simple as that, the problems raised by these insurgencies would have been arguably much less intractable.

Yet another American commentator, looking at the British operations in Malaya, pointed out that we were especially careful in ordering our language to describe the situation, avoiding 'ordinary Anglo-Saxon words'. The Malayan situation was not 'a war', rather in legal terms a 'state of emergency' with the military acting in support of the government and the police. The scene was in many respects paradoxical. In practical terms we were 'fighting the Reds in Malaya', at the same time trading with them in Hong Kong, talking with them in Peking and 'shooting them dead in Korea'. The British did not 'wage war' but conducted 'operations'.

In retrospect this was arguably a profoundly sensible and pragmatic approach which avoided the mistakes made by the French and the Americans in Vietnam, both increasingly entangled to their ultimate disadvantage, in full-scale warfare, eventual defeat and humiliation. But whimsical American comment was much mistaken in insisting not long after the institution of the 'state of emergency' that Malaya would be 'cleaned up within two or three years at the latest', an observation lamentably wide of the mark. A better prediction was that the British would win and the '*how*' of the winning would prove to be of considerable significance, not least for military training and doctrine and not least for lessons in 'How to Stay Alive Despite Guerrillas in Your Neighbourhood'. This jaunty note in *U.S. Army Combat Forces Journal* was indeed intended as a compliment to the 'inventiveness and heroism' of British civilians, pro-British Chinese and Malay foremen in contriving to stay alive where 'peace and war, murder and infantry, prosperity and terror' went hand in hand.

Donald Mackay's book, written from his experience as planter and soldier, is itself an example of that genre: the business of staying alive. But it also conveys, as indeed have many others, what a protracted affair the Emergency proved to be, which at this distance in time comes as something of a surprise. As a survivor and participant he is entitled to treat himself as his own 'primary source'.

The book as a whole is a review of the origins, course and conclusion of the Emergency. On this reading the chances of Communist success at the outset looked very promising. The military wing of the Party, the Malayan Peoples Anti-British Army under Chin Peng, had managed to concentrate 5,000 guerillas in the jungle, supported by the Min Yuen, an alternative government in waiting; but while it waited it was committed to producing intelligence, supplies and recruits.

Meanwhile Revolution in China was about to be consummated, a potential source of help to the Communists in Malaya. However, such help would be superfluous if as the Communists anticipated the British were defeated before the *Kuomintang* collapsed. The British position at this juncture was one of 'disarray and weakness', a condition compounded by the operation of the new-found Constitution of the Federation of Malaya which seemed purpose built to 'frustrate decisive action' at large. At home Lord Listowel, Secretary of State for the Colonies - how extraordinarily dated that sounds - gave out assurance that there was no cause for alarm. Only in 1950, two years after the declaration of the Emergency, was the Malaya Committee of the Cabinet set up in London, though the Administration in Malaya demonstrated that its inherent strength was greater than its obvious deficiencies, its basic structure sound in most respects. British weaknesses notwithstanding, Chin Peng's expectation of a Communist 'walk-over' did not materialise. The British 'trump card' was the position of the Malays, committed to eventual independence but unwilling to see the departing British replaced by the Chinese. Chinese-inspired insurrection remained for all practical purposes a Chinese phenomenon.

The police was reinforced as was the army, though Donald Mackay finds General Boucher's first use of that military reinforcement including the Guards Brigade less than impressive. Chin Peng was not without his problems, re-designating his force, the Malayan Races' Liberation Army, to preclude perception of the insurgency as exclusively Chinese in character. Enter 'the squatters', the Chinese squatters, rural Chinese communities. Registration and resettlement of the Chinese rural population proved to be enormously complex but evidently highly successful policies. The Communist response followed what the author describes as a 'descent from guerrilla war to pure terrorism'. This was a compound of attempts at cowing the masses, manifestations of ingrained pathological cruelty and a brutal alternative to a faltering military guerrilla campaign.

The appointment of Lieutenant-General Sir Harold Briggs is recognised for what it was, a major turning point and the implementation of the 'Briggs plan'. Here was the foundation of eventual British success, implementing co-ordination and co-operation from the very top to the bottom, producing an effective command structure. Yet early euphoria soon faded. Richard Clutterbuck in *The Long, Long War* recorded that in 1950 'we were undoubtedly losing the war'. How then did we go on to win? No magic wand was waved. Hard work and professionalism replaced grand gestures and 'sweeping strategic manoeuvres'. The essence of the 'Briggs ideology' was that the support of the whole population was needed, that of the Chinese in particular, but to gain such support the first vital step had to be to win the actual war on the ground.

Change on the British side, when it came, was quite dramatic. In 1951, with the change of government at home, Oliver Lyttleton took over the Colonial Office. The surprising choice (though apparently not the first one) for the position of High Commissioner and Director of Operations in Malaya, was Lieutenant-General Sir Gerald Templer. The General's mandate was clear: to bring the country to independence and to implement the steps necessary to effect this. Within a little more than two years, when General Templer left Malaya, the resettlement programme was almost complete, thus denying the Min Yuen their previous hold. Food controls were more effective, the police increasingly efficient, the war in the jungle waged with greater success, the military battle well on the way to being won.

To whom should the laurels go, if laurels there be? Donald Mackay acknowledges the achievements of General Templer but is inclined to assign the greatest credit for ultimate success to Sir Henry Gurney. Chin Peng's strategy was flawed from the outset. He seriously underestimated Communist weakness and further eroded what strength he commanded by moving into the jungle, thereby stranding his supporters. This left the security forces free to cut Chin Peng's links with his base. The programme of political and military action, what one American analyst called General Briggs' 'sociological strategy', beginning with resettlement which involved half a million people and culminating with Independence under the 1957 constitution, literally cut the ground from under the feet of the Communists. The British Army, swelled with National Servicemen, proved to be adept at jungle fighting, as subsequently did the Police, outclassing the Communists at their own preferred and much vaunted style of warfare.

It might be argued that all this was 'long ago and far away', of little consequence now, and that in any event what really triumphed was de-colonisation. This account commendably does not elevate the Malaya experience into some fount of supreme knowledge in countering modern guerrilla warfare, though it is at pains to emphasise the importance of having punctured the myth, or the presumption, that communist guerrilla insurgency would always succeed. Two other points are worth noting. The Communists failed to internationalise their struggle in Malaya, the prospect of receiving assistance from Communist China foreclosed when Thailand joined SEATO. Equally their attempts to win by political manoeuvre were blocked in August 1957 with Malayan independence and the conclusion of a defence agreement which secured the continued presence of British, Australian and New Zealand forces within the country. Both the front door and the back door had been bolted and given the circumstances firmly barred.

The Malayan Emergency has been the subject of much distinguished writing and revealing research. Yet there is space for a timely reminder of what transpired in this protracted campaign. Donald Mackay's account has all the feel of the country, intimations of first-hand experience and a sober account of eventual success without any excess of triumphalism. For those like myself who were not there but who waved fellow National Servicemen 'off East', this is an illuminating learning exercise. For those who did serve at whatever level and ultimately prevailed there is understanding, explanation and suitably measured justifiable acclaim.

John Erickson
University of Edinburgh
April 1997

ACKNOWLEDGEMENTS

There are many problems in trying to write with perspective about the Malaya Campaign nearly 50 years after the event. Much of the primary material is still held to be confidential and much is inaccessible in files and records in Malaysia. There are, however, many who served there who have been prepared to share with me their clear and perceptive memories of much that happened, and I am grateful to all those who helped me so generously.

I must in particular thank Lieutenant Colonel D'Arcy Mander, who commanded 1st Bn Green Howards from 1949, and RSM Mick Winter, also of the Green Howards, who has sadly died since I started to put this account together. Two other Green Howards who were most successful officers in the 'Subalterns' war were Field Marshal Sir Nigel Bagnall, latterly Chief of Defence Staff, and Captain Humphrey Thornton-Berry, and both have been liberal with their time in explaining how they went about things. My thanks go to them, as well as to Bill Douglas and Gordon Wilmot, both officers in the Royal Scots Fusiliers, who served in the rather odd conditions up on the Thailand border. Desmond Neill, whom I have known for many years, never ceases to be able to provide me with new anecdotes about his time as Chinese Affairs Officer in Pahang, and I am delighted that the preparations for this book have brought me to make contact again with Raymond Hands and Nick Gent (Sir Edward Gent's son) who were colleagues of mine in the past, but have not let that stand in the way of giving me generous advice and information.

Much of what I have written draws on my own experience in Malaya in the middle 1950s as a planter and very briefly as a soldier, and it would be wrong not to acknowledge the part played in my education by colleagues and friends from the Kluang and Kajang areas who shared bottles of 'Tiger' beer with me, as well as experiences and opinions, in clubs and resthouses and bars too many to admit to.

Finally, I should record my obligation to my brother, Lieutenant Colonel Hugh Mackay, Royal Highland Fusiliers, who was ADC to General Urquhart at the time of Lyttleton's visit – it is true to say that without his intervention I would never have gone to Malaya in the first place.

To all these, and the Government officers and academics and journalists and soldiers who have laboured to produce definitive reports and appreciations and analyses over the years, I gladly acknowledge my indebtedness: the errors and misconceptions in this book I can truly claim as my own.

Donald Mackay
January 1997

GLOSSARY

Atap Palm leaf thatch.

Balai Polis Police Station (see also *Rumah Passung*).

Barang Luggage, goods and chattels, personal bits and pieces, virtually anything you want it to mean – a most useful word.

Belukar Dense undergrowth or secondary jungle, often where light has been let into more established areas by felling or burning.

Changkol A large hoe, a necessary substitute for a spade where workers do not wear boots or shoes.

Cicak Small insect-eating lizard (pronounced 'cheecha').

'Colosseum' British-style bar in Kuala Lumpur, frequented by planters and European businessmen.

CPI Communist Party of India.

CT Communist Terrorist. The usual and ultimately authorised name for members of both the MRLA (qv) and armed members of the Min Yuen (qv).

Coolie Manual worker/labourer. Now regarded as pejorative, but in 1948 generally used by the workers to describe their own status.

'Dog' ('Spotted Dog') The Selangor Club, in Kuala Lumpur.

Dyak Native of Sarawak, in Borneo.

Force 136 Special force raised in the Far East after the fall of Singapore in 1942, on the same lines as SOE in Europe. Provided support for the MPAJA and was intended to spearhead the British assault on Malaya that was pre-empted by the Japanese surrender.

Istana Palace.

Kampong	Malay village. 'Kampong Malays' was a phrase used rather loosely to designate rural Malays, and Malay workers whether resident in villages or not.
Kempetai	Japanese secret police.
Kongsi	Chinese word for an association or joint business enterprise, often carried on by family or clan members. Hence, a business, or the place or building in which the business is carried on, or where the family live – often the same place.
Ladang	Cleared area under cultivation.
Lalang	Elephant grass *(Imperata cylindrica)*. Dense coarse grass with growth habit similar to couch-grass, with creeping roots. Capable of reaching a height of four or five feet. Where it takes over it will choke everything else, and cleared areas covered with *lalang* were common, especially in poor or worked-out soil.
MCA	Malayan Chinese Association.
MCP	Malayan Communist Party.
MIC	Malayan Indian Congress.
MPABA	Malayan Peoples' Anti-British Army.
MPAJA	Malayan Peoples' Anti-Japanese Army.
MRLA	Malayan Races Liberation Army.
Mata Mata	Malay policeman (literally 'eyes').
Mentri Besar	Prime Minister (of an individual State). The plural is properly *'Mentri Mentri Besar'* but for simplicity *'Mentris Besar'* is used throughout this text.
Min Yuen	MCP's undercover organisation in the villages and towns. (Short for Min Chung Yuen Thong's 'People-Movement').
OCPD	Officer Commanding Police District.

OSPC	Officer Superintending Police Circle.
Orang Asli	Aborigine. The word in common use in 1948, *'Sakai'* (literally 'servant' or 'subject'), is now rightly regarded as pejorative.
PMFTU	Pan-Malayan Federation of Trades Unions.
Padang	Open space in town or village, especially a grassed area, roughly equivalent to 'village green'.
Parang	Broad-bladed heavy chopping knife or machete, used both as a tool (in place of an axe) and as a weapon.
Penghulu	Village headman.
Punai	Green pigeon.
Sakai	See *Orang Asli*.
Stengah	Whisky and soda.
Towkay	Chinese businessman-proprietor.
Tuan	'Sir' – polite form of address to any man of position whether European or not.
Tunku	Prince.
UMNO	United Malay Nationalist Organisation.
Ulu	The Interior – 'up-country'. (Often wrongly used by British and Commonwealth soldiers as a synonym for *'hutan'* = jungle.)

Federation of Malaya, 1948.

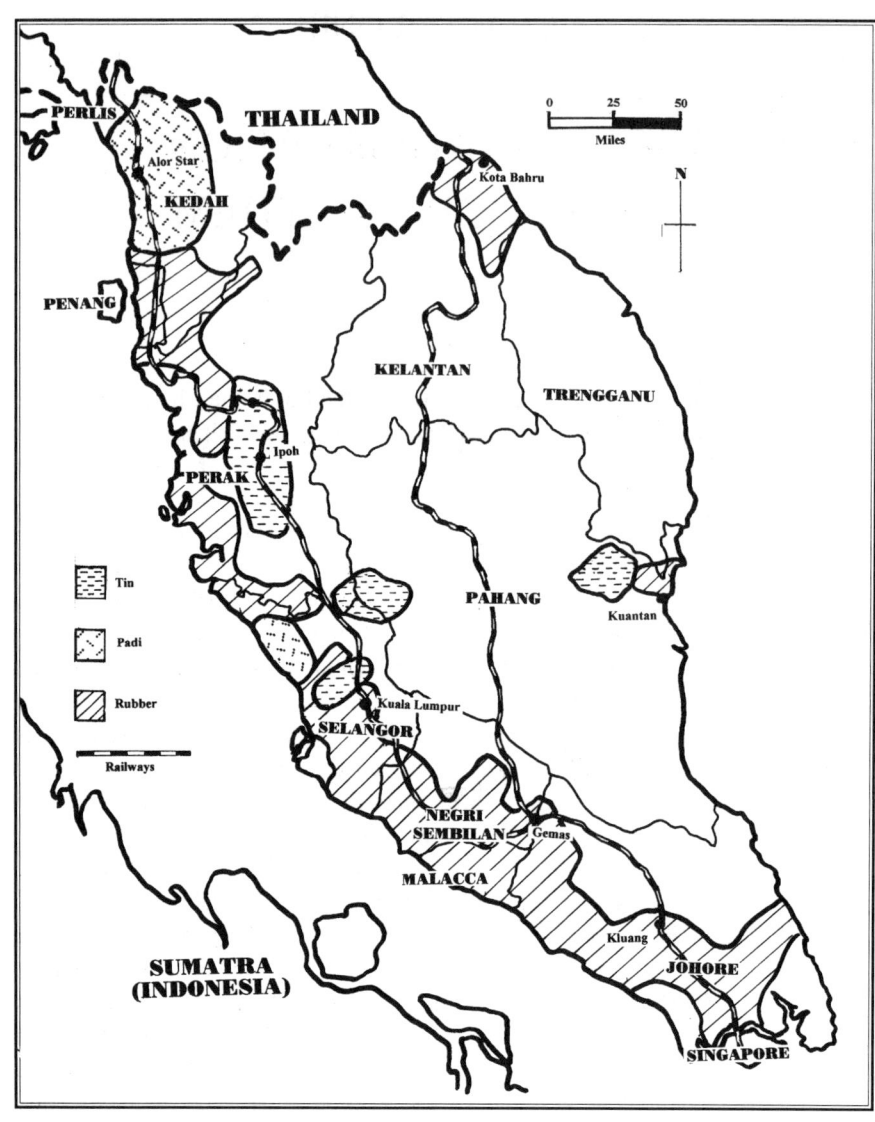

Federation of Malaya, 1948: Principal Areas of Production.

CHAPTER ONE

VIOLENCE, DISRUPTION AND BLOODY MAYHEM

On Thursday, 17 June 1948 – the Year of the Rat in the Chinese calendar – readers of the *Straits Times*, Malaya's leading English language newspaper, woke to the sensational headlines that they had been dreading for so long. 'Five Estate Murders on One Day – Three Europeans Killed: Gurkhas Rushed to Scene'. The three Europeans had been brutally murdered, the *Straits Times* reported, on the previous day, Wednesday, 16 June, on two rubber estates in the Sungei Siput district of Perak in northern Malaya, 18 miles from the State Capital, Ipoh. At about 9 o'clock in the morning Mr J M Allison, the Manager of Sungei Siput Estate, and his Assistant Manager, Mr I D Christian, had been tommy-gunned after having had their hands tied behind their backs. John Allison was 55; Ian Christian was only 21, and had served as a Gurkha officer before becoming a planter. He had been at Sungei Siput Estate for only a month and was due to transfer to Kantan Estate the very next day as Acting Manager. Witnesses reported that a gang of 12 'bandits' had surrounded the Estate office, seized both Allison and Christian, and demanded their pistols. Christian did not have one, and Allison's was in his bungalow, about a hundred yards from the office. The two were pinioned, frogmarched to the bungalow where Allison's gun was found, then after a few minutes they were marched back to the Estate office, where they were tied to chairs on the verandah. The horrified clerks were made to move away, and Allison and Christian were 'executed', bullets being pumped into their heads and bodies at point-blank range. The 'bandits' had taken $1,000 from the safe, but to make sure that there was no misunderstanding, that there should be no notion that the murders were simply part of a robbery, the leader of the execution squad explained to Tan Ah Joo, the Chief Clerk, that what they were about was killing Europeans. 'We will kill all Europeans', he said before the squad cycled away, leaving the bodies of Allison and Christian slumped in their own blood on the verandah. There was no sense of hurry or fear in their withdrawal; they took time out on the way to set fire to the rubber store. Half an hour before this, and ten miles away, on Elphil Estate, a similar scene had just been played out. Mr Arthur Walker was in his office by the main gate, sorting out some paperwork, while in the main office next to his the Estate's Chief Clerk, Mr A N Kumaran, was also at work; from his desk he could see the main gate and got a clear view of the three Chinese who

1

rode up on bicycles. 'I heard Mr Walker's dog bark and Mr Walker try to pacify it', Kumaran reported later, 'then I heard a Chinese say, "*tabek Tuan*" ("Good day, Sir"). Mr Walker responded to the greeting. Almost immediately afterwards I heard two shots. I ran out of the room into the main road. From there I saw two Chinese enter Mr Walker's room and fire more shots. They then came out, mounted their bicycles and rode off.' Walker had been shot through the head and chest, but although his safe keys lay on the floor, nothing had been taken from the safe.

Through the stilted phrases of Kumaran's statement it is still possible to realise something of the appalling shock of this sudden and cold-blooded killing. The story is the more poignant since the Walkers were just about to go home to the UK on long leave: at the very moment when her husband was dying, Mrs Walker was in the nearby township of Kuala Kangsar doing some last minute shopping for the voyage. If the killers had come a few days later they might well have failed to find their target.

The two other killings reported by the *Straits Times* that day were of a Chinese on Senai Estate near Johore Bahru in the south of Malaya, and another Chinese, a contractor, on an estate near Taiping. Sadly, the news of either of these two murders would not have caused much surprise to the breakfast-time reader of the *Straits Times*. Reports of violence, disruption and bloody mayhem had become commonplace in its columns over the last few months, and it was nothing unusual to read of squalid deaths like these. On the same page as its lead story on 17 June, the *Straits Times* recorded 13 victims of gunmen since the beginning of May, in places from Malacca and Port Dickson to Bahau, from Rengam and Layang Layang in Johore to Batang Berjuntai in Selangor, not to mention several who had been wounded or beaten-up in these and dozens of other incidents. The report ends laconically, 'Now to this list must be added yesterday's outrages'.

But of all the outrages that were becoming so usual a part of life in post war Malaya, it was the murders of John Allison, Ian Christian and Arthur Walker that brought the country up short. These were different; they were a declaration of war, nothing less. They were deliberately staged so as to make it clear that they were acts of political terrorism, meant to be seen as a demonstration of power and brutality. They were intended to precipitate Government reaction, and in that they certainly succeeded: what they did precipitate was one of the longest counter-insurgency campaigns ever fought, a campaign which was so unusual in its outcome as to be almost unique. Virtually alone among all the countries in South East Asia that were to be the targets of Communist insurgency, Malaya survived. Amid all the dominoes that were to fall, Malaya stood. To understand why, it is necessary to go back in time, back to the Second World War and even before. And it is necessary, too, to get a 'feel' for the country, its peoples, and its history.

CHAPTER TWO

THE BATTLEFIELD MAPPED OUT

Two days after the fall of Singapore to the Japanese in 1942, Winston Churchill came to the Commons to face angry and sombre recrimination from all sides of the House. He was assailed by friend and foe alike and none was more ardent in his fury than the Member for South Ayrshire, Mr A Sloan. Mr Sloan coupled his attack on the Prime Minister with a swingeing denunciation of those 'vultures and scoundrels' who had 'exploited the bodies and souls of the natives of the Far East', and went on, rather inconsequentially, to comment that 'Malaya and Singapore were merely names of far-off places in foreign lands. They conveyed little to the average mind.' Never mind that this comment was no more than a pallid echo of Neville Chamberlain's famous dismissal of the Czechs (the rest of Sloan's speech made it clear that he was not of an original turn of mind) – what he said was painfully true then, and remained so when the war was over. In 1948 most people in Britain knew virtually nothing about Malaya, and what little they did know made uncomfortable thinking. The military debacle in the face of the Japanese invasion in 1941, the sinking of the *Prince of Wales* and the *Repulse*, the fall of 'impregnable' Singapore and the ignominious surrender of thousands of half-trained troops, newly landed apparently for the express purpose of spending the rest of the war enduring the squalor and brutality of Changi, the Siam railway or the copper mines of Japan; all these were woeful thoughts. Much better to keep one's attentions nearer to home, even if that did mean the prospect of the Attlee Government and struggling to keep warm with a gas fire that glowed two inches up the elements if you were lucky.

Even before the war, and the disgrace of defeat by an oriental nation believed to exist by making cheap imitations of Western products, knowledge of Malaya had probably been confined to reading the works of Somerset Maugham. Malaya, it seemed, was a place where passionate women lived a life of cushioned ease, waited on by soft-footed flunkeys, and shot their menfolk after misunderstandings about letters, or it was where men solemnly changed into dinner jackets in the middle of nowhere, and read eight-week old copies of *The Times* in strict rotation; and all this while the burning sun and teeming monsoon rain played box and cox, taking it in turns to beat down on the primitive palm-thatch roofs. Noel Coward, safe in his cool suite in the Raffles hotel, could make witty jibes about 'mad dogs and Englishmen':

the reality wasn't exactly like that.

On the face of it, Malaya is one of the most beautiful tropical countries in the world – anyone who has been there will sooner or later come round to telling you that – but in many ways its beauty is only skin-deep. It is the southernmost part of the continent of South East Asia, and lies east of Greenwich by about 120 degrees or so; not quite on the other side of the world, but not far from it. From the Isthmus of Kra in the north (the border with Thailand), it extends east of southwards for about 400 miles to Cape Rumenia, just east of Singapore and just north of the Equator. It hangs from the great Indo-Chinese landmass like a pendant jewel, almost a perfect teardrop in shape, being about 200 miles from east to west at its widest point. Its climate is tropical without being too extreme, temperatures in the lowlands varying around 85-90 degrees Fahrenheit during the day and falling to the 70s at night. Humidity is high, there are heavy but short-lived showers almost every day, and this rain becomes torrential and lasts for days during the two monsoon periods each year.

Geographically speaking, the country is divided into two unequal parts by a 'backbone' range of mountains about 300 miles long and up to 35 miles wide. In the centre of this range, much of the country is over 4,000 feet, while the two highest peaks are over 7,000 feet. The bulk of the landmass lies to the east of this range, and is largely undeveloped. Steep slopes are deeply scored by streams and rivers, and over-all lies the natural jungle, a high continuous rainforest rich in a profusion of trees and creepers. Many of the trees are a variety of teak, which are harvested enthusiastically wherever access is possible. The spaces that are opened to light and air by this logging are quickly overgrown by *belukar* which just as quickly grows into secondary jungle, an almost impossible tangle that only slowly returns to the original primaeval state. Throughout this jungle there are orchids, aroids and ferns of all descriptions; different types of lianes, including the rattan, which those who know their Malaya call *rotan* (and recognise as being useful for an infinite variety of purposes, from making furniture to beating criminals); and then there is the local building material, bamboo, which grows in clumps that can often best be measured by the acre, and can only be hacked through with the heaviest and sharpest blade. One rather undistinguished-looking tree – undistinguished that is, until it grows to its full height – is the *angsana*, often reputed to be the *senna*, from which Victorian pharmacists and Nannies derived that wonderful, all-purpose specific, the sennapod.

This jungle is alive with noise and movement. An odd thing about a lot of the wild animals found there is that they tend to be smaller than their kin elsewhere: the Malayan elephant, for example, is usually smaller than the Indian elephant, but is otherwise genetically identical. The same is true of tigers, rhinoceros and several different species of deer, possibly because, although the jungle looks so lush, the underlying soil is not that rich in natural nutrients, and the greater animals at the top of the food chain find it hard to thrive. Other lesser animals inhabit the jungle in profusion, however, and they seem to flourish in rich variety: civets, monkeys, lemurs, rats and a whole host of others. One of the finest sights imaginable is to see a colony of flying foxes, enormous fruit bats with a wingspan of as much as five feet, circling with an unexpected grace black against the setting sun, before going about their evening's foraging.

Paradoxically, some species can reach an extraordinary size. Giant frogs are much regarded as the source of a square meal, by humans as well as by other predators. There are snakes, including cobra and python, as well as a glamorous but dangerous beauty called a sealing-wax snake, which has iridescent scales in a mosaic of bright colours, just like the pencils covered in dabs of different-coloured sealing-wax that you used to make as a child. The rivers, swamps and ponds teem with fish, which provide a welcome addition to the diet of crocodiles when the supply of incautious game is not enough. Everywhere there are birds, birds by the thousand, birds of every colour, shape and size, bulbuls and orioles, cuckoo-shrikes and minivets, kingfishers that fish the streams and pools, and kingfishers that comb the grasslands and verges for grasshoppers, hawks and mynahs and butcher-birds and parakeets and green *punai* that make excellent pigeon pie, all adding to the incredible variety and cacophony that seems to fill the Malayan countryside. For a European it can come as quite a shock to hear what seems to be a farmyard Rhode Island Red cockerel crowing in the middle of the most inaccessible jungle, until you remember that the jungle fowl is the ancestor of Western domestic poultry. Even at night there is seldom silence: there is one maddening bird, a nightjar that is universally known as the 'tock-tock' bird, and has been known to drive insomniacs nearly insane by its continuing intermittent 'tocking'. Even the most intelligent people seem to find it impossible to resist counting along with the 'tocks' and trying to stop at exactly the same time as the wretched bird.

And then there are the insects. There are nine hundred species of butterflies, spiders, beetles and ants (including a half-inch red beast that bites like the very devil if it gets down inside your shirt) and all in such variety as to keep the most blasé entomologist enraptured. Leave the beaten track for a while, sit down for a few minutes virtually anywhere where there is undergrowth, and it will be only a moment or two before you will begin to sense a surreptitious movement in the nearby leafmould: leeches looping like caterpillars towards the smell of your blood. In 1948 the problem of mosquitoes was still high on the list, but even on a more mundane level, insects could seem to be unpleasantly important. One little black beetle, for instance, looks totally innocuous but is protected by its ability to squirt out a jet of foul-smelling liquid, like a skunk, whenever it is threatened. This can make a big difference to the flavour of your whisky when the wretched thing decides to drown itself in it. One of nature's lines of defence against intrusive flying insects is the gecko, a charming little lizard that will move in from the jungle and live behind the pictures in the house, coming out in the evening to hunt all the flying nuisances that are attracted by the lights. Their characteristic call is a clucking noise, which accounts for their Malay name, *cicak*, and they have a rather disconcerting habit of forgetting sometimes to maintain the suction between the big pads on their fingertips and the ceiling, so that they fall off with a plop on to the floor.

Wherever you go in Malaya you are never far from the jungle, and it is hard not to be aware of its presence. Despite its beauty and variety it looms behind the thin veneer of human living, a brooding and dangerous mass that is never quite to be trusted. It is not impassable – the Japanese forces showed that in 1941 – but movement is very difficult and slow, especially for formed bodies of troops. Its hazards can be legion: bites from insects and leeches can turn septic in a matter of hours, fungal skin complaints can immobilise a man in two or three days, razor-sharp leaves and stiletto thorns can cut and slash the skin in a way that leads inevitably to infection if treatment is not prompt and thorough. Malaria is endemic, and always there is the wet. Being constantly damp soon leads to sickness and debility, and, strange though it may sound, there is even the problem of cold, especially at night a thousand feet or so up the side of a mountain. This jungle was to dominate the course of events in Malaya from 1948 onwards – it dominated the way people lived and where they worked, it dominated the thoughts and plans and hopes of those on each side of the conflict, and in the end it dominated the way the campaign was fought and won.

There *were* roads into this jungle, and through it – just a few, and these were mostly estate and logging tracks, crudely engineered from dirt and laterite gravel, that quickly became a quagmire in wet weather. There was a railway, too – a cranky branch line that left the main north-south track at Gemas on the northern border of Johore and wound its erratic way north eastwards through Pahang up to Tumpat on the Thai border. Large areas of this jungle massif had never even been surveyed and mapped. And yet however inhospitable this jungle might be there were still people who lived there. A few thousand aborigines eked out a semi-nomadic living by hunting small game, fishing and growing poor crops in ragged little 'slash and burn' clearings. It was barely a subsistence living, and in 1948 these *orang asli* were a dying race, debilitated by disease and malnutrition. They were a shy and primitive people, with little ambition to join the modern world. All in all they were regarded as a rather inconvenient curiosity by everyone except a few dedicated Government officers who were rewarded for their sensitive and devoted care by being thought rather more than mildly eccentric.

That was the jungle – and then there was the rest of Malaya, a relatively narrow strip down the western side of the country. Apart from the developed areas of Kelantan and Trengganu in the extreme and rather isolated north-east near the Thai border, it was in this western strip that practically the whole of the population was crammed and most of the towns and villages were situated. In this strip were the main railway, an all-weather road system that connected all the main centres, an effective telephone network, and virtually all the country's wealth. Here were most of the country's 700 tin mines, mostly dredges using gravel pumps to extract the tin ore from alluvial deposits.[1] Perhaps even more important than the tin industry, however, was rubber: 33 million acres producing high-grade natural rubber for which the synthetic butadienes were not yet an adequate substitute. To any visitor these rubber estates must surely be one of the most impressive sights – mile after mile of trees arranged in mathematically aligned rows like the serried pillars of some vast Byzantine basilica, stretching seemingly into infinity. The rubber tree – *Hevea Brasiliensis* – was introduced to Malaya late in the nineteenth century, from a quantity of stolen seed smuggled out of Brazil and germinated at Kew, but in just over 50 years the industry had grown to dominate Malaya's economy. It had materially changed the country's social structure and had established Malaya's importance in the world as by far the largest supplier of a vital strategic raw material.

In this western strip, too, were concentrated nearly all of the country's other agricultural ventures: coconuts, oil palm, pineapples, rice and the small-holdings that grew the vegetables and produce that fed so many of the towns and villages, mines and estates. There was one coal mine, at Batu Arang, that was to play an important role in the industrial troubles of 1947 and early 1948, and there was some industry – for the most part light engineering.

Thus the picture in 1948 was one of a large, inhospitable jungle-clad wilderness covering some 80 per cent of the country on the one hand, and on the other a mosaic of all the country's vibrant activities co-existing within a relatively small area. In this 'developed' strip, movement and communication were good, by the standards of the day, and given the resources, policing and control were relatively easy. In the jungle, by contrast, movement was difficult and slow, communications were virtually nonexistent, and subsistence without at least some outside support was impossible. This geographical division of the country into two 'blocs' was to be an important factor in the way each side was to try to develop the campaign between 1948 and 1960. Even more important was to be the ethnic make-up of the population.

Firstly, there were the Malays, who saw themselves, with justification, as the indigenous people and the rightful possessors of the land. In 1948 there were just under two and a half million of them, making up the largest single ethnic grouping, living a largely agrarian way of life, showing little interest in commerce, and usually staunchly feudal, owing allegiance to the Sultans who had ruled the individual states since the Middle Ages. They were even more staunchly Islamic, although it has to be said that, for most Malays, their faith sat fairly lightly upon them, at least to outward appearances – it would have been hard to find a race more politely tolerant of other cultural habits and beliefs. Among the British they were generally thought to be too easy-going, even to the point of fecklessness, although this rather patronising view was not often shared by those who knew them well, and who usually regarded them with great, if somewhat exasperated, affection. It is not clear whether that affection was returned or not: people with such perfect manners can be hard to read clearly, and it seems likely that the Malays looked on the British more with amused acceptance than admiration or devotion. After all, the British were merely the latest in a succession of foreign colonial rulers, following the Hindu-Javanese Empire of Majapahit, the Portuguese and the Dutch, each of whom had had their day, changed things a little, and then passed on into history. Even the British had not held sway for long: some states had come under British influence as recently as 1910, well within living memory of all but the young.[2]

Even so, it was the British who had had the greatest effect on the country; on its economy, its legal system, its social and cultural make-up, the Malay Rulers and their people, as well as on the Chinese, the Indians and all the countless other peoples who had come to make a living in Malaya and out of Malaya.

Rivalling the Malays, in numbers and in many other ways, were the Chinese. Even before Francis Light founded the Honourable East India Company's trading station on the island of Penang in 1786, there had been a thin trickle of Chinese immigration into the Malay states, through Malacca and the tiny east coast ports that had received merchant traders from South China for generations. Mostly these Chinese were Cantonese, and they came to trade and to work the tin and lead that they found in such abundance, for example in the area around what was then the insignificant settlement at Kuala Lumpur in the state of Selangor.[3]

With the commercial development that followed the British flag, this Chinese immigration became a flood. Chinese traders came to live, and deal, in the Straits Settlements ports of Penang, Malacca and Singapore. Forbidden to bring their womenfolk with them, they took local Malay girls to wife, developed a distinct and rich life-style and became very proud of being 'the Queens Chinese'. Their descendants, the 'Nonyas', or 'Babas', are thin on the ground these days, but still struggle to hold aloof from other ethnic Chinese. Soon after the arrival of these capable and cultured people, many of whom possessed great energy and business skill, and became wealthy in consequence, there was an influx of indentured coolie labour brought in to work in the tin mines. They served as building labourers and stevedores, generally doing all the hard, unpleasant work that the smiling Malays could not see the necessity for (let alone remotely contemplate doing). These coolies were for the most part the poorest of the poor, illiterate Hokkien or Hakka, who were yet keen to break out of the cage of indentured work as soon as possible, and to become independent. It wasn't long before much of such light engineering as there was, and a major part of the local commerce, as well as many of the services such as vehicle repair were in the hands of second generation Chinese, self-reliant and very aware of their cultural heritage. In 1948 Chinese families that might have been settled in Malaya for two or three generations still saw themselves as Nanyang ('Overseas') Chinese, not Malayans, and many still remitted money regularly to relatives in China. In the 1947 Census the number of adult Chinese was recorded as just under two million, not far short of the number of Malays, and this number was constantly being refreshed by further immigration as work opportunities presented themselves, as well as by the traditionally ardent Chinese attitude to producing large families as an insurance against the tribulations of old age. Overall the Chinese were still outnumbered by the indigenous Malays, but the trends showed that that might not be the case for much longer. Furthermore, in the south-western States, and in Penang and Singapore, the Chinese predominated, both in numbers and in influence exercised by right of financial muscle. From the Malay point of view it was just as well that these incomers did not have the right to vote, and could not also dominate politics.

In 1948, therefore, these were the two major racial groupings: Malays and Chinese. However, that was not the end of the story, for Malaya then (and now) was a kaleidoscope of ethnic groups, all co-existing in a way that would gladden the modern 'politically correct' race-relations expert's heart if the situation could be taken at face value. To provide labour for the rubber estates, there had been a policy of recruiting in Southern India – what is now called Tamil Nadhu – over many decades. This immigration had been Government-sponsored, was surrounded by legal safeguards, and was directed in the main towards European employers, who applied paternalistic if not generous policies. In 1948 there were some 570,000 Indians recorded as resident in Malaya, mostly Tamil labourers, and mostly living in rural areas in company-owned line-sites. They had arrived from India with high hopes, for even the hard work and relatively poor pay on the rubber estates were infinitely better than anything they could expect at home. A Tamil who worked hard could go back to India a prosperous man, that is provided he hadn't drunk his savings in the meantime. He had every reason to look on the Government as a benefactor and in any event probably held a rather uncritical attitude of loyalty and subservience to the Raj. His links with India remained strong and many remitted money regularly.

There were other Indians in Malaya, too. Malayalams and Telegus, also from South India, dominated the estate clerical and supervisory systems, and looked down from their greatly superior educational and cultural heights on their Tamil cousins. Chettiars set up shops, Bengalis lent money under complicated systems of interest that always left the debtor deeper in debt, no matter how much he paid, Sikhs were glad to provide bank guards and security and even some ranks of the Police, where their imposing presence and great skill at whacking ankles with staves could be most profitably employed. Many of the higher-caste Indians in Malaya had been educated through the English language, and held posts that kept them close to Government and the British. Unlike the Chinese, they seemed to relish the complexities of the legal system and became adept at using litigation to achieve advantage, even when that entailed opposing the Government. Certainly, if generalities are ever justifiably made about any community, it can be said that the Indians understood the Colonial legal system more clearly than the Chinese, and recognised that illegal pressures would be harshly dealt with. However, politically they were never either as significant or as aggressive as the Chinese, and it is curious that a people who are notoriously fond of politics and Trade Union activities should not have taken up the Communist cause with much greater enthusiasm. Some did, but not many.

Besides the Malays, the Chinese and the Indians, there were others, of course. There were the British: as the Colonial Power, the British filled the upper echelons of Government, Civil Service, Police and such utilities as the Public Works Department, Posts and Telephones, and so on. The great majority of planters were British and most of the larger tin mines were British managed, as were the big trading and management houses such as Harrison and Crosfield, Jardines, Guthries and Dunlop. Then, too, there were British doctors and dentists, British lawyers and even British clergy of all denominations. Yet, although they always seemed to be everywhere, and were very definitely at the top of all the heaps that mattered, there were never all that many Britons: perhaps 35,000, leaving aside the Armed Forces, all trying to recreate a British way of life amidst the lush green, the humidity and the heat, and all professing no greater ambition than eventually to be able to go home to the UK. A surprising number didn't really mean that, though, and a significant factor in the 12 years' campaign to defeat the Communists was the commitment of so many of the 'ordinary' Britons to the country and its people. The same has also to be said for the Dutch, French, Armenians, Americans, and half-a-dozen other nationalities that had been attracted to do business in this most welcoming of lands.

As can be seen, then, there was nothing simple about the ethnic picture in Malaya in those years immediately after the Second World War. It was certainly not a case of a European Colonial power exercising unwanted control over a homogeneous and independence-minded native population. The Federation of Malaya in 1948 was hardly homogeneous, and much of what it was and what it stood for had been contrived by the British with the acquiescence if not the enthusiastic support of large numbers of the people. As will be seen later, Britain did not in any case hold untrammelled power, and there were bitter divisions among the governed, many of whom did not even regard themselves as committed to Malaya in the first place.

So, as we paint in the background to events in 1948 and after, there emerge from amongst a mass of sometimes confusing detail, two factors which were to condition the course of the Emergency. Firstly, there is the topography: specifically the division of the country into a relatively small developed 'strip' on the western side, teeming with activity, fertile and productive, well served with roads, railway and communications; and the remainder, nearly 80 per cent of the landmass, a sombre, jungle-covered 'massif', virtually undeveloped and home to a few thousand aborigines who scratched a meagre living from an inhospitable environment.

Secondly, there is the ethnic make-up of the population, a population divided by history, culture and religion into groupings that did little to intermingle, were often suspicious and resentful of each other, and in many cases turned to other countries and philosophies for their inspiration and strength. It was a mixture that could be lethal. Against the background of militant Communism fishing in the troubled waters of South East Asia's rejection of Western colonialism, lethal was what it very nearly turned out to be.

CHAPTER THREE

THE FIRST STEPS TO CHAOS
– THE COLLAPSE OF A MYTH

By early 1948, the ground in Malaya could hardly have been more fertile for insurrection. Until the War any stirrings of nationalism or resentment of colonial rule had for the most part been held in check by the British reputation and ineffable assumption of the right to rule. Until the surrender to the Japanese it had hardly crossed the mind of any except the maddest dreamers that the British Empire might be overthrown; but, in the course of a few weeks in 1941, the legend had been destroyed. Speaking in the same debate as the vitriolic Mr Sloan, Captain Lionel Gammins, MP, had put his finger on what was destined to be one of the most important long-term effects of the capitulation:

> Do not let us underestimate the significance of that event. Our contact with Asia has been a long and on the whole honourable one, and during all those years the Union Jack has never once been lowered. The story of that scene at Fort Canning will reverberate in the bazaars of India, on the plains of China and in the Islands of the South Seas when everyone of us has long since been dead and gone.

He was pitilessly right. After the War the returning officials and Police, the planters and miners and businessmen who only wanted to restore things to their pre-war state as quickly as possible found it hard to comprehend how completely the British had lost face. In 1941 they had been very obviously and ignominiously defeated and disgraced. Now, in 1945, they had come back, blithely assuming that they could take up where they had left off. But no-one in Malaya had seen them win anything, not a battle, not a war; they were back, so it seemed, through no merit of their own, but because of victories won by others on distant battlefields. Shamed and debunked, what right had they now to overrule the Sultans, to dictate to the Chinese where they might live and at what they might work? What authority had the British to import Indians to labour on the rubber estates, and then send them back home when they had outlived their usefulness? What right had they to take up the top posts in industry and commerce, to dispense justice, to impose taxes or to raise troops? Truly, the King Emperor was seen to be very lightly dressed, even if it was too risky to suspect that he might have no clothes at all. Suddenly all the ambitions of the pre-war years that had seemed such impossible dreams, the pan-Malayan federations, the Marxist utopias, South Seas Chinese hegemony, the restoration of the Sultanates to their former power, all these and many other dispensations were now perhaps achievable. Whatever their intentions, the British were in for a hard time regaining face, and showing that the lion was not toothless after all.

One of the most sensitive problems that had to be dealt with was the position of the Malay Rulers. To some extent, all of them had collaborated with the Japanese, some by default, some by speaking out in ways that they were to claim afterwards were dictated to them by the occupying power, some a great deal more enthusiastically even than that. Their justification lay, in their view, in the British failure to honour their Treaty obligations: the Rulers had ceded their powers (not always entirely voluntarily) in return for British guarantees that they would be protected against invasion or subjugation by a foreign power. Against the Japanese, however, the British had just folded up. By contrast, the Japanese had endorsed the supremacy of the Malays amongst the races under occupation, had fostered their distrust and dislike of the Chinese, and had welcomed their active co-operation (particularly the Police) with the occupying security forces. Now the Rulers and their subjects realised that they had backed the wrong horse, and waited nervously to see whether they would be forgiven.

For the Chinese, the Japanese occupation had been an unadulterated horror. The *Kempetai* had supervised a programme of brutality, torture and arbitrary execution against whole communities, and this programme had been implemented with casual efficiency by the Imperial Forces whenever there was nothing better to do. Thousands of Chinese fled to the fringes of the jungle, where they squatted on any land they could occupy. Faced with adversity they had responded in the traditional Chinese way, by drawing the walls of clan, family and secret society around themselves, resisting all authority except the imperative of their own survival, and trusting no-one. That distrust now applied just as much to the returning British as to anyone else. There was no reason to think that the British would do anything for the Chinese – best to keep themselves to themselves and struggle for their own ends.

However, even amongst the British all was far from well. There is something of the seedy atmosphere of a Bourbon restoration in the picture presented by the reimposed British regime in the first two or three years after the War. The Civil Service was understaffed, many officials were in poor health following years of captivity and all seemed desperately jaded. The same was also true of the European officers in the Police Force, which was in any case also badly under strength. Morale was poor, and was not improved by the almost paranoid antagonism between those who had conscientiously obeyed orders to stay put in face of the Japanese occupation, and had had to endure the misery of the prison camps in consequence, and those who, for one reason or another, had got out, and returned in 1945 wearing all the badges of success and prosperity.

For the civilians returning to try to restore their businesses and their livelihoods things were no better. Many planters, for instance, who had suffered appalling deprivation as prisoners, returned to their estates to find that even survival was a nightmare. Bungalows were in ruins or had been looted down to the bare walls, and not even the most basic of human necessities was easily to be found, let alone the little comforts that made a European lifestyle remotely possible. In Kuala Lumpur the top brass thought they were suffering in almost equal measure. At King's House, when there was entertaining to be done, crockery and cutlery had to be borrowed from neighbours, and a guest at one of the High Commissioner's cocktail parties in 1946 remembers the drinks being served in brown 'Tiger' beer bottles with the necks carefully cut off.

Throughout Malaya there were many who found it impossible to conceive how the War had changed things, and could think only in terms of turning the clock back, of restoring the old culture of autocratic privilege. Against this background, the task of rebuilding was daunting. There was so much to do, everything that could possibly be ruined *was* ruined, everything needed restoration or replacement. The economy was in tatters, systems of national and local government were broken down and ineffectual. In a rather erratic attempt at a 'scorched earth' policy in the face of the Japanese invasion in 1941, plant and machinery at the tin mines and rubber estates had been smashed, rubber stocks burnt and vehicles put out of action. Under the Japanese, things had got even worse. Many acres of rubber had been felled, tin mines were abandoned and by 1945 rice production was down so badly that even the most basic allocation could not be supplied without imports; all this at a time when there was virtually nothing to generate foreign exchange. Just to tackle one problem, that of getting the rubber industry back into production, meant a massive and wearisome task of finding management from the Forces or from prison camps or hospitals, and returning them to estates which were often totally isolated and where the labour force had disappeared to the four winds. It meant struggling to find supplies of such apparently trivial items as *changkols* and millions of latex collecting cups and tapping knives, not to mention buckets and coagulating tanks and all the other paraphernalia needed to do the everyday work in field and factory and smokehouse. The problems were as basic as that, and it was much the same across the board, throughout industry and commerce. Production lines had been smashed or scrapped or dismantled; vehicles could not move for lack of spares; all but the essential railway tracks had been allowed to fall into disuse, or, worse, cannibalised to build or maintain other tracks; the telephone system worked only spasmodically, and the public power supply was intermittent at the best of times.

Into this uncertain social and political scene the British Government dropped a constitutional bombshell. A new Labour administration under Clement Attlee had little stomach for a return to the pre-war regime, the 'politically-correct' thinking of the day being that a measured progression towards full democracy, which ought 'eventually' to lead to indepenaence, was the right way forward. What is more, the instrument of this policy was already to hand. As early as 1942, with the surrender to the Japanese only weeks old, the Colonial Office had turned its thoughts to the question of how Malaya might best be governed when Japan was defeated.[1] The Eastern Department, under the direction of its Head, the Colonial Office's senior specialist in Malayan matters, Mr Edward Gent, was set to work drawing up a new constitution. Almost immediately he found himself facing conflict. On the one hand, the Foreign Office wanted to dictate a structure which would mollify the Americans in their urgent pursuit of the dismantling of the British Empire. On the other, his own masters were insisting that British authority should not be compromised to any significant extent, although convincing protestations about independence in the long term were certainly to be made. How Gent was to balance these two conflicting demands was not clear. Neither for the first time nor for the last was he faced with reconciling the irreconcilable. One difficulty was that, although Gent had a fine academic knowledge of the situation in Malaya, he had little practical experience.[2] In the main, he had to rely on his study of minutes and correspondence, as well as contacts with old 'Malaya hands' whose experience was not recent.[3] Gent's tidy mind recoiled from what he saw as the untidy and anomalous structures that had sufficed until now, and his solution to the problem of conflicting pressures was to seize this opportunity to rationalise things on a neat and tidy basis.

What he eventually proposed, and what the British Government agreed should be imposed, was the Malayan Union. In essence this new constitution was an attempt at a fairly traditional colonial system, where a Governor appointed by London held almost total executive power, but worked with a notionally 'democratic' Council which might in time be given a parliamentary gloss. Citizenship was to be given to all, Malays, Chinese, Indians, as well as to all the ragtag and bobtail of other ethnic groups who could claim *jus soli*. The promise was given of votes for all, at some time unspecified in the future, and the Malayan Union was to comprise all the Malay States, as well as the old Crown Colonies of Penang and Malacca.[4] The Sultans were denuded of such little power as they still had, reduced to mere social and religious figureheads in the states that they and their forebears had ruled as autocrats since the thirteenth century or before.

The enforcer sent to 'negotiate' this new constitution was one Sir Harold MacMichael. He was not really a very good choice. A former Governor of Tanganyika and High Commissioner of Palestine, he was by temperament and experience a dictator rather than a negotiator, and cloaked a harsh determination to get his own way in every particular beneath a correct and urbane manner. He was also extremely vain: on taking up this appointment as 'Special Representative of HMG' he demanded that he should be sworn of the Privy Council, so that he might be styled 'Right Honourable', and also that he might travel to Malaya in one of His Majesty's warships, 'the larger the better'. His list of vanities did not stop there, but the Colonial Office was unsympathetic, and he got none of them.[5] In his resolve to secure the agreement of the Rulers to their own extinction, MacMichael was brutal and devious in his methods, and conceded not an inch. Rulers who hesitated to sign were threatened with everything from deposition to close arrest while their conduct under the Japanese was scrutinised. The Sultan of Kelantan was required to sign a copy of the treaty, in which his name and titles had been left blank, so that if he refused he could be set aside, and time would not be wasted drawing up a new copy for whoever might be appointed to succeed him.[6]

The Sultans were all duly cowed into signing, conscious that their enthusiastic co-operation with the Japanese had done little to strengthen their position. MacMichael left, well pleased with himself and what he had achieved, and Edward Gent, newly knighted, was appointed the first Governor of the Malayan Union, charged with the impossible task of making it all work. The siren of the ship bearing MacMichael off to his new appointment as Governor of Malta had barely died away when the Rulers began to realise the enormity of what had been done to them. They boycotted Gent's inauguration, and they and their subjects settled down sullenly to make sure that the whole deal came unstuck as soon as possible. They did not have long to wait. In fact, the Malayan Union lasted only a few months. Faced with the realities on the ground, Gent very quickly grasped that the Sultans could not be expected to accept the virtual annexation of their realms, nor the enfranchisement of three million non Malays. Far from making the Union work he had to take on the thankless task of persuading the Colonial Office, and the Attlee Government, that a bad mistake had been made, and of hurriedly cobbling together a replacement constitution. The result was the Federation of Malaya, a structure that to all intents and purposes turned the clock back to the old pre-war system that Gent, from his desk in London, had seen as being untidy and unsuitable. A large measure of power was handed back to the Rulers, at least for internal matters;[7] though each had to accept a British Adviser whose advice, by and large, had to be taken. There was to be a unified Malayan Civil Service and Police Force, and the Federal Administration was headed by a High Commissioner appointed by the Colonial Office. The High Commissioner could take advice from a nominated Legislative Council of 57 members, (although he was not bound to accept that advice) and, except in an emergency, he must pass legislation through that Council.

This constitution did do something to mollify the Malays, though the whole sorry episode had not done much to restore their love and trust for the British, nor ease their resentment and suspicion of the Chinese. In their turn, the Chinese, who had been looking forward to being enfranchised under the Malayan Union, now found themselves smartly disenfranchised again, and were not impressed. The ground for insurrection became that much the more fertile.

As if these were not troubles enough, Gent and his officials found themselves under severe pressure to introduce political and social reforms that reflected the values of the Labour Government in London. Emphasis was to be placed on schooling, a sensible and very welcome move, particularly for the Chinese, for whom education had always been the way out of poverty and rootlessness. Less welcome to the expatriate managers of industry and commerce was the active encouragement to be given to reforming and expanding the Trade Unions. Each industry was to have its own union (sometimes more than one), each State its Federation of Unions, and overall the Pan-Malayan Federation of Trades Unions was to hold sway, in a macabre imitation of the TUC in Britain with which Labour MPs felt comfortably familiar. For the planter, used to an autocratic and paternalistic relationship with his labour force, the idea that he might have to negotiate with shop stewards and the like was quite horrifying. There was no chance that the Unions would help in leading to industrial harmony, but for those who were interested in promoting unrest they offered a wonderful opening to power. Yet more fertile ground!

Nor was Gent able to concentrate his undivided attention on the internal affairs of his fledgling Federation, however much the deplorable situation might have warranted it. In one South East Asian country after another resurgent nationalism was showing an unnerving readiness to cross borders. French Indo-China was deeply unstable and was already beginning to break into the ferment that was to infect it and its neighbours for close to three decades, the Dutch East Indies were riven by civil war, and everywhere the prospect looked threatening. Most ominous of all, in China Mao Tse Tung was clearly winning the war against the Kuomintang forces of the elderly and corrupt self-styled 'Generalissimo' Chiang Kai Shek, and no one could tell how soon he might be in a position to start spreading the Revolution to other lands. Already there were signs of this in Malaya: amongst the Chinese community, supporters of Mao and the Kuomintang were already at each others' throats and the killing had started.

A High Commissioner of great charm and drive might have been able to work within this unpromising and immensely complex situation to achieve what was needed. Sadly, to many of the people that he had to deal with, Edward Gent seemed to lack either warmth or incisiveness, although he brought to his task many other admirable qualities. He had an excellent academic mind, gaining a double First at Oxford, and a rugger Blue as well – his height must have given him a commanding presence in the scrum. During the First World War he won a Military Cross as a junior officer, and then a DSO as a 23-year-old Lieutenant Colonel in 1918, commanding a Battalion of the DCLI. There can be no doubting his courage. When he took up his appointment, in April 1946, he brought with him a lifetime's experience in the Colonial Service, much of it gained while working on the problems of Malaya. On the face of it, he was typical of the best kind of Colonial administrator, clever, widely experienced, well versed in the priestly mysteries of the Colonial Office and surely ideally suited to the task of returning Malaya to normality and laying the foundations of greater things to come. With all the advantages of hindsight, it is easy to criticise him for falling short of these expectations, for being indecisive or rigidly unimaginative, for taking an apparent relish in sticking to the letter of the rule book, whatever the circumstances. But hard work and a meticulous regard for system, rules and precedents were the prerequisites in the Colonial Service; Gent would have had that dinned into him over the years, along with the suspicion that anyone who showed flair and originality might find a question mark against his name.

Descriptions of him as 'courteous and stiff' ring true. He found it difficult to empathise with either the Malay Rulers or the leaders of the Chinese Community, nor did he find much greater rapport with expatriate planters, miners and the like. In their attitudes to their workers and to him, Gent found them to be selfish, unco-operative and unduly demanding, and they responded in kind: he became richly unpopular with the European community.[8]

When Gent was appointed, he can have been in no doubt that he faced an appalling task in returning the widespread desolation to something like the peaceful prosperity of the pre-war years. What he was entirely unprepared for was the assault by international Communism. If he had little notion of how to cope with that, he cannot truthfully be blamed – in 1948 he was not alone in lacking answers to questions that no-one had ever asked before.

CHAPTER FOUR

A HISTORY OF SUBVERSION

At this point, it is necessary to go back over the Malayan Communist Party's history and see how it had come to be such an important player in this confused and turbulent scene.

At the second World Congress of the Comintern, in July 1920, Lenin himself had put a high degree of priority on work in the colonial territories of the East, and it was not long before this directive was translated into an active attempt to set up a subversive Communist organisation in the Straits Settlements and Malaya. Alas for Russian ambitions, this attempt was at first laughably unsuccessful. Too many of the would-be leaders of the Revolution were ineffectual academics, interested only in intellectual debate, while the more down-to-earth members found themselves struggling to make headway against a quietly efficient Special Branch who knew all about dealing with secret subversion, and were determined to pinch out this little budding plant before it became established. The Inspector General of the Straits Settlements Police, René Onraet, among his other preoccupations,[1] took a leading role in raids on offices, illegal printing presses and bomb-making factories, and the Courts showed no compunction in deporting those identified as ring-leaders.

In 1931 a Frenchman posing as a commercial traveller for a firm in Paris entered Singapore under the name of Serge Lafranc. It was a clumsy and naive attempt at deception: a simple check with the Sûreté showed that the firm in Paris did not exist, and Lafranc was unmasked as Joseph Ducroux, a French Communist already known to the police. He and those with whom he had made contact were arrested and charged with being members of an unlawful society, and Ducroux was sent to gaol for 18 months. René Onraet was worried that what seemed to him to be a very lenient sentence would send the wrong signals to those who were trying to import Communism and unrest into Malaya, but in fact the Communist effort was stopped in its tracks, at least for the time being. It was to be nearly ten years before Communism was to emerge again as a significant force in the politics of Malaya and the Straits Settlements.

In the aftermath of Ducroux's arrest, the clearing up of the South Seas branch of the Communist Party extended as far as Hong Kong, where one fish who was pulled in was a Vietnamese, Nguyen Ai Quok, one of the original founding members of the French Communist Party, who was better known under his preferred codename, Ho Chi Minh ('the Enlightened One'). Another Vietnamese slipped through the net, though, a clever, energetic young man called Loi Tak, who was already beginning to make a name for himself in revolutionary circles. He was allowed to re-emerge in Singapore, in what looked like an uncharacteristic piece of carelessness on the part of Onraet and his Special Branch, and very soon began to make his mark amidst the broken pieces of the Malayan Communist Party (MCP), as it now had become. Quietly and unobtrusively he and the remaining Party leaders set about rebuilding. Although they took care at the beginning to attract as little attention as possible, Onraet kept his eye on them, and from time to time the raids and arrests were resumed. However, while other ring leaders were being gaoled and deported, Loi Tak flourished, although it was his outstanding ability rather than default that soon saw him appointed to the top position in the Party, Secretary General. By the outbreak of war he had remodelled the MCP on orthodox subversive lines as a small but relatively effective organisation, well placed to enter the political battleground of disruption and revolution.

Then came the War, and with it the making of the Party. In 1941 the MCP was still an illegal organisation, with its members liable to arrest and deportation. When the Japanese invaded Malaya, Loi Tak offered the services of the Party in the battle against them, and the British, desperate for help from however unlikely a source, were pleased to accept. No talk now of illegality. Lieutenant Colonel J M L Gavin, RE, had been charged with setting up No. 101 Special Training School in Singapore to train 'stay behind' forces who might go into the jungle and fight a guerrilla war against the occupying Japanese, and at a ludicrously conspiratorial meeting on 18 December 1941 (at which Loi Tak and his colleague lurked behind dark glasses), Colonel Gavin's Second-in-Command, Major F Spencer Chapman, together with a representative of the Special Branch, agreed to accept as many young Chinese as the School could cope with. Three days later Spencer Chapman himself gave the opening lecture to the first draft. Time was desperately short, but in the few weeks before the surrender of Singapore on 15 February 1942 some 200 of what Spencer Chapman described as 'probably the best material we ever had at the School' were given a rudimentary training in the use of small arms, explosives and demolition, and were introduced to some of the skills of living and moving in the jungle. This pitifully small force became the nucleus of what was eventually to become known as the Malayan Peoples Anti-Japanese Army (MPAJA) and by the end of the War its numbers had grown to something over 7,000. With a little, rather illusory, help from a few courageous but desperately ill-equipped British officers such as Spencer Chapman himself, the MPAJA had carved out camps for themselves in the jungle, armed themselves as best they might from what the retreating British had abandoned, as well as from the Japanese, organised themselves into what they called 'regiments' (ten in all), and settled down to hold aloft the flag of resistance. Not even the majority of those recruited into the MPAJA were Communists, at least not when they went into the jungle, but the MCP made no bones about the fact that its ultimate aim was to prepare the way for a Communist state after the war, and much of the rank and file guerrilla's time in the well-concealed jungle camps was spent soaking up indoctrination and Marxist-Leninist dialectic. Political commissars held important positions in each formation, alongside and often outranking the military commanders, and by 1945 the MPAJA was quite clearly a Communist force, the military wing of the MCP. When, at long last, aircraft operating from Ceylon found enough range to drop supplies and to infiltrate small squads of specialists from Force 136 to provide guidance and radio communications, the MPAJA could claim to be an effective resistance force, well motivated, reasonably well trained, and, thanks to these supply drops, well equipped and well armed. A great source of strength was the supporting organisation that had been built up in the towns and villages, charged with providing food, medicines, information and recruits. The MPAJA and its undercover supply operation was roughly responsive to a rather cumbersome and pedantic central command exercised by the MCP Central Committee through a network of Regional Committees and undercover cells.

With the Japanese surrender in 1945, the MPAJA emerged from the jungle to a hero's welcome, at least from the Chinese community. Before British troops returned and the British Military Authority took up government, there was an opportunity for the MPAJA to take over large parts of local administration. District Committees were formed, rough justice was meeted out to those deemed to have collaborated (and, be it said, a great many private scores were settled too), and for a few weeks it appeared to everyone that the aim of displacing the Colonial regime was well on the way to being achieved.

But then the British returned in force, and somehow the Revolution was postponed. After some indecision the MPAJA handed back the arms issued by the British, plus a healthy surplus acquired during the campaign, a representative contingent went proudly to London to march in the Victory Parade, and the rank and file were sent home to return to peaceful pursuits. Each guerrilla received a small gratuity, and most followed the normal practice of servicemen in the aftermath of war, and formed Old Comrades Associations, for mutual support and self-help, as well as for talking, drinking and, being Chinese, gambling. What the MPAJA and the MCP got out of the War was the reputation of having fought and beaten the Japanese. Out of sight, out of mind, the British were not seen as having contributed to the Japanese defeat in any way, and they returned to Malaya with their reputation as the losers of 1941 and 1942 intact. The Japanese had drummed the British out of sight in 1941, and, so local opinion went, the MPAJA and the MCP had gone on to beat the Japanese; surely, then, the MCP must have the beating of the British if only they had had a go, instead of tamely disbanding? There were many who were puzzled that Loi Tak seemed content to miss such a golden opportunity.

Whatever may have been Loi Tak's reasons for avoiding armed insurrection in 1945, the MCP had by no means given up the idea of displacing the Colonial power, however. The Party was now recognised, and policy was to use its hard-won legitimacy and reputation to underwrite a conventional Communist campaign of subversion, encouraging and infiltrating labour organisations and unions, fostering violence and fraud, and promoting civil unrest.

There was one major underlying problem, though. By an accident of history – or, rather, several accidents of history – Communism in Malaya had become a largely Chinese concern. There had been a time when it might have been rooted in Western sources, and appealed to all the 'subject' races. Pan-Malayan nationalism might then have been harnessed, although from the example of Indonesia and Burma it seems that any movement of that kind might have resisted becoming part of International Communism. As it was, Malayan Communism was conditioned by two factors: increasingly the MCP would look to China rather than Russia for policy and spiritual sustenance; and the opportunities for advancing the cause of Revolution would be seen as arising from within the Chinese community rather than the country as a whole.

Amongst the Chinese there were attractive avenues that opened invitingly, uniquely suited to the nature and structure of the Chinese community. Education has always been a passionate concern of the Chinese, particularly the coolie classes, who have seen in it the key to an escape from their poverty. The Chinese schools were crammed with avid and ambitious students, and provided not just a golden opportunity to indoctrinate the young with Marxist-Leninist ideology, but also a marvellous source of recruits to 'the Cause'. Beyond the schools there were the Labour unions, inviting infiltration. Given the background of the Chinese, especially the recent immigrants, they found it natural to coalesce into 'self-help' societies and such-like secret and secretive associations, and it did not take much effort to imbue trade unionism with some of the ethos and glamour of such facsimiles of the Triads. What the MCP could offer was organisation and a theme – a central direction – and, initially at any event, this involvement was very welcome. Soon, however, the Party became bogged down by the number and variety of 'clubs' that it was expected to co-ordinate. There seems to be something overwhelmingly attractive to the Chinese psyche in complicated and pedantic bureaucratic structures, and the problem was made worse by the ignorance and inexperience of junior Party officials, who did their best to promote their own status through a proliferation of committees and councils.

In the central matter, though, of spreading disaffection in the workplace, Communist penetration of the Labour unions was quickly effective, and it was here that the first running battles between the Government and the MCP were fought. The pre-war General Labour Union had been reorganised into two components, the Singapore Federation of Trades Unions and the Pan-Malayan Federation of Trades Unions (PMFTU). Through each, the MCP sought to maintain control over the individual unions, manipulating elections to committees and official posts and infiltrating Party activists into branches. When appeals to quite valid feelings of dissatisfaction with wages or conditions of employment were not enough to mobilise strikes, then extortion, threats and physical violence were usually enough to bring the membership out. Increasingly, on the estates, in the tin mines, and in the docks, the MCP were able to orchestrate strikes, stoppages, sabotage of machinery and plant, and assaults on managers and supervisors. One particularly fruitful source of disaffection was the coal mine at Batu Arang, where conditions were frightful.

To this mounting campaign of disruption and violence, the Government reacted by clamping down as best it could: new legislation banned from office in a union anyone who could not show that he had been a bona-fide worker in the relevant industry for at least three years, union offices were raided and seditious material was seized, and the Police were prodded into taking action against the PMFTU and the State Federations of Trades Unions at the slightest hint that their activities might be unlawful under the Societies Ordinance. Newspapers' licences to publish were withdrawn in response to articles that were deemed to be seditious, and printers were gaoled for printing inflammatory pamphlets. The most cogent sanction of all was deportation: any dissident who could not prove a legal claim to residence could be deported, and in the case of Chinese members of the MCP that meant to the Kuomintang China of Chiang Kai Shek. This, for an avowed Communist, was not an encouraging career move. In fact, these measures were more effective than was realised, but at the time it seemed to the British administration that the battle was still being lost and post-war Malaya looked as though it was being reduced to chaos by a subversive foe that could not be gripped or stopped. The prospects were getting steadily more dismal.

Then, in March 1947, an organisational cataclysm threw the MCP back on its heels. Loi Tak, the Secretary General, disappeared. So did most of the Party funds.

CHAPTER FIVE

'ONE MAY SMILE AND SMILE AND BE A VILLAIN'

In all the events of the months leading up to the declaration of the Emergency, the defection of Loi Tak was perhaps the most momentous, since in its way it was to shape the policies and destinies of both sides in the conflict, and to lead both part-sightedly into war.

And yet we know so little about the man.[1] His origins are so obscure as to be opaque: a Vietnamese, a known associate of Ho Chi Minh in Hong Kong, as early as 1934 a man with a reputation, no-one in fact knows where he came from, how he became a Communist, nor even whether his reputation was well founded or merely a figment of his own imagination. He claimed to have been trained both in Russia and in France, and both claims are possible. When he slipped into Singapore after the Ducroux incident, though, nobody bothered to ask whether his credentials and experience were all that he portrayed them to be – the rump MCP was in such disarray that anyone who could demonstrate energy and commitment, and seemed to know how the Party apparat might be restored, was surely God-sent. Loi Tak was welcomed with enthusiasm, in spite of the fact that he spoke little of any Chinese dialect, and never learnt to read or write Chinese. It did not take him long to show that he knew what he was about, and everyone soon appreciated his formidable organising power.

He was instrumental in restructuring the Party on a cell system, and by 1939 he had risen so successfully through the hierarchy that he was elected Secretary General. One factor in this dramatic rise to power was his consistent luck: avoiding arrest in Hong Kong was only the beginning of what seemed to be a charmed career. Time and time again Onraet's raids on the MCP's offices and printing presses and meetings missed Loi Tak himself, while scooping up his Party rivals.

This luck even persisted throughout the War. When the Germans invaded Russia in 1941, Comintern policy was put into reverse, and Communist parties around the world were told to co-operate with governments opposed to the Axis powers. This change came just in time to allow Loi Tak to negotiate the deal with the British that eventually led to the formation of the MPAJA, yet Loi Tak himself never went into the jungle. He stayed in Singapore, and masterminded the Communist resistance without even apparently making any very great attempt at concealment – and still his luck held good. It seemed possible for him to drive about the country without serious hindrance from the Japanese security forces, who yet found nothing like the same difficulty in laying hands on his senior colleagues. In August 1942, for instance, the whole of the Central Committee of the MCP was in full session when it was raided by the Japanese: the only person to avoid arrest was Loi Tak, who had been delayed on the way to the meeting. As if that were not enough, within the month his luck held again. The leading commanders and commissars from the MPAJA in the jungle were called to a meeting at Batu Caves, just north of Kuala Lumpur, a meeting which Loi Tak was again supposed to attend. Once again he was delayed and did not arrive until too late: the Japanese were there in good time, however, and over 90 of the Communist guerrilla leadership were 'disposed of' in the gun battle that ensued.

So it was that by the end of the war Loi Tak was in a position of virtually unassailable authority in the MCP. He had a golden reputation for being lucky, which in itself was a tremendous asset amongst the often deeply superstitious Chinese that made up the rank and file of the Party, and he was effectively without rival in the hierarchy. It was Loi Tak who decided what the policy was to be towards the restored British Colonial regime in the immediate post-war era, it was Loi Tak who was to design the programme of manipulation of the Labour unions and set in train the campaign of civil unrest which was to characterise the period leading up to the Emergency, and it was Loi Tak who was to loom over the threat of renewed guerrilla war that was posed by the clandestine cadres of the MPAJA that had been maintained in the towns and villages, together with their arms dumps and camps in the jungle.

Nevertheless, this paragon was not entirely without critics in the Party. His policies were not universally acceptable to the emerging young Turks, many of whom, such as Chin Peng, the Party Secretary for Perak, wanted outright war; and, more importantly, the whole business of his incredible charmed life was coming under scrutiny. Was it really possible that he should have been able to travel the country throughout the war in total immunity, without hindrance from either the Malay Police or the Japanese? How did it come about that he was so often conveniently 'delayed' when vital meetings that he had himself convened were raided by the Security forces? Was it possible that his devotion to the Cause was rather less than wholehearted? Worse than all that, could it be that he had in fact been a double agent for the Japanese?

By early in 1947 these questions had become too pressing to ignore, especially since there seemed to be irregularities in the management of the Party's funds, and Loi Tak was summoned to a meeting of the Central Committee to explain himself. The meeting was scheduled for March 1947, and it was destined to be the last engagement that Loi Tak was to miss for unexplained reasons. He has never been seen since, as far as we know,[2] and the MCP funds have never been recovered either.

What has become clear since is that not only did Loi Tak act as an agent for the Japanese during the War, but he had also been operated as a double agent by the British Special Branch from the time that he appeared in Singapore in 1934. Indeed, the probability is that even before then he had been trained and operated by the French in Indochina, and the French had passed him on to the British when it seemed possible that he had been 'blown', at the time of Ho Chi Minh's arrest in Hong Kong. There is nothing inherently unlikely in the idea that a double agent might achieve the highest position in a target organisation, especially if the case officer who is running him can speed up the process by a few selective arrests and deportations – Onraet was certainly capable of that. In this case, it means that the British were presiding over a security triumph that was as important, not to say dazzling, in its context as, for example, the Russian management of Kim Philby. In effect, the Special Branch had been running not only some extremely effective anti-Communist activities, but also the MCP itself, so Loi Tak's demise was as much a serious loss to the British as it was to the Communists, although it must have been on the cards all along. What had been a classic intelligence coup had come to a sudden end, and at a highly critical time Colonel Dalley, who was now filling Onraet's shoes in charge of Intelligence, had to try to rebuild his net within the MCP. From a situation in which he might even have been very largely in control of the direction of Communist policy, he had now to try to penetrate once more the Party at a high enough level just to get an inkling of what was going on.

For the Party, though, the problem was far more serious. Apart from the financial mess that Loi Tak left behind, and the appalling loss of face that the whole of the Leadership had suffered, policy and plans were alike in ruins, and everything that Loi Tak had had a hand in must be treated as suspect. A new Secretary General must be appointed, in haste and without fanfare, the whole organisation must be scrutinised and, if need be, purged and reshuffled, and new policies must be adopted that might rebuild morale and self-esteem by discrediting what had gone before. That meant that from now on the argument for armed struggle was to dominate MCP thinking. Loi Tak's defection was to set the scene for a radical shift of gear during the time that led up to the murders of 16 June 1948. He might no longer be present on stage in person, but even in his absence he was to dominate events during those 15 months almost as surely as he had during the last 15 years.

CHAPTER SIX

THE IMPULSE TO ARMED STRUGGLE

The first thing the MCP had to do was to find a new Secretary General. So it was that Chin Peng, the Party Secretary for Perak, finally found himself at the head of his Party, at a time and in circumstances that he probably would not have picked if he had had the choice.[1] Yet, although he was faced with some urgent problems, there were also some glittering opportunities.

First, the problems. Morale had been badly shaken by Loi Tak's defection, and there was a pressing need to construct a plausible account of why it was possible for such a thing to happen, an account which might help restore lost face, as well as cement Chin Peng's new-found authority. Such an exercise was certain to be painful, but it provided the opportunity to bury the past and make a new start: new policies could be made to appear as wise rejections of previous mistakes, rather than symptoms of vacillation and uncertainty. Chin Peng understood this very clearly, although the Central Committee's report on the 'Wright Affair'[2] took nearly nine months to prepare – it did not see the light of day until December 1947, and final publication did not take place until May 1948.

When it came, it did all that could be expected of it. Loi Tak was to blame for all the Party's ills, he was an internal renegade, a traitor who had conspired with the enemy, betrayed the Revolution and embezzled Party funds: all without doubt true, but the report went further. His dictatorial way of running the Party's affairs had weakened the Party leadership, relaxed discipline and promoted confusion, turning the Party into a weak, incompetent organisation.[3] Something was needed to restore the confidence of 'the comrades who think that our past work was done in vain'. At this point, it becomes clear that the report is going to signal a shift in policy.

The truth was that Loi Tak's policy of working through such traditional channels of civil unrest as schools and colleges, trade unions and secret societies was showing worrying signs of failure. To be sure, strikes were still fairly easy to foment, thanks at least in part to the intransigence and incompetence of much of management; industrial unrest, minor riots and upheavals could still be engineered; and, despite new legislation, it was still possible to arrange a continued flow of inflammatory propaganda in the Chinese-language press. But increasingly the industrial and social climate was becoming unhelpful. The British administration might be despondent about the effectiveness of the measures taken, but in fact they were beginning to hurt the MCP dissidents to a serious extent. In particular, the fear of deportation was preventing many who might otherwise have been active in the cause from being more than passive fellow travellers and the poverty of the immediate post-war years, which had held out such promise to the would-be revolutionaries, was being replaced by prosperity in a way that no-one had ever thought possible. United States' policy was to stockpile strategic raw materials, and rubber and tin prices were in consequence climbing to unprecedented heights, with some at least of the flowing cash trickling down into the pockets of estate workers, small shopkeepers and the like faster than anyone could have hoped. Perhaps the grounds for Revolution were not quite as fertile as they had seemed at the start.

At the same time, and in part as a result of the rapidly improving social conditions, the PMFTU and the State Federations of Trades Unions were beginning to run into money problems. It was becoming difficult to persuade the membership to part with hard-earned dues when there now seemed to be so many better things to be done with the money, and in consequence extortion was employed to try to keep the cash coming in. As the higher officials became accustomed to the benefits of legal status and political power, and started to vote themselves the trappings of successful Western society, disaffection grew among Party activists. 'Even as communists, the rank and file, whenever they were dissatisfied with their lot, appear to have clung to the Chinese propensity to expect corruption among those in high office.'[4] Money was short, they were told, they must work harder to extract cash from the workers; yet in some mysterious way cars, chauffeurs and modern European-style homes could all be paid for out of Party funds. Loi Tak's defection merely confirmed some very gloomy suspicions – something must be done.

That something was to move to armed struggle. Even before Loi Tak's defection there were many in the Party (Chin Peng himself amongst them) who had argued vigorously that this was the only way forward. They did so, not out of desperation, and the hope of restoring the drive and enthusiasm of the Movement, but out of deeply-held ideological conviction and in full confidence of victory. Although nearly two years would pass before Mao Tse Tung finally clinched his hold on mainland China, the Communist success there was already written on the wall for all to see, and the tide of victorious revolution seemed bound to lap over the whole of South East Asia. Increasingly, young revolutionaries were finding it compelling to turn to Mao rather than Stalin for their inspiration, and that was particularly true when the revolutionaries were Chinese. Chauvinism is deeply entrenched among the Chinese, and Mao was able to offer a specifically Chinese philosophy of revolution, besides providing a manual of insurgent strategy and tactics that was guaranteed to bring victory if followed painstakingly and with determination. Mao had said that 'power grows from the barrel of the gun', and if that was so, then it was in the barrel of the gun that power must be sought, nowhere else. Mao taught that armed struggle was not just the means to an end but an end in itself, the spiritual force that unites the workers and drives them forward; that force must therefore be harnessed to overcome the staleness and sense of failure that was engulfing the Movement.

So Chin Peng, faced with the need to do something drastic to restore the revolution and realising that the MCP's campaign of political unrest was in danger of running out of momentum, turned to his own deeply-held belief that the way forward must lie in violence. To reinforce that belief was the appreciation that everything that was needed to go to war lay readily to hand. When the MPAJA had been disbanded, all the arms that had been received from the British had notionally been handed in – in fact, more had been returned than the British had ever issued in the first place. What was *not* handed in was the mass of weapons and ammunition that the MPAJA had collected during the War, either taken from the Japanese and their local collaborators, or gleaned from the abandoned wreckage of the battlefield as the British and Australian forces withdrew towards Singapore.[5] These arms had been gathered in secret caches, lovingly tended, and held for just this situation. Cadres of the MPAJA itself had been kept in being, fostered under the guise of Old Comrades Associations and self-help societies, the undercover support organisation, the Min Yuen, had been maintained in the villages and towns, and the command structure was in place. In the jungle, well-ordered camps capable of holding 200 or 300 guerrillas had been built and kept in good repair, well concealed yet within easy striking distance of roads and targets. The will to war was strong, the plan was good and assured of success, the means were there, and experienced well-organised forces could be mobilised and brought into action almost in the instant. All that was needed was to give the order.

Then, if there had been any doubt in Chin Peng's mind, the final factor fell into place. In February 1948, two Communist front organisations, the World Federation of Democratic Youth and the International Union of Students, sponsored a conference in Calcutta: the 'Conference of Youth and Students of South East Asia Fighting for Freedom and Independence'. Despite its windy and self-important title, this Conference was well attended by delegates from all the principal Communist parties and fellow-travelling organisations throughout South East Asia. They found themselves faced with an appropriately high-flown programme that on the face of it consisted largely of hot air and wordy rhetoric. On the opening day the keynote address was given by a Vietnamese delegate, Le Nam, who waxed lyrical about the anti-Imperialist struggle in his own country. The formal sessions that followed continued in a strongly militant vein, and the ideological justification for violence as the only way to achieve freedom in colonial countries was rammed home again and again. Great attention was given to a Yugoslav delegation, whose rather surprising presence at a conference to talk about South East Asia was explained by the example they offered of a state whose proletariat had already pursued revolution successfully through armed struggle.

The really important agenda, however, was not what was covered in the plenary sessions, but what went on behind the scenes. In the background, behind the two sponsoring organisations, stood the Soviet Union. Red hegemony had been clamped down on in Eastern Europe in 1945, and ever since then the Russian aim had been to extend and tighten their hold by whatever means came to hand. This policy had culminated in the formation of the German Democratic Republic as a puppet of Moscow, and the attempt to blockade Berlin, an attempt that had finally come up against surprising and firm resistance. The Berlin airlift was pouring supplies into the besieged city in a volume that ensured that Berlin would not be reduced, the Marshall Plan was fast restoring the economies of the Western European countries and the USA, France and Britain were making it clear that any further attempts at expansion would be met by force. Already the diplomatic negotiations were under way that would result a year later in the setting up of the NATO joint command. The line was being drawn clearly in the sand, and the Soviet Union was in urgent need of some diversionary activity to deflect the attention of the Western powers.

Despite all that, however, it does not seem that Russia came to the Conference with a cut and dried plan for insurrection, or with detailed orders for the individual Communist parties concerned. It was a well-tried Soviet technique to fish in troubled waters, and South East Asian waters were already quite sufficiently troubled to give them all the opportunity they could wish. There was no need to risk a rebuff by assuming a heavy handed authority; judicious encouragement should be enough. In the event, the call to action fell on most receptive ears. Directly after the Calcutta Conference the Second Congress of the Communist Party of India took place – from 28 February to 6 March – and this was attended by what have been described as the 'professionals' of the South East Asia parties.[6] Soon after, the CPI itself became actively involved in insurgency, 'taking over' what had previously been a non-Communist uprising in Telengana; and almost simultaneously armed insurrection broke out or was stepped up in French Indo-China, Burma, the Philippines and the Dutch East Indies. Co-ordinated policies and plans may have been lacking, and many of these independence movements were not initially overtly Communist ideologies, but the Russians must have been well pleased with their efforts to set South East Asia alight.[7]

For Chin Peng the appeal was a clarion: all his political instincts led him in the direction of armed struggle; in the aftermath of the Loi Tak affair the best interests of the Party would be served if a new and dramatic policy were to be adopted; and now Russia, still the Alma Mater of international revolution, had sent the fiery cross round South East Asia. The weeks until the end of May were filled with heady activity, organising the mobilisation of forces, activating the Min Yuen, and directing the move into the jungle and the launch of the military campaign. Instructions were sent out to all MPAJA Associations, ordering a review of membership, destruction of all documents and records that were not absolutely essential and the sale of all property that could be turned into cash. The senior officers that made up the Military Council of the MPAJA (now imaginatively retitled the Malayan Peoples Anti-British Army) were joined by the Central Committee members of the MCP in a secret camp in the jungle in Pahang, for a planning meeting at which final decisions could be taken and orders given.[8] Prominent MCP officials disappeared from their usual haunts (some of them to escape arrest, and some whose enthusiasm for Chin Peng's policy was less than 100 per cent never to be seen again). Some local Government Officers reported rumours that ex-members of the MPAJA had been called up for training in the jungle.[9]

Documents captured later suggest that the new wave of terror was not supposed to start until later in the year, in September, and that the murderers at Sungei Siput and in Johore had jumped the gun. That is certainly possible, as control and communication were to be major problems for the MCP and the MPABA throughout the 12 years of the campaign, but even if the violence started a little too early, nothing was lost: in fact, in the short term the results were highly satisfactory from Chin Peng's point of view.

With all the advantages of hindsight it is easy to be critical of Gent and his handling of the situation. Certainly there seemed to be an appalling lack of urgency about the way he reacted to the events that had led up to the MCP's de facto declaration of war, and even in the days immediately afterwards. The representatives of the planters, industry and even some of his own officials had felt it necessary to put him under increasing pressure as the tension grew and the violence got worse. On 25 May three Chinese who had complained about intimidation had been shot, and a European estate manager had been stabbed and wounded. On 2 June there had been a running gun battle between Police and what was described as a Chinese murder squad, and in the following week there was a series of attempted murders – three more Chinese died. By 11 June the Police were setting up road blocks and searching vehicles, and on 12 June three Kuomintang supporters of Chiang Kai Shek were shot in Johore. In all, over a period of three weeks leading up to the killings on the Elphil and Sungei Siput estates, there were ten murders and three European estate managers were attacked. It is not surprising that those most at risk felt that something must be done.

In fact, the Government had done something, but was getting bogged down in bureaucracy and dissension. The PMFTU and the State Federations TUs had been deregistered, and senior Government officers had attended many earnest meetings to discuss what else might be done. On 8 June Gent himself had met European members of the planting, mining and commercial communities, and patiently explained why he was limited in what he might do: there were physical and practical difficulties in catching terrorists, the Police lacked transport and radios, the military garrison consisted largely of half-trained Gurkhas whose Government insisted as a condition of allowing recruitment in Nepal that they should not be used in aid of the Civil Power on strike-breaking or normal Police duties; and so on and so forth. All of this was true, but Gent's well-attested dislike for what he regarded as the pampered and self-pitying European community no doubt did little to disturb the composure with which he told them some of the facts of life. The European representatives were not impressed by Gent's exposition. They were the ones who were going to face the terrorism which by now everyone saw coming, and when Gent asked sarcastically whether they expected him to provide armed guards for every estate and bungalow, the answer was, yes, that was just what they did expect. There was no meeting of minds, but then there had not been any for some months. Gent's feelings of contempt for the planting and commercial communities were reciprocated with some warmth.

Yet in a way, Gent's attitude was by his lights fully justified. His background and training as a Colonial administrator had taught him never to run the risk of overreacting, always to be reluctant to jettison precedent, and to be careful not to step outside the normal confines of Civil Law. Above all, he must never court the danger of inflating what might still be just a minor 'Empire skirmish' into a crisis that might earn him a rebuke from his Colonial Office masters.

To declare an emergency would be to trigger all sorts of problems – problems of costs and compensation, problems of voided insurance policies and of law, and above all the practical problems of control of military and Police activities. Nor was he getting all the help and advice that he might have expected from colleagues – the quality of the intelligence reports, for instance, that he was getting from Lieutenant Colonel John Dalley, his Director of the Malayan Security Service, was suspect to say the least. Dalley was one of those strange characters that seem so often to be thrown up by the dark forces of Intelligence work, a secret man inhabiting a world of conspiracy and distrust, contemptuous of superiors and at the same time suspicious and defensive in his personality and aggressive in his relationships with others. Before the War he had made a name for himself by breaking up a subversive Malay political organisation, and had fed on this success throughout his subsequent career, showing an almost paranoid interest in the possibility of further trouble amongst the Malays. In 1941 he had raised and led DALFORCE, a detachment of locally-recruited Chinese, whose original function had been to act as an observer corps, patrolling the mangrove swamps on Singapore Island as scouts against a possible Japanese landing. Dalley had transformed them into a surprisingly effective fighting force, and although already middle-aged, had proved himself to be a tough and skilful commander of irregular troops. With some understatement, he has been described as a man of unconventional views.[10] Having lost his main asset in the MCP, Loi Tak, it is not surprising that Dalley should have found it difficult to report with as much certainty as he had in the past, but, being the man he was, he was not going to let that put him off. His briefings began to show signs of bluster, but worse than that, he started to hedge his bets – so, for instance, he saw nothing incongruous in saying that he saw no immediate threat, and, in the same report, that the situation was highly dangerous. Much of what he wrote about the MCP's dispositions was reasonably accurate, but there was a strange lack of urgency about his interpretation of their intentions. As late as 14 June 1948, two days before the murders at Sungei Siput, his appreciation was that it was unlikely that the Communist Party would attempt a full-scale trial of strength. In the same report he further diluted the impact by referring again to the dangers of Malay nationalism and illegal immigration from Java and Sumatra. Perhaps it is no wonder that Gent found it difficult to pay much attention to Dalley's briefings.

But Gent had another cross to bear: the ever-looming presence of the British Commissioner for South East Asia, Malcolm MacDonald. MacDonald roosted in Singapore (or, more accurately, in Bukit Serene, a royal villa provided for him by the Sultan of Johore, just over the Causeway in Johore Bahru), and was responsible for co-ordinating British policy throughout the region. He was an able man, a politician by background and inclination rather than an administrator or governor, whose character seems to have been moulded by his upbringing in the shadow of his father, Ramsay MacDonald. He was observed to be very ambitious, both politically and personally. There is a fine line between co-ordinating and interfering in a job like MacDonald's, and it would have taken a more sensitive and self-effacing man than he to have drawn that line when faced with the problems of the fledgling Federation of Malaya. Gent found MacDonald's presence galling and unhelpful, especially when he claimed to see his way through the complexities that baffled Gent himself. That MacDonald was there at all was evidence of the touching faith amongst politicians even then that when organisation and decision-making are proving troublesome, the answer to the problem is to insert another politician into the mechanism, preferably with terms of reference that allow him to make plausible noises without taking the risk of being held responsible for anything that goes wrong. If nothing more, lines of communication might have been considerably less blurred without MacDonald's intervention.

Perhaps, too, Gent had 'frozen'. He was coming to the end of a courageous and on the whole successful career. Like many colonial civil servants and governors of that time he had come over the years to identify as much with the governed as with the Empire, and he believed passionately that independence must be the ultimate goal. Over the past couple of years, since his appointment in 1946, he had designed and instituted the Malayan Union, and then watched it being strangled by the intransigence of the Malays, the apathy of the Chinese, and the old-fashioned greed and insensitivity of the expatriot community. On a purely personal level, life at Kings House had often been uncomfortable and uncongenial, exacerbated by Malcolm MacDonald's intervention. In 1948 there were no precedents to offer guidance about how to combat a Communist insurgency. Try as he might, Gent could not see any clear way forward.

The murders on 16 June finally forced his hand, yet still the action that he took was cautious, or half-hearted, depending on your point of view. He declared a State of Emergency in parts of Perak and Johore, which was extended to the whole of both States the following day. Eventually, on 18 June, the Emergency was imposed on the whole of the Federation of Malaya. The stock panoply of measures was applied: the Police were given special powers of arrest and detention, search and seizure of vehicles, boats, documents and any items that might be used as weapons. The death penalty was to be exacted for the unauthorised possession of firearms or explosives, buildings could be seized, curfews imposed and particular areas might be closed. Again, the European planters and commercial managers were unimpressed. They wanted guns, they wanted troops to guard the mines and rubber factories; above all, they wanted some evidence of confident and decisive action. Quite what that action might be is not all that clear, but such was the state of Gent's standing that whatever he did must almost certainly be thought inadequate. 'Govern or get out!' was the headline in the *Straits Times*. Saying that, the newspaper spoke for virtually every member of the expatriot community.

Malcolm MacDonald was not the one to miss such an opportunity. He sent a copy of Dalley's report to London, suggesting again that Gent was not up to the job and should be dismissed.[11] Then, on 22 June, he met Gent in Kuala Lumpur, accompanied by Gimpson, the Governor of Singapore, General Wade (GOC Malaya) and the Commissioner of Police, Langworthy. The first item on the agenda was the latest intelligence report from Dalley, giving an estimate of the MPABA's strength, which was accepted as realistic (which it almost certainly was), but no coherent forecast of the insurgents' intentions. Discussion therefore soon moved on to what was to be done, and once again Gent and MacDonald were at loggerheads. MacDonald, rightly anxious that the Communists should not be allowed to close down the mines and plantations and drive the European managers and officials out of the rural areas, wanted a rapid deployment of all available Police and Army units to act as static guards. Gent and Wade feared that this would cede manoeuvre totally to the MPABA, and wanted to take a longer view, using the Army to strike at the guerrillas when and where they could be found. Nothing could be agreed, and eventually Gent exploded. The minutes of the meeting surely record an expurgated version of what was in fact a blazing row. Gent reminded everyone (and that particularly meant MacDonald) that responsibility and authority were his alone, that he wasn't going to have his hands tied by any committee, as MacDonald had proposed, that the measures that he had decided upon would be put into effect, and that Wade and Langworthy could do as they were told. The implication that MacDonald could mind his own business was not spelt out in the minutes but was clearly understood. In the event, MacDonald was probably right and Gent wrong, but a more tactful and less obviously ambitious man than MacDonald might have found a way of reaching consensus without forcing Gent to put out the 'Keep Off the Grass' signs.

MacDonald very soon had the upper hand, however. While all this had been going on in Kuala Lumpur, the Colonial Secretary in London was being lobbied by a delegation 'representing all Malayan interests' asking for Gent to be replaced, and when MacDonald cabled London after the meeting on 22 June, saying that Gent really must go, his advice fell on receptive ears. When he was recalled 'for consultation' Gent no longer had the spirit to fight, and left Singapore on the night of 28/29 June, knowing in his heart that his career was ended. His flight was delayed in Colombo by a piece of bureaucratic bumbledom, and eventually this gallant but outmoded servant of the Empire was offered an onward passage in a converted Second

World War aircraft, a York freighter. On the morning of 4 July this aircraft was in collision with another over London airport, and all on board were killed.

CHAPTER SEVEN

STRENGTHS, WEAKNESSES, OPPORTUNITIES AND THREATS

Perhaps Chin Peng saw the death of Sir Edward Gent as a good omen – not that he needed omens to convince him that the course that he had taken so far was the right one. Everything was going well. True, the mobilisation and move into the jungle had presented problems: many of the 'volunteers' had been disappointingly reluctant to volunteer after all, and pressure had had to be exerted. Communications had already shown themselves to be a nightmare, and there were some rather worrying indications that discipline might turn out to be a problem, particularly amongst those units of the MPABA that were more interested in mayhem than Marx. However, to Chin Peng these were relatively minor hitches. His position was strong, his plan was tried and tested, goals were clear and readily achievable. Rural industry – rubber, palm oil, tin mining – was to be disrupted, and the Europeans driven off the land into the major towns. When that had been achieved Liberated Areas would be set up, as laid down in Mao Tse Tung's instruction manual. Long-term goals were less clear, but time enough to think about them when 'Stage One' was complete. The military wing of the Party, the MPABA, had successfully concentrated some 5,000 guerrillas in the jungle, in relatively sophisticated camps each capable of holding at least 100 and sometimes many more troops. These camps were carefully sited so as to be difficult for any security forces to find and attack, and yet strategically well placed to pursue their campaign objectives, while retaining access to their logistical support in the towns and villages.

This support was provided by the Min Yuen, which was already an active and committed under-cover organisation, at its peak numbering as many as 150,000 members penetrating nearly every Chinese community, town, village and *kongsi* in the Federation. It was intended that the Min Yuen should eventually provide the alternative government when the British administration crumbled, but in the meantime its function was to produce intelligence and supplies, as well as the recruits that would be needed to make good the inevitable MPABA casualties as the campaign progressed.

Directing this campaign, the Party and the Military High Command came together in an interlocking organisation of Committees and headquarters which may have been involuted and bureaucratic, but was in place and working. Morale was high, and the guerrillas basked in the reflected glory of the wartime success of the MPAJA as being the force which had taken on the enemy face to face and won. In addition, there were the triumphant forces of Revolution in China which could be called on for help, although there would surely be no need for that: before Mao had finally disposed of the Kuomintang, the campaign against the British in Malaya would be won. Against this façade of strength the British position seemed one of disarray and weakness. The Constitution of the Federation of Malaya had barely settled down after the debacle of the Malayan Union, but was already showing that it might have been purpose- made to frustrate decisive action. Virtually every policy had to be driven through each State's legislature, Sultans, whose capacity and commitment were often doubtful, had to be lobbied with great sensitivity, and State *Mentris Besar*, who owed their loyalty entirely to their Rulers, had to be persuaded that their distrust of the colonial administration was outmoded. That administration in any event was largely makeshift. When Gent left, the Chief Secretary, Sir Alec Newboult, had taken over as Officer Administering the Government, acting as High Commissioner until a replacement might be appointed. Alongside Newboult there was thus an acting Chief Secretary, besides an acting Attorney General and an acting Financial Secretary. Langworthy, the Commissioner of Police, had resigned due to ill health almost immediately after the Emergency had been declared, leaving the Police in the hands of an acting Commissioner. Almost without exception the leading figures in this stopgap administration were either tired and dispirited men, or temporary appointments pitchforked into office at short notice – often they were both.

Answering questions in Parliament in London, Lord Listowel, the Minister of State for the Colonies, had reassured Members that there was no cause for alarm, since both the Police and the Army were at more than adequate strength for the job – an appallingly complacent terminological inexactitude. In fact, the great majority of senior and middle ranking Civil Servants and Police officers who had spent such brutal and dispiriting years in Japanese concentration camps were still in poor health, and morale remained low. This was particularly true of the Police, where officers who had obeyed orders to stay at their posts in 1941 and had endured the miseries of the Railway or Changi in consequence, could hardly bear to be in the same room as those who had escaped, and 'had a good war'. Compounding these problems, both the Civil Service and the Police were under establishment, despite Listowel's mendacious assurances to Parliament,[1] and Police equipment fell woefully short of what was needed – there were few radios, arms were antiquated and there were no armoured vehicles.

On paper, the Army was in rather better shape. In June 1948 there were ten infantry battalions in the Federation: six battalions of Gurkhas, 1st and 2nd Battalions the Malay Regiment, and two British battalions, 2nd KOYLI in the North Sub district and 1st Seaforths in Johore. In addition, there was 26th Field Regt. RA, and the 1st Battalion Devonshire Regiment stationed in Singapore could be made available immediately, provided there was no trouble in Singapore itself. However, all the battalions were under strength, some seriously so, and numbers were not made up for over a year – often not even then. More worryingly, training standards were inadequate, particularly in the Gurkha battalions where the proportion of recruits was high.[2] Again, standards of equipment were not more than adequate, and a lack of armoured cars was an important deficiency.

Nor did the Army command structure hold out much hope for decisive and successful action. Lieutenant General Boucher had only taken up his appointment a few days beforehand, replacing General Wade. His previous experience had been entirely of warfare in Europe, a characteristic that he shared with nearly all his senior commanders, and one which would condition tactics and plans for many months to come. It is true that he had had some limited experience of operations against Greek partisans, but the lessons learnt from this were not to prove entirely helpful.[3] His own reporting lines were not clear: as Acting High Commissioner, Newboult was responsible for security and defence, yet Boucher reported not to him, but to GOC-in-C, Far Eastern Land Forces (FARELF), based in Singapore. In that context he was expected to be much more concerned with the worsening situation throughout South East Asia, and thus with the defence of Malaya against outside threats, than with internal security. These outside threats continued to absorb much of the attention of the Defence Staff until as late as the middle of the 1950s.

In the air there were similar weaknesses. The Air Officer Commanding could deploy one squadron of *Spitfires*, plus a squadron of *Sunderland* flying boats if anyone could think of an operational use to which they might be put against guerrillas in the jungle. And that was all, except for some *Auster* photo reconnaissance aircraft and a handful of *Dakota* transport planes. The AOC himself reported to the Air Ministry via an exclusively RAF chain of command that did not recognise any urgent need for co-operation with the Army – it seemed that little had been learned since 1941, when just this kind of chaotic lack of co-ordination had led directly to so many of the British failures.

Intelligence remained a crucial weakness. The Special Branch was efficient within its limitations but was pitifully small and of military intelligence there was no vestige. While Dalley could give a fairly good estimate of the numbers that Chin Peng had been able to mobilise in the jungle, he had little idea of how the MPABA was organised or where its units were deployed, let alone of future intentions: he compensated for these deficiencies, however, by putting forward vigorous suggestions about operations that the Security forces should undertake.

Direction from the Colonial Office was at the same time both detailed and woolly. No serious attempt to organise any constructive input or support from London was to take place until the formation of the Malaya Committee of the Cabinet in April 1950, nearly two years after the Emergency had been declared, and in the meantime a hopeful directive, 'to restore law and order' was the most cogent policy statement the administration had to work on. The original, rather vague, statements of intent, that the constitutions of the Malayan Union and then the Federation might eventually lead to independence, seemed to have been forgotten; many doubted that they had ever been meant to be taken seriously in the first place.

As the battlelines were drawn, the communities amongst whom the war was to be waged started to take up their positions. It was to be expected that the Malays might still be sullen and unco-operative. The Chinese were at best neutral, at worst anti-Government. There were virtually no Chinese in the Police or the Army, and the Rulers had resisted the recruitment of any but ethnic Malays to the Malayan Civil Service, something that was much resented, particularly by the Straits Settlements Chinese. Politically, such organisations as the Chinese Chambers of Commerce remained firmly on the fence – perhaps understandably. To add to the Government's problems, the success of the Communists in mainland China was closing the door on what had been one of the Government's most feared and effective sanctions against dissident Chinese, the threat of deportation.

With confidence, then, that the cards were stacked high in their favour, the regiments of the MPABA set out to bring in the Revolution. Estates and mines were attacked,[4] planters and miners were ambushed, Police stations were surrounded and captured. While there were some casualties in these actions, the effect on the Police was marked: all too often the demoralised policemen surrendered themselves and their armouries with depressing readiness. In Kedah it was found necessary to close Police stations that it would be difficult to defend, if only to cut down on the number of arms lost to the enemy.

Very early in the proceedings the MPABA had found it advisable to form what were rather vaingloriously called 'Blood and Steel' units – specialist companies whose stock-in-trade was terror. Not only did these units provide a useful outlet for those Party members whose enthusiasm for brutality, torture and murder was embarrassingly close to the pathological; they had already proved their worth in persuading reluctant comrades to go into the jungle and fight for the cause. Now that battle had been joined their skill was turned to executing 'traitors', and to intimidation and extortion, as they terrorised their compatriots into providing food, medicines and information. They also became involved in crudely effective fundraising through payroll robberies and raids on commercial organisations which were often Chinese-owned.[5]

Early in the morning of 13 July 1948, the MPABA returned to a favourite stamping ground, the coal mine at Batu Arang. Some of the attackers were uniformed MPABA guerrillas, led by one Siu Mah who would become famous later in the Emergency for a far more important action, while others were recognisably members of the mine's own work-force. The Police station in the town was attacked by one group while another combed the town itself, killing three Chinese who were accused of being members of the Kuomintang, together with two mine employees. A few minutes later the Kuala Lumpur train was held up at the railway station, while passengers and staff were robbed. In the mine itself, plant and machinery were blown up or smashed, a bus was ambushed on the road nearby and the driver shot and wounded, trucks were set on fire, and explosives and detonators were taken. The attackers, possibly 80 in number, suffered no casualties and withdrew successfully.

On the same day, in Kajang, Selangor, one man was murdered in the market in plain view, without anyone apparently noticing that anything untoward was going on. At Langkap in Perak the Police station came under fire in the small hours of the morning but the Communists were driven off after a brisk engagement. Estate bungalows and factories were attacked, ambushes were laid – and so it went on.

The most significant action of those early days took place at Gua Musang. Gua Musang – the name means 'Cave of the Civet cat' – is a small, remote railway township in Ulu Kelantan, about 100 miles south of Kuala Krai. On the eastern side of the town stands Bukit Gua Musang, a sheer limestone massif towering over the town and railway track to a height of 400 feet. Apart from that there is little to distinguish the place from any one of hundreds of small rural settlements up and down the country. Even today it is totally remote. During the Japanese occupation it had become to some extent a 'safe house' for the guerrillas of the MPAJA because of its isolation, and because the population was almost entirely Chinese and therefore could be relied on not to co-operate with the Japanese; not that the Japanese showed very much interest in anything that went on there.

By the end of June 1948, the guerrillas' presence was brooding over the whole place once more. In the nearby village of Bertam the police had taken off their uniforms and were refusing to undertake any duties, while in Gua Musang itself the population had mostly fled some way down the river. Recognising that there was a threat of attack, the Police post had been reinforced to the tune of one Inspector and four constables, a total of 14 in all, armed with Sten guns, rifles and a couple of revolvers. To make good the lack of a radio set the *penghulu* of Pulai, the neighbouring township, was issued with a bicycle – quite where he was supposed to pedal, or whom he was supposed to tell if the MPABA did attack, is not at this remove quite clear.

The question is academic, in any case. On the morning of 1 July, when the MPABA did put in the expected assault, the *penghulu*, along with the majority of his fellow citizens, joined in the attack with some vigour. The Police put up a token resistance, but when threatened with grenades from the limestone cliff surrendered the post and its armoury. None of the Police were wounded, each was given a cup of coffee and a few dollars, and the battle was over. The whole story illustrates perfectly the appalling state of preparedness and Police morale at the time, and is in marked contrast to the countless examples of great gallantry shown in later months and years, very often by the self-same constables who performed so badly at the start.

Gua Musang was declared a 'liberated area' in accordance with Mao's precepts, and its new rulers set about doing what rulers all over the world have down since the dawn of time – they collected taxes. The locals were told, not that Gua Musang was the first of what should be many liberated areas, but that it was almost the last. The Communist triumph was all but complete, Kuala Lumpur had already fallen, and those *Spitfires* which by now were so busy in the air above the town were explained as Chinese aircraft, operating in solidarity with the Comrades. Five days later, with support from those self-same *Spitfires*, a combined force of soldiers and Police reached Gua Musang, there was a short engagement, and the MPABA contingent together with the not very military enthusiasts from Pulai were bundled into the jungle. The relieving force lost one officer and six other ranks killed. The MCP's first and only 'liberated area' had been unceremoniously and peremptorily returned to lawful government.

The defeat at Gua Musang was not the only reverse that the insurgents suffered during those first few weeks of the Emergency. Three days after the assault on Batu Arang, an informer tipped off the Police in Kuala Lumpur that there was to be a meeting of important Party officials near Kajang, about 18 miles to the south. At dawn the following day, 16 July, a Special Force patrol of 14 police, led by a very colourful British Superintendent called W F Stafford, found the place that the informant had described, a wooden hut half-concealed in *lalang* on a hillside about a mile outside Kajang. As the patrol approached the hut they were seen by a woman, who screamed, whereupon three men hurled themselves out of the hut, firing revolvers as they tried to scatter. They did not get far: two were shot and killed, the third wounded and captured. Inside the hut the Police found six women, some maps and a quantity of arms and ammunition. One of the dead men was identified as Lau Yew, the Chairman of the MCP's Military Committee and overall commander of the MPABA. His wife was amongst the prisoners. As Stafford took the steps needed to clear up after the action, calling forward transport for his prisoners, bagging up the arms and ammunition, and setting fire to the hut, his patrol was counter-attacked by a large force of Communists, perhaps 40 or more. In the ensuing fire-fight five of the women prisoners and the wounded man were killed, in circumstances that remain slightly baffling to this day. Lau Yew's body disappeared, and so did his wife. When Stafford and his tiny patrol charged the very much larger Communist force, the terrorists melted away, leaving three dead.

The death of Lau Yew was a bitter blow to Chin Peng and the military ecommand of the MCP. During the war Lau Yew had been one of the few truly competent military leaders in the MPAJA, and in the reconstructed MPABA he was the only senior official with military experience and ability – he was irreplaceable, and the organisation never fully recovered from his loss. Chin Peng had never been on active service in the jungle,[6] and relied heavily on Lau Yew to compensate for his own lack of knowledge and experience. Now he had to find someone else, and there was no one. From that day the Military Committee of the MCP withered.

As early as the end of 1948 – within only a few weeks of the start of it all – it was beginning to dawn on Chin Peng that the Revolution was not going to be the walkover that he and his colleagues had expected. At Gua Musang the Security Forces had shown a totally unforeseen speed of reaction and determination, and had demonstrated quite conclusively the inadequacy of the MPABA regiments when confronted by trained troops. Liberated areas were off the menu for the time being. The Communist campaign had been intense: by the end of 1948, during a total of 1,274 incidents, 149 members of the Security Forces had been killed and 211 wounded. Over 300 civilians of all races had been killed, while 90 were missing – but all this had been at a cost. During the same period 374 terrorists had been killed, 263 captured and 56 had surrendered.[7] The imbalance in this equation was worrying.

Rather more worrying was the lack of evidence that the attacks on estates, mines and rural communities were having the expected results. Rural life was not being broken up as predicted and with very few exceptions the planters and miners had armed themselves as best they might, fortified their bungalows, and stayed put. Clearly something was going wrong – it was time for a rethink.

CHAPTER EIGHT

'ALL OVER BAR THE SHOUTING'

The most important problem facing Chin Peng was that he had completely misread the situation. The picture of Communist strength and British weakness was superficial: what he had expected, what he had planned for, was a virtual walkover, and in that he was sadly mistaken. In some respects the Colonial Government *was* dangerously vulnerable, but those weaknesses concealed a vital underlying robustness. Firstly, there was the character and structure of the administration itself. Although in 1948 some officials were of poor quality, and many posts were vacant, the essential structure was sound. It was based on experience of colonial government throughout the Empire, and was a system that had proved itself over the centuries throughout the world. Officials were uncorrupt and many of them were later to demonstrate a high degree of loyalty and courage in carrying out their duties in the face of terrorism. The rather complicated Federal constitution and the relationship with the Sultans may sometimes have made decision-making and implementation a long-winded process, but at bottom each of the parties to government knew the rules: it was the British writ that ran. 'The British Adviser ruled and the Malay Ruler advised.'[1] In other ways, too, this rather peculiar constitution could be seen as a strength: because the appearance of power was retained by the Sultans, a large part of the population could be happy in the belief that colonialism sat lightly. They could look upon the British more as benevolent senior partners, rather than as foreign rulers to be deposed.

The position of the Malays was a trump card in the British hand. The Rulers found that the new Federal constitution was infinitely more acceptable than the defunct Malayan Union, and in a troubled world were not going to be rushed into any further changes for the time being, especially in the name of some illusory 'independence' that more probably meant the exchange of one foreign regime for another. They shared with their subjects a distrust and contempt for the Chinese that dictated that a Chinese-inspired insurrection of whatever political complexion would remain just that, an almost entirely Chinese phenomenon. While the Malays might have independence as a long-term goal, they had no wish to see the British merely replaced by the Chinese. Almost to a man they united against the MCP in support of the Government, which meant that something like fifty per cent of the population was committed to the defeat of Communism right from the start of the campaign.[2] What is more, this 50 per cent comprised not only the indigenous ethnic majority of the country as a whole, but also the native backbone of the Armed Forces, the Police and the Civil Service.[3] As a result, the Colonial Administration could in good conscience hold itself as representing the constitutional wishes of the majority, and the MCP's claim to speak 'for the people' was clearly specious.

To this position of constitutional and political strength the British administration could add other assets. For instance, if at the local level the administration had some difficulty in penetrating to the smallest villages and settlements, then there were the managers – of mines, plantations and other rural enterprises – who were able and willing to take responsibility for extending Government authority, often into even the most isolated areas. All spoke local languages such as Malay and Tamil, and many had military training.[4] However the Government found little initial difficulty in raising fresh troops and Police, to a number that substantially outweighed any effort that could be deployed by the MPABA. As a first step towards this expansion, an astonishingly large force of full-time, paid, volunteer Special Constables was raised and equipped in a very short time, a force which almost immediately did much to resolve the problem of static defence for a host of targets that might be vulnerable to assault by the MPABA, while not dissipating the military strength that was needed to seek out and destroy the insurgents in the jungle. Within a week of the declaration of the Emergency, regulations were published authorising the setting up of this new force. It was originally envisaged as consisting of about 15,000 men, but this figure was soon increased and within three months 24,000 men had been recruited.[5] To start with, virtually anyone who could pass the rather skimpy system of scrutiny set up by the Commissioner of Police was accepted, and the guards that were already being employed by planters and miners were swept up, as were former Volunteers, ex-Police and the Malay Regiment. Not all were of high quality – Harrison and Crosfield had drawn on the advice of Colonel Dalley to recruit guards for their estates from amongst some of the shadier characters in Singapore, and it was to take some time to unwind some of the problems caused by the rather original approach to their duties of some of these brethren.

In the meantime, all were grist to the mill, all were given some sketchy military training, by officers and NCOs seconded from the Army, by ex-Army personnel dug out of civilian jobs, and by the estate managers themselves. Arms were initially a problem, and issues were at first restricted to a pitifully low level, but all posts could be supplied with something, and it was not long before the problem was resolved by imports from the USA and Britain. Nearly all these volunteer Special Constables were Malays, an early indication of how the ethnic and cultural make-up of the Federation's population was to have a crucial effect on the campaign.

The regular Police, too, could be reinforced in much the same way, although the pace of expansion was slower. However, more recruits than usual could be accepted, and the rather leisurely initial training programme was speeded up, from a year to five months, so that by the end of the year numbers had risen to nearly 13,000.[6] One of the lucky circumstances that greatly helped the Government's unexpectedly decisive and vigorous response to the Communist declaration of war was the fact that earlier in 1948 Great Britain had yielded up her Mandate in Palestine. Apart from the relief that this gave to overstretched resources, it was to have a great effect on the British management of the Emergency, not least in the immediate availability of 500 ex-Palestine Police sergeants who could be recruited and posted as Police Lieutenants to knock the Special Constabulary into better shape. Their robust if rather unconventional approach to police work against terrorists had an immediate effect in boosting the efficiency and morale of the Special Constables, as well as the bar receipts in their local clubs.

The Army was just as vigorous in its response, even if still rather undirected. Even before Gent's declaration of a State of Emergency in June, two operations, PEPPER and HAYSTACK, had been mounted in the north to clear the rump of a Kuomintang force that had degenerated into straightforward banditry. Although these operations had been inconclusive, valuable experience of jungle patrolling and supply had been gained.[7]

In August 1948, 2 Guards Brigade, consisting of three virtually full-strength battalions, arrived in Malaya direct from the UK – a posting which gave some indication of the seriousness with which the situation was regarded, since this was the first time that any members of the Household Brigade had been deployed outside the British Isles in what was notionally peace time. Sadly, the provision for jungle and counter-insurgency training was abysmal in those very early days, consisting almost entirely of 'finding out by doing', and these new troops did not become fully operational until November, although their presence hampered the MPABA's initiative. Probably a more significant reinforcement was the arrival of 4th Hussars, whose armoured cars filled an important gap.[8] More reinforcements could be found, and soon were. However, true to the well-established British tradition of fighting a war with the weapons, strategy and tactics of the last, General Boucher embarked on a series of futile large-scale operations which achieved virtually nothing worthwhile, except possibly the acclimatisation and frustration of the troops involved. He compounded that failure by holding forth in committee about his intention to do such things as would be the terror of the earth.[9] While all this thrashing about in the jungle was going on, though, right at the beginning of the campaign, his subordinate commanders had adopted a much more successful technique: small bodies of locally recruited men, Police and Army, led by ex-Force 136 officers or Police with good experience of operating in the jungle, many of them with local knowledge of the terrain, likely camp sites and even of the Communist personnel they were fighting, were put into the jungle to harry the MPABA formations just where they thought they were secure. These 'Ferret Force' units each numbered about 14 or 15 men, were lightly armed and equipped, were prepared to subsist on very basic rations, and were proud of their ability to move relatively quickly. They usually operated against

MPABA units condiderably stronger than their own, and had some notable successes. However, in November 1948, after five months in which they had contributed almost the only effective aggressive activity by the Government forces, they were disbanded – for reasons that no-one to this day can plausibly explain.

The availability of ex-Palestine personnel also meant that some sort of shift could be made to put right the dreadful weakness in the Security Forces Intelligence organisation. Even before Gent's departure, MacDonald had been pressing for something to be done to put Intelligence on a war footing. When Langworthy, the Commissioner of Police, resigned within days of the declaration of the Emergency, Colonel W N Gray, the former Inspector General of Palestine Police, was available to replace him almost immediately, and he made it an urgent priority to try to strengthen the Intelligence operation. In the short term little could be done to tackle the lack of Chinese-speaking Special Branch officers, and this was to remain a problem for years. However, experienced military and Police Intelligence officers could be drafted in in the hope of getting the organisation right and setting in place the systems for analysing and disseminating information, officers whose experience against Irgun and the Stern Gang was unique.

Then, too, the economy of Malaya was thriving. By 1948 much of the damage done during the Japanese occupation had been made good, and growing world demand for tin and rubber meant that Malaya was becoming rich. This wealth had two effects: firstly, the average citizen was considerably better off than he had ever been before, and took a jaundiced view of Communist exhortations to make sacrifices for a more prosperous future; and, even more importantly, the Government had ample revenue to fund whatever was necessary to fight the war.[10] More than all these Government assets, though, the matter of morale has to be considered. At the outset of the campaign Chin Peng had been convinced that the resistance of the Colonial Government and the expatriate establishment would fold after a fairly short time. He looked to the way the Raj in India had collapsed just a year before, and could not believe that the British would be any more resolute in such an unimportant little territory as Malaya, especially since they had shown such incompetence and lack of will in the face of the Japanese attack seven years previously. But as has been seen, that was not all what had happened. In the event, Chin Peng was taken by surprise by the way that the expatriot civilian population in the rural areas had not reacted to terrorism according to the book – far from deserting the estates and the mines and flocking to the towns, they had armed themselves, fortified their bungalows and coolie-lines, and carried on.

The British Government, too, while still shilly-shallying in a way that was most unhelpful to those trying to deal with the crisis on the ground, had yet shown itself in general terms remarkably determined to restore law and order – there could be no question of abandoning such an important net dollar earner as the Federation of Malaya when Britain's economy was in such a mess. What's more, the public at home was in no mood to let the Communists have their way. The Cold War was already mobilising opinion, and there was none of that immediate television coverage that was to bring the horrors of the Vietnam campaign into American homes 15 years later. There seemed to be general acceptance of the idea that British soldiers might have to be committed to a colonial war, and even the National Servicemen who would have to bear the brunt of the battle seemed almost to relish the situation – active service in Malaya was certainly a better bet than counting blankets in Catterick or sitting in a cold wet hole on Lüneburg Heath.

To sum up, the Colonial Government's position was in some ways appallingly weak, but against these weaknesses there were some vital strengths to be set in the balance:

- in Malaya, civilian hearts and minds were more than 50 per cent won, and morale was much better than the MCP had believed;
- rapid expansion of the Security Forces to the required level was easy. The forces available were reliable, could be equipped more than adequately and could be trained very quickly to at least a minimum standard;
- capable and experienced leaders, administrators, officers and intelligence experts could be found and deployed readily – and what they decided to do could be made to happen (eventually);
- as far as anyone could be said to know how to deal with an insurgency, the British in Malaya had the relevant experience;
- the operation could be funded;
- the British Government at home, and the people, were determined to win.

Whether Chin Peng saw the British position in those terms or not is hard to tell. What he could not disguise from himself was that just as the British position of apparent weakness concealed some important strengths, so his own apparent strengths were offset by some crucial weaknesses. The army that he had led into the jungle was not anything like the effective force that its reputation claimed. It had proved distressingly difficult to mobilise the Old Comrades of the MPAJA, a large number of whom had never been motivated by the Communist ideology in the first place: they had fought in 1942 because they hated the Japanese, China's traditional enemy, not to bring in some half-understood Marxist millennium. Since the War many had been lost to prosperity and commercial success – in fact, of the estimated 5,000 guerrillas who went into the jungle in 1948, less than 1,000 had served with the MPAJA or had any training, or even experience of living in the jungle, let alone of fighting in it. The remainder had been recruited within the last three years from among the dissatisfied, the inadequate, or the very young. For the most part they were motivated by a confused mixture of envy and greed rather than by any burning desire to free their country, not that many of them in any case thought of Malaya as their country. However, even if the entire force been made up of wartime veterans things might not have been very different. The truth is that, in spite of its reputation, the MPAJA had not achieved anything very much – in fact, for the most part the Japanese had been able to ignore them.[11] Once in the jungle, the MCP and its field commanders had made little secret of the fact that the objective was not so much to defeat the Japanese as to prepare for the Revolution when it was all over. Much of the ordinary rank and file's time, therefore, was spent in camp, studying dialectic, singing rousing revolutionary songs, and just keeping house. Merely staying in being was a struggle, and it had become more and more necessary (and pleasurable) to resort to terrorism to extort from the Chinese villagers the food, medicines and information that they needed to survive, rather than court trouble from the Japanese. In this respect it is significant that, from the landings in the North to the end of the War, the Japanese lost a total of 2,300 killed in Malaya. During the same time the MPAJA executed 2,800 'traitors' – i.e. Chinese who failed to give them support.

The 1,000 or so MPAJA veterans who did go into the jungle in 1948 were thus a rather mixed blessing. At best they contributed experience of living and moving in the jungle, together with some commitment to the Revolutionary cause; at worst they brought with them an attitude of idleness and complacency, together with a tendency to see terrorism and brutality as a first resort whenever in difficulty. Sadly for Chin Peng, his subordinate commanders were not experienced or able enough to compensate for these weaknesses, and the death of Lau Yew so soon after the start of the campaign was the more sharply felt. The MPABA inherited too much of the old MPAJA's culture, and very soon poor morale was to become a major problem.[12]

When the Central Committee of the MCP decided to accept Russian encouragement and turn to violence, moving their 'regiments' into the jungle was not the only option, but it seems to have been the only one seriously considered. It did seem to draw on the experience of the military wing of the Party, however mistaken that belief may have been, but the decision reveals an awful sterility in Chin Peng's understanding and reflects a pedantic and uncomprehending attempt to apply Mao Tse Tung's precepts of guerrilla warfare in an environment where those precepts were totally inappropriate. Ironically, Mao's writings had always stressed that it was not possible to apply Russian solutions in China, yet Chin Peng and his colleagues saw nothing incongruous in trying to apply Chinese solutions in Malaya.

By early in 1949 Chin Peng had realised that his strategy was badly flawed, that the tool in his hand was blunt and ineffective, and his enemy was not to be defeated anything like as easily as he had thought. It was time to rethink everything. In March he convened another planning meeting in the jungle of Pahang, in a mood of much more sober consideration than the euphoria of nine months ago, and in April the Regiments of the MPABA moved deeper into the jungle, leaving the Min Yuen to keep up as much pressure as they could. The Security Forces noted the decline in the number of terrorist incidents, and took comfort: voices were even to be heard in 'The Dog' and in the bar at the 'Colosseum', saying that it was all over bar the shouting.

CHAPTER NINE

THINKING AGAIN

If proof were needed that Chin Peng tended to think as a bureaucrat rather than a guerrilla commander, it might seem to be provided by the first decision that flowed from the MCP's reappraisal: from now on the MPABA was to be known as the Malayan Races' Liberation Army (MRLA). However, what was apparently a typical piece of public relations irrelevance in fact showed that the MCP was beginning to recognise one of its biggest drawbacks, the essentially Chinese nature of the movement, to the exclusion of the Malays and other races. The old name, the Malayan Peoples' Anti-British Army, had been deliberately chosen to identify the revolutionary forces with the prestige of the wartime MPAJA, and that in turn had been designed to call up overtones of Mao's forces fighting against the occupying Japanese in China. Unfortunately what it did, though, was to remind everyone that not all the peoples of Malaya had supported the MPAJA, that to many it had been the MPAJA rather than the Japanese that had been the threat – not a very successful ploy when trying to position the revolution as a movement of the masses. Time was to show that just changing the name would not be enough.

There was also the need to do something about the poor standard of training and equipment. During the initial move into the jungle it had proved difficult to retrieve all the arms that had been stashed away, much ammunition had deteriorated and was unreliable, the guerrillas themselves had not adapted quickly to jungle conditions and were baffled and depressed by the problems of subsistence and movement. Big formations, sometimes consisting of as many as 300 guerrillas, had tried to manoeuvre and deploy, and had mostly failed. Many of the casualties sustained by the MCP forces in the early days of the campaign had been inflicted by small, aggressively-led Government squads, acting quickly and decisively, and it was clear that the MRLA would have to become faster and better led.

And then there remained the appalling problem of communications. Even if the MRLA had had effective radio, there would have been no possibility of establishing an efficient and secure net.[1] Any soldier who struggled through a day's march in the jungle with a heavy set on his back or with what seemed like a ton's dead weight of spare batteries in addition to all the rest of his arms and kit, only to find when the patrol bedded down in the evening that signals were completely blanked out and there was no way of getting into his company net, would be well placed to give a pungent if unscientific explanation of the frustration of trying to operate a radio net in jungle-covered hill country. In any case, even if the MRLA had been technically able to set up radio communications, it would have been only too easy for the Security forces to eavesdrop.

Telephones were also not an option, as there were none in the jungle, so the solution was to set up a courier system. Using the Min Yuen, that did not present too many problems at first. Messages could be carried by seemingly innocent civilians, passed from hand to hand, with all the panoply of cut-outs and dead-letter drops needed for security. Later, this courier network was to become very vulnerable to penetration by Special Branch, but in the early days, it seemed to answer well enough – well enough, that is, except for the unconscionable time that everything took. Delays were so bad that the system soon degenerated into virtual paralysis; operational orders could take weeks to get from Central to the field commanders and sometimes never arrived at all, while general directives and policy instructions could take as much as a year to penetrate to each Party member. The chances of organising well co-ordinated operations, bringing together enough guerrillas to ensure local superiority, and dazzling the Security forces with speed and certainty of manoeuvre, were nil. It was to prove an insuperable problem. Chin Peng's troops were deployed on their chosen ground throughout the country, yet he could not give effective command.

The solution found was to set quotas. Each unit commander was given a quota of activity for each month – so many trains derailed, so many ambushes, so many rubber trees slashed, so many planters or soldiers or policemen murdered, so many 'traitors' executed, and so on. In case there might be local reasons why it might prove hard to achieve the quota in one category, the unit commander could substitute incidents in another, so long as his overall total was fulfilled. If he could not murder enough planters then 'traitors' might be executed as an acceptable alternative. If his nerve failed him, so that he did not feel it was a good idea to attack the local Police station, then a few thousand rubber trees slashed would keep the books straight. Of course, it was no real solution at all, and was in effect an admission that central control was impossible. MRLA forces could not be concentrated against vital targets, and there could be no systematic pattern of guerrilla war, and attacks would effectively be random; the Revolution stood on the brink of the slippery slope that would end in hopeless terrorism. More and more it would be the Min Yuen that would prove the effective arm of the campaign. Much of what Chin Peng was thinking was revealed to the Security forces when the Special Branch got possession of a Communist publication, *Present Day Situation and Duties*, which constituted an appreciation of the problems facing the MRLA. It had been produced late in 1948, and in all probability the Special Branch saw it sooner than many of the MRLA's outlying units. What it demonstrated was the dawning of realism – the realisation that the MRLA was relatively weak, that the mobilisation had been chaotic and that units were only just beginning to achieve operational efficiency, and that the Security forces were not going to be easily overcome. As might be expected, confidence was expressed in the final outcome, especially since the international situation was favourable to the MCP's struggle, although it was noted that work amongst the Malays had not so far been successful. Determination was essential, since the struggle would be slow, painful and hard.

This reappraisal brought into focus another problem. By choosing to move his forces into the the jungle Chin Peng had brought into play one vital piece: the rural Chinese community that everyone called 'the squatters'.

Even before the War, landhunger amongst the poorer Chinese had driven many to squat illegally, on Malay Reservation land and in clearings hacked out of the jungle, eking out a living by small-scale farming, vegetable growing and rearing such livestock as pigs and poultry. During the War this movement on to the land had become a flood, encouraged by the occupying Japanese who saw in it some kind of solution to the Chinese 'problem', as well as a way of boosting food production. By definition, most of these squatter settlements were as remote as possible from authority, with poor communications with the rest of the community, and were miles from Police stations, schools, hospitals or civil government. Some consisted of two or three families living in primitive wooden shacks, without water or sanitation, others of larger groups, still in primitive wooden buildings but organised into something recognisable as hamlets or villages. All lived in constant fear of eviction. A measure of the size of the squatter problem is that in 1948 no-one really knew how many of them there were, but everyone agreed that the number was at least 400,000. Some estimates were as high as half a million – perhaps as many as a quarter of the whole Chinese population of the Federation, sprawling over vast areas of what was properly Malay Reservation land, or Forest Reserve, or land designated for mining and agricultural development. Many had even moved on to land that had been privately-owned plantation until felled by the Japanese.

Their very insecurity made the squatters deeply suspicious of authority, an attitude which was often warmly reciprocated by the District Officers who had to try to impose that authority. After the War the powers-that-be had shied away from doing anything about them, even though they were richly disliked by the Malays who saw their incursions and the speed with which they bred as the foundation of an alien peasantry that would soon dominate the countryside. The State Rulers and *Mentris Besar* were constantly putting pressure on the administration in Kuala Lumpur to do something about the squatters, and as much as anything it was the idea that they might be given equal citizenship that had led the Sultans to wreck the Malayan Union. Nevertheless, by the middle of 1948, little had been done. One or two Chinese Affairs Officers had written worried reports drawing attention to the growing problem and proposing solutions that were rather more sympathetic than the Malay Rulers' ideas, but that was that.

Once in their jungle camps, and separated from the urban communities of the western lowlands of Malaya, it was to these *kongsis* and squatter villages that the MRLA had to turn for food, medicines, information and recruits. On the face of it, the squatter villages were a natural constituency for the Communists, and Chin Peng could be confident that he would get the support that he needed. If he could not, he was in deep trouble – if the Security forces could block off that support, his strategic position would be dire. The whole campaign could turn on this: whoever dominated the squatters dominated the war. They had become the vital ground of the battlefield.

Present Day Situation and Duties made it clear that the MCP fully understood the importance of the squatters to their cause, and proposed that these 'rural masses' must be prodded into compromising themselves vis-à-vis the Security Forces, so as to provoke attacks and 'galling restrictions' that would turn them firmly against British imperialism. It was recognised that this policy would, in all probability, have to be forced on the squatters 'resolutely and ruthlessly', that in consequence the Party could not look to be popular amongst them, and that those Chinese who joined unsympathetic organisations would have be ruthlessly smashed. The pious hope was expressed, however, that not too many would have to be murdered. Some hope – here was a ready supply of 'traitors' who might fill the quotas of hard-pressed unit commanders. Not surprisingly, while the overall number of incidents fell for a while, the number of Chinese murdered held up remarkably. The importance of the squatters was not lost on the Government either. As the makeshift administration struggled to cope with all the decisions that had to be made in an impossible rush, discussion returned time and again to the problem of what to do about the squatters. With Gent dead and no permanent replacement for him apparently in prospect, MacDonald took a large part in the deliberations, and it was during these months that he went far to justify his appointment. He made an attempt to grasp the nettle of the squatter problem, and also imposed sound policy in resolving an early 'political' problem that was showing every sign of destroying the thrust of the Government's embryo plans before they were even under way. The new Commissioner of Police, Nicol Gray, fresh from Palestine, found himself battling with the Army for the direction of operations, and was glad to have a ready ally in MacDonald, who backed him vigorously in asserting that the Police must always be the directing force, whatever might be the weaknesses in Police strength and organisation for the time being. This concept, the supremacy of the Civil Power, was to be the guiding principle throughout the Emergency, even if at times it was unpalatable to soldiers such as Boucher, who tended to be understandably frustrated when they saw what little gains they had been able to make thrown away by idleness and incompetence amongst the 'Civil'.

New measures to help the Police were pushed through the Legislative Council with unprecedented speed. The Printing Presses Bill, which decreed that no newspaper could legally be published without a permit, was enacted in one day. Police powers of search, detention and controlling the movement of goods and people were strengthened. Powers of collective detention and punishment (Regulation 17D), and the deportation of detainees who could not establish Federal citizenship or prove that they were British subjects born in Malaya, were clearly designed with the prime object of bearing heavily on the Chinese community. Most draconian of all, the illegal carrying of firearms became subject to a mandatory death penalty.

Yet with all this agonising over policy, all this rushed legislative activity, what MacDonald and Newboult and Grey and Boucher found themselves facing over and over again was the urgent and ugly problem – what was to be done about the squatters? The Malay Rulers and their officials had few doubts. The squatters were a menace, with no legal right to be where they were. All that was necessary was to evict them, send them packing and burn all their *kongsis* so that they could not resettle. If they had nowhere that they might legally go, then the newly enacted regulations providing for deportation could be brought into play. True, many District Officers were exhibiting incomprehensible scruples about implementing a policy that would, in fact, not be very different from the terrorism so cheerfully advocated by Chin Peng, but surely the Army and the Police could be made responsible – where was the problem? On balance, however, MacDonald and Newboult preferred to explore less drastic options. More legislation was designed, and in particular the foundations were laid for a scheme of registration, under which all adults would have to carry identity cards. Much thought was also given to the possibility of recruiting more Chinese-speaking officials who might the more effectively bring Government rule to isolated areas. Useful measures, all of them, although none really getting to the root of the problem – but as yet it seemed that no-one was thinking of resettlement as an active policy.

While these deliberations were going on, the troops and Police on the ground were beginning to evolve their own approach, one that recommended itself hugely to the Malay Rulers, as well as to the other owners of land that was being illegally occupied. In the absence of any clear directive from above, and exasperated, no doubt, by the knowledge that they were dealing with people who were often active supporters of the MRLA, Army and Police squads were dispensing with such trivialities as the need for evidence and, quite literally, fighting fire with fire. Jalong, Lintang, Tronoh, Hailam Kang are among the names that appear briefly in the war diaries and incident books, names of squatter settlements and *kongsis* where the Police or Army, or combined squads of both, evicted the occupants and torched the buildings.

Perhaps the most notorious of these incidents happened at Kachau, in the Kajang Police District of Selangor. Kachau was quite a large village of its kind, with some 50 houses and about 600 inhabitants, established before the war, and with a well justified reputation as a centre for all kinds of trouble. There really is no doubt that the MRLA was finding very active support there. Even during the war it had been a refuge for guerrillas, arms had been dropped there in quantity and never been recovered, and everyone knew that there were MRLA units operating in the immediate area that depended on Kachau for supply and intelligence – as evidence, the Security forces had recently found packaging from shops in Kachau in a deserted MRLA camp.

During the night of 1/2 November 1948, guerrillas attacked Dominion Estate near Kachau, and burnt down the factory. Led by the OCPD, Kajang, the Police responded swiftly, and by first light on 2 November the village had ceased to exist. Official reports after the event did little to clarify what had really happened, being clearly aimed at covering up a brutal and illegal act, and it took a matter of years before the truth came out. There seems to have been no attempt at anything remotely like an investigation; in the pitch dark the Police surrounded the village, the OCPD called the villagers out and gave them 30 minutes to get their belongings out, and then the wooden buildings were set on fire. No matter that 30 minutes were nowhere near enough, and that many of the houses were still full of their owners' property when they went up in flames; such was the heat that everything that *had* been got out and stacked in the roadway caught fire as well, and by daybreak the villagers were all destitute. The OCPD's sympathy was not stretched, however. The villagers were brusquely told that they were now free to leave and that no-one was to return to Kachau. Conscious of a job well done, the OCPD went back to Kajang for breakfast, leaving the villagers to find their own solution to the problem of homelessness. Not all of them had been Communist activists, some in fact had been providing information to the Security forces. These must have felt much encouraged in their endeavours.

The OCPD was not commended for his action, and left the Police soon afterwards in rather obscure circumstances. His superior officer, though, did report that whatever the legality of what had been done, the operation was justified since it had had a significant deterrent effect. Instead of the compensation that some of the villagers were claiming, he recommended that anyone who made a fuss should be put in a detention camp.

Higher authority was less blimpish. Kachau was recognised as being nothing more than a reprisal, and the whole affair was seen as being dangerously counter-productive. The frustration of having to deal with such blatantly Communist settlements was understood, but illegal tit-for-tats were not the answer. Indecision could not go on: a clear policy to deal with the squatters, properly resourced, was essential.

Late in October 1948, four months after the death of Sir Edward Gent, with the problem of the squatters still unsolved, a new High Commissioner came to Malaya.

CHAPTER TEN

A WHITE KNIGHT RIDES IN

Sir Henry Gurney was a man apparently cast in the same mould as Sir Edward Gent – what John Buchan called 'being of the same totem'. A Wykehamist, aged 50 at the time of his appointment, he had served with distinction in the 60th Rifles during the First World War, being wounded just before the Armistice. After the War he had gone up as a scholar to University College, Oxford, and had then entered the Colonial Service, perhaps not the most sparkling recruit of his year, but with a good academic record and a passion for golf that never left him. Apart from a brief and not very happy spell in Jamaica he was to spend most of his time until 1946 in Africa, where he built a sound but unobtrusive career, culminating in his appointment as Chief Secretary to the East African Governors' Conference, based in Kenya. During this time he gained a reputation for tact, sound judgement and quiet competence, and particularly drew respect for his ability to get on with politicians, soldiers and civil servants alike, however their demands might conflict. All who dealt with him noted his imperturbability, although his Wykehamist reserve and good manners were often interpreted as diffidence and remoteness.

Then, in 1947, he was plucked from the comparative calm of Nairobi to become Chief Secretary in Palestine, and found himself once again trying to deal with both the 'Civil' and the Army, at a time when terrorism was reaching a peak, no-one had very much idea about what was to be done, and the soldiers, particularly, were in a mood to go out and wreak bloody vengeance on anyone they could find for their sufferings at the hands of the Stern Gang and Irgun. Sir Alan Cunningham, the High Commissioner, himself a soldier, was on record as greatly admiring the way in which Gurney managed to restrain the field commanders from taking military reprisals for terrorist outrages. His knighthood was richly deserved.

After the tragic air crash that killed Sir Edward Gent there was a brief period of consternation in the Colonial Office, and then Gurney, who was on leave following the end of the Palestine Mandate, was asked to accept what must have looked suspiciously like the poisoned chalice. He did not want it. What he wanted was to go back to an academic life at Oxford, where he had been offered the chance to supervise courses for Colonial Service probationers. His hesitation was the more understandable since there were already undercurrents of opinion suggesting that he was not the right sort of man for the job, that what was needed was a soldier – the problem was seen by many as being largely military, especially in Army circles. In time, though, he overcame his doubts and accepted that his duty lay in Malaya. Despite his brand-new stamp of honour as KCMG, there must have been many moments over the next three years when he doubted whether he had made the right decision.

On the face of it, then, a man cast in the same traditional Colonial Office mould as Gent, in fact Gurney was very different. His bent was not truly academic, he was a pragmatist with recent experience of riding the troika of Army, Police and Civil authority at a time of brutal terrorism, and with an excellent track record of dealing with complex political and social sensitivities. Once again, Palestine had proved a wonderful source of talent for the Colonial Office. It is hard to believe that a better qualified man could have been found to meet the challenge of that hour.

However, if Gurney had not wanted Malaya, by the same token the Malay Rulers didn't want Gurney. They were worried that, coming from Palestine, he would see the Malayan problem as simply being one of reconciling the differences of two communities, the Chinese and the Malays, and granting them the same equivalence as had been given under the British Mandate to Jews and Arabs. While they did not go so far as to boycott Gurney's inauguration as they had Gent's, they made it clear that he was going to have to work hard to dispel the clouds of suspicion about British intentions that still swirled around the royal *istanas* up and down the country. No-one knew what the Chinese community really thought about his appointment, if only because there was not as yet any coherent representation of anything that could be described as a Chinese community. The British civilians held their breath – at least now there was a proper High Commissioner again – but Gurney was very definitely on probation.

In this atmosphere of distrust, Gurney looked to his priorities. The military situation seemed to be relatively under control. Troop reinforcements were flowing in, and, despite the naïve and primitive approach to training, the newly arrived soldiers were becoming more effective, learning the hard way at least some of the skills of living and moving in the jungle. Although the number of terrorist incidents remained disturbingly high (in the region of 50 a week), they were noticeably lower than at the beginning of the campaign earlier in the year, and General Boucher could claim this reduction as evidence for the success of his plan. At the end of July 1948, Boucher had explained to the Legislative Council what he intended to do, and it seemed to make sense. As more troops became available, he planned to pit them against the MRLA concentrations, breaking these up, and forcing them further back into the jungle. Then the Army, acting in concert with the Police, would follow them in, harass them and keep them on the move, denying them food, rest and recruits, and making them split up into ever smaller units. Sadly, the larger forces that Boucher had at his disposal allowed him to continue to try to achieve these very logical objectives by mounting large sweeps, sometimes involving formations at nearly brigade strength, even though some at least of the officers on his staff were beginning to appreciate that operations on this scale were largely ineffectual. In truth, although some casualties were inflicted on the MRLA, particularly on the 4th Regiment in south Johore, they were seldom more than a handful and were totally disproportionate to the effort required. For the most part, the MRLA units that were the targets shifted camp until the noise and strife were over, and then went back to their old stamping grounds – if their camps had been destroyed, a couple of days were all that it took to build a new one. Of course, one of the major weaknesses in the Security forces' approach was that locating their targets was almost always a matter of guesswork, as the vestigial military intelligence could provide virtually no accurate picture of terrorist dispositions. Still, big operations gave the comforting illusion of activity, and, in any case, what else was there to do? In these circumstances, the dissolution of the successful 'Ferret Forces' appeared a sorry mistake. Boucher's concentration on big formation operations may have set back the development of truly effective counter-insurgency tactics by several months, if not years.

In point of fact the MRLA Regiments were beginning to realise that it was no bad thing to go along with Boucher's plan and split up into smaller units of their own accord. With Chairman Mao's primer in hand, Chin Peng was still issuing policy directives that hankered after concentration of his forces, to the point where battle might be offered by large bodies of formed troops, as was later to be the case in Vietnam. However, the awful problem that the MRLA had with communications, as well as the poor quality of training and equipment in the individual units, meant that to the local commanders there was no attraction in trying to deploy and control the size of groups that Chin Peng wanted, the sort of formations that had originally attacked Batu Arang and Gua Musang. They were just too cumbersome. Smaller units could move faster and with less chance of being gripped, and they could be just as effective as companies of two or three hundred in most of the actions which the MRLA was trying to carry out. An advantage was that they would be less vulnerable to attack from the air: the skill that the Army and the RAF were showing in joint ground support actions had come as a considerable shock to MRLA officers who were totally ignorant of any concepts of the use of air superiority. The Air Officer Commanding had newly had his hand strengthened by the arrival of *Beaufighters* from Ceylon, and these, with the handful of rocket-firing *Spitfires* already in theatre, had caused considerable mayhem amongst MRLA units that had been caught on the move in the open. (Some of the casualty figures claimed for these undoubtedly successful actions have to be taken with a considerable pinch of salt, however. It was always MRLA practice to carry off their dead whenever possible, and some confident claims clearly owed more to statistical probability than to actual body counts.)

To Gurney, then, it looked as though the Army's strategy was developing in the right direction, and he could leave soldiering to the soldiers. The Police were a different matter. Although in policy terms Gray was entirely right to insist that control of the counter-insurgency effort must be a civil concern, with the Army acting in aid of the

Civil Power, in practice he was on very thin ice. The Police were in a mess. It was not just a question of numbers, equipment, training, or dispositions. Morale was so low that it was not possible to maintain Police posts in vulnerable areas. In four months of confronting armed terrorism senior officers had not buried their differences, and while some junior officers at OCPD level had shown themselves ready for some highly suspect operations, there was reluctance to get involved in aggressive and well directed activity. Gray had found to his horror that many Police stations still had the comfortable habit of closing at six o'clock every evening, to reopen the following morning at eight, and in some places they even closed for the weekend as well. The whole culture was wrong. When Boucher and his soldiers argued that they should be making the decisions, it was hard to convince anyone that control should continue to lie with the ramshackle and dismal operation that Gray had inherited, but at this point there was little that Gurney could do to put things right. He could sympathise with Gray and insist that the policy of Police primacy in the direction of affairs must stand, but beyond that it was up to Gray himself. The equipment that he had demanded, especially arms and radio, was beginning to arrive. Police recruits were flooding in, and training programmes were being streamlined to bring the new men – and women – into active service just as quickly as possible. Only time and leadership would dispel the accidie that frustrated so much of what the Police were called upon to do. Gray was a hard enough man to do what was needed, and was best left to get on with it, at least until other matters had been dealt with. At this point, neither Gurney nor Gray appear to have recognised the need to do something about the appalling gaps that persisted in the Security forces' Intelligence operations.

These considerations left the squatter problem at the top of Gurney's list of immediate priorities. Even before Gurney arrived in Kuala Lumpur to take up his appointment, it had been recognised that the problem of the squatters could not be swept under the carpet much longer. In July, the British Adviser in Kedah reported that the Malay authorities were getting rather more than restive about the lack of action being taken against people who were mostly roosting illegally on land which was designated as Malay Reserve. The Sultan and his *Mentri Besar* were mainly concerned, he said, that the Chinese, who already dominated the commercial life of the State, should not be allowed to dominate the rural life as well, and the fact that the squatters were supporting the Communists only lent urgency to their fears. They wanted them out, and that meant right out – off the land and out of Kedah. Resettlement was not a possibility.

The Adviser on Chinese Affairs in Pahang submitted a report in the same month, making many of the same points, but recommending a much less trenchant solution. It was important that the rights and aspirations of the Chinese should be recognised, they must be treated with considerably more sensitivity than heretofore if they were not to be driven irrevocably into the Communist camp, and some sort of resettlement that offered them security of land tenure was the only way forward.

In his report to the Legislative Council on 27 July, Boucher took up a not dissimilar position to the British Adviser of Kedah. Quite accurately, he assessed the role that the squatters were designated to play in Chin Peng's plan, and promised greater toughness in dealing with them. However, he did not specify what form that toughness was to take, and as has already been seen, some at least of his subordinates interpreted his intentions as giving them licence to go outside the law. Not that they really had to. Under the new Regulations clearances were perfectly possible within the law, and both the Police and the Army found that they could apply Boucher's 'get tough' policy with undiminished enthusiasm, provided they took care to avoid too much scrutiny by the civil authorities. HQ, Malaya, went so far as to issue orders that once a decision to evict had been taken, the civil authorities were *not* to be informed. For the Army, the squatters were the enemy, and to be treated as such. There is just a suspicion that some soldiers were beginning to see the civil authorities in the same light. Squeezed between the doves and the hawks, and seeing that endless agonised discussions and reviews were getting nowhere, MacDonald had eventually seized on the politician's solution, and proposed setting up a committee to examine the whole question and make proposals.

When Gurney arrived, he found that this Squatters Committee had already started its work. It sat under the chairmanship of the Chief Secretary, Sir Alec Newboult, and consisted of nine officials, one Chinese, three Malays, and five Europeans, an intriguing balance. Sadly, in the best traditions of Malayan bureaucracy it appeared to be operating without any real sense of urgency, so, knowing that it was imperative to get things moving, Gurney gave Newboult a deadline of early in the New Year to complete the Committee's work and report. The pressure he was exerting was underlined almost at once by two events that stood out, even from the frightfulness that had characterised the Emergency right from the start. In one, on 19 January 1949, the Security forces moved in on the squatter *kongsis* and Chinese-owned mines at Hailam Kang, in Johore, destroying nearly 150 houses, and detaining over 600 people. Those who felt that this kind of draconian action was excessive, and counter-productive into the bargain, were confounded at least in the short term by the fact that the evictions worked. Hailam Kang had been used for some months by the 4th Regiment, MRLA, as a safe base area for its operations in South Johore, and it was quite clear that most of the squatters who were conniving in this were doing so of their own free will. The destruction of Hailam Kang forced 4th Regiment to disperse into smaller sub units, and subsequent aggressive patrolling by 1st Seaforths pushed many of these squads into leaving the area altogether. It did not take long for most of them to find their way back, however, when the first flurry of activity was over, and in the long run South Johore remained a hotbed of terrorist activity, with the MRLA able to reap the benefit of a strong sense of grievance and fear amongst the remaining squatters. Both doves and hawks could claim some support for their views, but it was beginning to dawn on the more farsighted District Officers and Police officers that a distinction was going to have to be made between villages such as Hailam Kang, whose people were actively supporting the Communist effort out of conviction, and the very many which were unprotected and whose villagers were forced to choose between co-operation and a particularly brutal death.

If some, at least, could be satisfied with what had happened at Hailam Kang, no-one could be happy with the other operation, which had been carried out a month earlier, on 11 and 12 December. A detachment of 2nd Battalion, Scots Guards, comprising 13 guardsmen under the command of a Lance Sergeant, had been patrolling the area round Sungei Remok Estate, near Batang Kali, about 30 miles north of Kuala Lumpur on the way towards Kuala Kubu Bahru. About mid-morning on Saturday, 11 December, they had fired shots at two men seen some 300 yards away on rising ground not far from a Chinese *kongsi*. As far as could be ascertained neither of the men was hit, and there was no positive identification of them as terrorists, although it was claimed afterwards that both were wearing some kind of uniform in jungle green. The area was noted for MRLA activity, and it is highly probable that the two men were terrorists, perhaps Min Yuen couriers.

After that rather inconclusive engagement the patrol continued on to its objective, a group of remote wooden buildings where rubber tappers and field labourers (both men and women) were quartered while they worked the area near the edge of the jungle. There was also a large hut which served as a store. The patrol rounded up everyone they could find, separated the men from the women, and set about interrogation. There is evidence that ammunition was found in the store, although some accounts say that only some detonators were found, kept, albeit illegally, for fishing. Either way, it is not surprising that the patrol commander was in a suspicious frame of mind, given the possibility that terrorists were in the area, and with the tension of the minor fracas earlier in the day still fresh in his mind.

By nightfall, the interrogations were still unfinished, and the Lance Sergeant's doubts had not been quelled, so the men who had been detained were shut in the store while the patrol posted sentries and tried to get some sleep. At dawn the following morning, the men were led out of the store. Twenty-four were shot dead; one, who had been held separately, survived. None of the women were harmed. The buildings were burnt, and the Army bulletin that was issued after the event reported laconically that 24 terrorists had been killed. In claiming to have carried out one of the most apparently successful actions in the campaign so far, the Army's report was unaccountably lacking in any kind of euphoria.

It is still not clear what really happened. The Police mounted an enquiry, which produced an anodyne report some ten days later that the men had been shot while trying to escape, although the question of whether they had been terrorists or Min Yuen was not addressed. (There was no evidence that they were: not one appeared anywhere on any Police 'wanted' list, although that might point to nothing more than the poverty of Police Intelligence at the time.) Even if it was true that they had tried to run away, that could not be construed as evidence of guilt, as was pointed out in the press at the time. Quite apart from the normal Chinese fear of anyone in authority, they had every reason to be terrified of the troops – they had been grilled for hours, and, according to some of their families who were not far away, some had been threatened by having unloaded weapons put to their heads and the triggers squeezed, a process now recognised as mental torture.

Overwhelmingly, however, the suspicion has to be that they were *not* shot while trying to escape, but were killed in cold blood. It is difficult otherwise to explain how it came about that all 24 were killed and none were wounded, despite the rather unconvincing lecture delivered to the Press afterwards by a senior Army officer about the effect of high-velocity weapons. No charges were brought against the sole survivor, who for some reason had been segregated right at the beginning, and who died some years later without giving his version of events. The families, who had not been far from what happened, later told various stories, some startlingly lurid, of earlier ambushes and killings, and arrests of Min Yuen smugglers, of detonators accidently set off by burning buildings, and of panicking troops thinking they were under fire and blazing away uncontrollably. Much later, on 1 February 1970, *The People* published a story in the wake of the American massacre at My Lai, which claimed that the report of an attempted escape was a cover-up, and that the 24 men had indeed been murdered in cold blood. *People* reporters found ex-Guardsmen who had been on the patrol to swear that this was so, though in these days of chequebook journalism even that kind of evidence has to be considered suspect, to say the least. But maybe – maybe this was the atrocity that has been claimed. At best, it seems to have been a ghastly mistake, the result of poor intelligence compounded by inadequate leadership and inexperienced and badly-trained troops who were deployed without any clear idea of what their aim was meant to be. At worst, it was all that it was claimed it to be, a brutal and callous reaction to men who, incomprehensibly, did not speak English, and whose fear seemed like dumb insolence. Either way, incidents like this, at Batang Kali, and those at Kachau and Hailam Kang, demonstrated very clearly that there needed to be a total reappraisal of the attitudes and policies of Government and Security Forces towards the rural Chinese communities. The Army and Police needed a definitive statement of aim, clear definitions of what might or might not be done, and senior officers must be made to accept responsibility for seeing that orders were carried out meticulously and with sensitivity. Above all, the political and social nettles of the squatter *kongsis* had to be grasped or those Chinese who were not actively committed would be driven into Chin Peng's camp. Batang Kali must not be ignored, even if it was, thankfully, a unique stain on the British record during the Emergency.

The report from the Squatters Committee could not be delayed, nor was it. Despite the inauspicious circumstances in which the Committee was set up, and the pressure under which it had to operate, the report was produced with admirable speed; and when it was submitted it constituted the most farsighted and significant policy proposal put forward at any stage of the Emergency. It was to condition the course of the entire campaign in virtually all its aspects, military, social and political, and in its acceptance and wholehearted application it was to plant the seeds of the victory that were to take so many weary years to come to fruition. It was also, be it said, a blueprint that would excite the interest, admiration and almost total lack of comprehension of most of the other powers involved in fighting Communist insurgency elsewhere in South East Asia for many years to come.

What the Committee proposed, in summary, was that wherever possible squatters should be resettled, and resettlement should ideally take place where they already were. Where resettlement was not possible in the existing area, for legal or technical reasons, then an alternative site should be found as near as possible to the original location. The important thing was that the resettled squatters should be given a secure legal title to occupy the land, and that the new villages should be a substantial improvement on the *kongsis* that were being replaced: they were to be provided urgently with Police stations, schools, clinics, water and electricity and, most importantly, with a high level of security. That entailed fencing and security lights, and as soon as possible the villagers were to be given the means of defending themselves by the raising and arming of a Home Guard. Potentially loyal squatters were to be offered the chance of a peaceful livelihood free from intimidation and administrative measures must be taken to reassert Government authority, especially by appointing more Chinese speaking officials and liaison officers. Squatters accepting resettlement should be helped with the movement of private property, chattels and livestock, and where it was not possible for them to take everything with them compensation must be paid for what had to be destroyed. Only if resettlement was refused should squatters become liable to summary eviction, with deportation (under the pseudonym 'repatriation') remaining the ultimate sanction.

Given the climate of opinion at the time, the legal situation and the sheer cost of such an undertaking, the proposal was an incredibly bold initiative. Until then, the Government and the Police had been prepared to contemplate the eviction and detention or deportation of up to 20,000 squatters. Now the States were being asked to move and rehouse 20 times that number. To the State governments the whole idea was quite quixotic: even if there had been a scintilla of willingness to cede title of good agricultural land to unwelcome immigrants, they were not prepared to accept the responsibility of putting the resettlement programme into action, for it was on the State governments that the main burden was to fall. Although the Federal Government might help with some of the costs, the Army and the Police would provide trucks to move people and their *barang*, and armed guards to provide security during the move itself, that was only the least part of it. The civil authorities would have to provide construction materials for the villages themselves, besides finding school teachers and medical dressers, sourcing good quality water, building chain link and barbed wire security fences, recruiting and appointing Chinese liaison officers, engineering roads and buying and installing electrical generators: doing all the thousand and one things, in short, that would make all the difference between success and failure for these 'new' villages. The new High Commissioner might endorse the plan, the policy itself might be imaginative, farsighted and statesmanlike, but those of the Rulers who were not stunned were appalled.

Four months after the report was published not a thing had been done, and Gurney was reduced to writing to each *Mentri Besar*, pleading for action and threatening reductions in military operations if things were not speeded up. Still there was a deafening silence, and Gurney was forced to accept that if his resettlement policy was to work he himself would have to drive it through. With the awful example of MacMichael before him, he realised that browbeating the Rulers would get him nowhere, and that what he faced was a tedious programme of negotiation, cajolery and tactful pressure. It was going to take a long time; even Gurney could not have thought that it was going to take the rest of his life.

CHAPTER ELEVEN

THE DESCENT INTO TERRORISM

Gurney had taken on a mammoth task in trying to negotiate and implement the resettlement programme – it was not even as though that was all he had to worry about. There was so much that must be tackled besides, in the field of emergency legislation and administration, quite apart from the thousand and one things that made up the day to day business of government. For example, one thing that had to be dealt with urgently was the condition of the agricultural workers on the larger estates. The security of the tin miners and planters themselves was being improved at least to some extent, but what about the workers? Most European-owned estates housed their labourers and tappers in small groups of buildings dispersed throughout the rubber, so that they could be near their tasks: typically a division of, say, 4,000 acres might have a main factory and office site, and as many as ten or more different line-sites, housing in total perhaps 400 workers with their families and live stock.[1] Spread out like this, and without perimeter fences or guards, they were just as vulnerable to Min Yuen and MRLA pressure as were the squatters, and the only answer was to concentrate them in newly-built line-sites where effective security could be provided. Easily said and obviously right, but the estate-owning companies in the City of London had to be persuaded that it had to be done quickly, and, what is more, funded out of profit, as the Government was not going to pay.

Even when that battle was won, the conditions of the workers still needed to be improved in so many other ways. Larger line-sites meant that the newly-formed trade unions could justifiably call for schools and clinics, besides such basic things as clean water and reasonable sewage treatment. As prosperity returned, Tamils wanted temples, Malays expected mosques, all to be paid for by the estates, and all the workers looked for the daily rate of pay to be improved and maternity benefit to be paid. There was even talk of heady matters like provident funds! The harsh reality was that old-fashioned draconian and authoritarian management styles had done much to create the climate in which the Communists had found it easy to engineer mayhem, and there had to be a complete change of culture. Some employers were enlightened and realistically concerned, but for many these ideas were unfamiliar and most unwelcome. Coping with the Emergency and running their businesses at daily risk to their own lives were problems enough, without having to adapt to such dangerously new ideas. To be fair, there could be no denying the need to improve the security of the factories and line sites, and in fact tin miners and planters themselves had been forthright in condemning a Government policy that provided the managers with Special Constables and weapons while leaving the workers to fend for themselves. But costs on the estates were high as many still struggled to repair the damage of the war years, and welfare provision on the scale looked for would be hard to fund without eating into shareholders' dividends and capital investment programmes.[2] Legislation could be used to force the issue, but again Gurney knew that he faced a long campaign to persuade the European companies that they could help themselves by improving workers' conditions, besides shortening the war. Another call on his tact and persistence.

Much of what had to be done was going to risk alienating just those people whose support had to be gained if the Communists were to be defeated. An important part of the Government's strategy was to deny the MRLA food and medicines, and that meant rationing, as well as a host of irritating restrictions on the movement and handling of anything that might help to sustain terrorists in the jungle. New regulations had to be drafted, limiting individuals as to how much rice they could have at any one time, and laying down that where it was possible to organise communal cooking, all meals had to be cooked and eaten centrally – it was to be an offence to be in possession of anything more than a very small amount of cooked food and no uncooked food might be retained at all. Shops, too, would be limited in the amount of produce that they might hold and the Police had to be given powers to check stocks and demand records of transactions. Tins must be punctured before being sold, goods in transit by road must be in sheeted lorries travelling in escorted convoys, and vehicle checks and searches were to be carried out at road blocks at every town or village, down to the smallest. Even bicycles were to be searched by the growing army of Special Constables, since medicines and small quantities of rice could be hidden in crossbars or frames or in the battery space in the back of the lamp. It is astonishing what can be concealed in or on a bicycle, given the Chinese genius for contrapting. All these regulations were to be crucial to the success of the Government's campaign, but it would take time, hard work and patience before they could be effectively implemented.

It was now, under the aegis of Gurney's new administration, that two measures were inaugurated which were to turn out to be amongst the most effective deployed against the MCP and its supporters. The National Registration regulation required that everyone, male and female, over the age of 12 should register with the authorities, and thereafter must carry at all times an identity card carrying the individual's name, photograph and thumbprint. In fact, the decision to impose registration had been taken in September 1948, before Gurney came on the scene. However, perhaps because the move was bound to be deeply unpopular at first, as well as being cumbersome and difficult to implement, nothing much had been achieved, except in two areas: on the Thai border Chinese (only) had been registered, and in Penang, where the difficulties were almost non-existent, it was thought that all qualifying adults had been caught up. Once more, Gurney found himself having to inject some urgency into matters. Teams were sent out to towns, villages, estates and squatter *kongsis* to carry out a crash programme of registration, village photographers were recruited to produce thousands of photographs (which, like all passport photos, bore only a passing and coincidental resemblance to the subject), planters and miners were appointed as Registration Officers, and estate clerical staff were dragooned into doing the paperwork and keeping the records.

Predictably, the Communists reacted with fury. The people were subjected to a flood of virulent propaganda: registration would allow the Government to conscript men for forced labour or to fight, taxes would be raised, rationing and restrictions on movement and personal freedom would become oppressive. Villagers were threatened with reprisals if they registered, workers were rounded up and their identity cards taken and destroyed, buses were ambushed and the passengers' cards confiscated and burned (with the buses). When that was not enough to put a halt to things, photographers and Registration Officers were murdered, often with great brutality, and so were people caught carrying the hated cards. It has to be said that Chin Peng was fully justified in being dismayed by the move, as an effectively implemented system of National Registration would be a major setback for him and his strategy. Identity cards made food rationing possible – no ID card, no food. Identity cards would allow the Police to control the movement of people and goods, which meant that the freedom of movement of the Min Yuen and their sympathisers' was severely curtailed, which, given the MCP's reliance on couriers, was to become a serious problem. On a psychological level, National Registration was seen by both Government and governed as an important step in the reimposition of authority, redefining the responsibility that each had to the other. Perhaps most importantly, without Registration the resettlement programme could never have been possible. It was vital that Chin Peng should not be allowed to strangle the National Registration scheme, and the Government's eventual success was the first real victory over the MCP.

The other measure that was introduced which was to prove so effective later in the campaign was the offer of bounties for the surrender, capture or killing of members of the MRLA, and it was, in a way, the product of a misapprehension. The fall-off in the number of incidents that followed Chin Peng's reappraisal exercise during the first few months of 1949 had convinced many on the Government side that the battle was well on the way to being won – MacDonald even went so far as to claim that the MRLA had already in effect been defeated, since their military aims were no longer achievable. A copy of an unusually frank appreciation of the MRLA's position, 'Our Opinion of the Battle', was found in a hastily vacated MRLA camp, and British Intelligence was much encouraged to read in it that Central seemed to be losing confidence. The appreciation said bluntly that the Communist campaign so far had been poorly planned and directed, popular support had not been aroused, and the

Security forces were being unexpectedly successful in discovering and destroying MRLA base camps. Other documents such as diaries that were captured in various operations during the early months of 1949 painted a similar picture of despondency amongst the Communist foot soldiers, and the Government's thoughts turned to how to cash in on this seeming war weariness. Terms for surrender began to be discussed.

It was out of these discussions that arose the decision to offer cash bounties to anyone who could engineer the surrender, capture or killing of named members of the Communist hierarchy. The amounts to be offered were relatively small, at least by comparison with the tariff which proved so attractive in later years,[3] and members of the Security forces were expressly excluded from getting any rewards under the scheme, but, even so, the principle was hotly argued. Some were deeply hostile, on ethical grounds, to the whole notion that money might be paid to people, in all probability themselves guilty of terrorism, to betray their leaders and associates. The pragmatists argued, on the other hand, that, however repugnant it might be to pay money to criminals to do what the law and their duty to society required of them in any event, if any of them could be persuaded to desert, and bring about the demise of any of their colleagues into the bargain, then the squalid means were justified by an end that surely was devoutly to be wished. In the end, the pragmatists won and although no offers were published until September 1949, bounties became an important tool in the psychological battle throughout the rest of the campaign, and brought about some astonishing results.

About this time, one other far-reaching decision was taken: from now on the enemy were to be known as 'Communist Terrorists' – 'CTs' for short.

Meanwhile, on the ground the campaign continued, although some subtle shifts were just beginning to become apparent in the way that both sides were tackling the battle. From time to time the MRLA still tried to engage in big formation actions (200 or 300 involved at a time), but increasingly they were coming to rely on much smaller units, and finding some success.

One thing that was happening was that the individual guerrilla was getting better at his job: a very high percentage of the 4,000 or so men and women who had gone into the jungle for the first time in early 1948 were quite unprepared for what they had to face, and were lacking in anything but the most basic skills in weapon handling, field-craft or tactics. Most were urban Chinese, and started by being as frightened of their new environment as they were of the Security forces. Now they were becoming used to living and moving in the jungle, their skill in field-craft and concealment was approaching excellence, and their battle procedures and drills were getting very practised. In the matter of setting ambushes and booby traps they were becoming lethally imaginative. They had learnt, for example, that it paid to ambush from an extended position along one side of a track or road, so that the whole length of a column or convoy could be engaged at one time, rather than the first two or three men or vehicles only. Breaking away from the terrorist fire positions, the ambushed troops would then find themselves amongst the booby traps that had been concealed on the other side of the track for just that purpose – sharpened bamboos were particularly effective, since once the unfortunate policeman or soldier had impaled himself, the stakes would flex to hold him, and inflict still worse injury and pain.

At this early stage of the Emergency the Security forces were prime targets, particularly when moving in soft skinned vehicles on relatively narrow roads and tracks, where the undergrowth extended right down to the verges. In one harrowing incident, 4th Hussars suffered a bad setback when they lost one officer and six troopers in an ambush near Sungei Siput. The situation was retrieved, to some extent, by 2nd Lieutenant John Sutro, who, at 19, was very newly commissioned and had only arrived in Malaya two weeks beforehand. Twice wounded, he engaged the enemy, and managed to extricate the remainder of his force, killing six Communists in the process – he was awarded the MC. In the short term, the effect of such incidents on Army morale was not good, however, and it came as a shock to many to realise that this war was going to be real; senior regimental officers and NCOs who had survived the War in Europe and now had to face all the strain again, instead of returning, as they might have hoped, to peacetime soldiering, sometimes found it hard to make the adjustment.

Later, the Police suffered a similar reverse, in a carefully prepared and most professionally executed ambush on a winding road in Negri Sembilan, on the way to Jelebu. Seventeen police were killed and nine wounded, including the two British Police officers. They were the victims of one of the larger operations that the MRLA were still carrying out: about 100 guerrillas were involved in the action, and, as far as is known, suffered no loss.

One skill that the guerrillas had learnt from Force 136 officers during the war against the Japanese was derailing trains, and the MRLA and Min Yuen resumed the practice with some enthusiasm and not a little success, at least to start with. In fact, it is not particularly difficult to derail a train, especially in countryside like Malaya, where the line runs for long distances through lonely, remote spaces which give saboteurs almost unlimited scope without much chance of their being disturbed in their work. Explosive is the most effective tool, of course, and can achieve the most gratifying results when applied carefully and knowledgeably to appropriate bridges and suchlike, but all that is really necessary is to remove a section of rail; since the MRLA could usually rely on the active help of Malayan Railways plate-laying workers who lived along the line, these derailments were an easy way of fulfilling the quota. An ambush by the side of the track would almost always cause a lot of casualties among the frightened passengers trying to escape from the wreckage, and there would probably also be a fire to help things along the way.

Greater reliance on the Min Yuen, operating in relatively small bands from villages and *kongsis*, to keep up the pressure, while the MRLA units regrouped and retrained deeper in the jungle, meant that the character of many of the incidents changed as well. Planters continued to be attacked, and many were killed. Planters remained a soft target, since however well guarded they might be by Special

Constables accompanying them on their rounds, the very nature of their job required that they should risk going to the dangerous parts of their estates, often miles away from help of any kind, right up to the jungle edge. Much of their work had to be done on foot, in any case, away from the limited protection afforded by a vehicle, and it really was not much help for the pundits to tell them that they must vary their routine. Tappers had to work their tasks on a regular, predictable pattern, and if you were going to supervise tappers, you had to be there when the tappers were working, so it did not take a high level of Intelligence amongst the terrorists to guess where a planter who had been targeted was most likely to be vulnerable. All any planter could do was to try to keep his eyes open, to stop his Special Constables from dawdling or going to sleep on their feet, and to hope that if anything happened there would be a split second in which he might find some kind of cover. One favourite CT trick was to fell a tree across one of the laterite gravel tracks that served as estate roads, and roll grenades under any vehicle that stopped, shooting up the occupants as they tried to get away. Unfortunately, fallen trees are not uncommon on rubber estates in the normal course of things, and the effect on the nerves of driving round the corner and finding the way blocked can be imagined. Most planters became very expert at driving quickly in reverse, but once back round the corner the question still had to be answered: what had brought the tree down, terrorists or termites?

The pressure on squatters, estate workers and the general public was no lighter. In headquarters and directorates up and down the land, the statistics of incidents were studied with all the dedication of investors scanning the *Financial Times*, and even small decreases in the numbers were hailed as successes by the officers who were trying to interpret the everyday patterns of conflict. But behind the bland statistics lay a picture of ordinary people quite literally fighting for their lives, and suffering appalling atrocities in the doing of it. On one estate, where tappers had refused to pay levies to the Min Yuen, three children were dismembered with *parangs* as their parents were forced to watch. More would die in the same way if the tappers persisted in their obstinacy, they were warned. More children were killed in Johore, some shot, one eight-year-old burnt to death with her family, to encourage others to toe the party line. The superintendent of the Serendah Boys Home for Orphans was murdered and the building burnt down, photographers who had helped with Registration were slashed and left in the sun to die, one *penghulu* who had showed insufficient enthusiasm for the cause had both arms crudely 'amputated' with a *parang*. At Kampar a grenade was tossed, apparently at random, into a circus tent: four died and 44 were wounded, all civilians. Three more died and several mourners were wounded when a burial at a Chinese cemetery was booby trapped. Apparently pointless murders were commonplace. Tappers on isolated tasks would be found with their throats cut, contractors who were supplying labour to estates were abducted and only found two or three days later when the smell led the Security forces to the trees to which they had been tied before being delicately sliced to ribbons and left to bleed to death.

The relish with which the Communists adopted terrorism and brutality, and directed them so much towards what ought to have been their own supporters, stemmed from a strange mixture of factors. It was partly habit: that was what the MPAJA had done during the War, and it seemed to have been successful then, so why change a tried technique? It was in part considered policy to cow the masses; it was to some extent the expression of a pathological cruelty that marked so many local commanders, who clearly enjoyed what they were doing very much; and it was partly because terrorism was beginning to seem the only alternative to continuing a guerrilla military campaign that was already proving much more difficult to win than anyone had anticipated, and was showing ominous signs of foundering. Overwhelmingly, though, the atrocities were a response to the attitude of the vast majority of the Chinese, rich and poor, *towkay* and coolie. Chin Peng's plan had depended on the masses rising in support of the Revolution, but they had done no such thing. Almost without exception they had climbed carefully and deliberately onto the fence and were waiting to see who would win the battle down below.

It was what Chin Peng, of all people, might have expected. Chinese cultural belief lays stress on authority that is exercised under the 'Mandate of Heaven', and it is impious to reject such authority. The belief was applied to the Emperors, for example, in a way strangely reminiscent of the Stuart doctrine of the 'Divine Right' of kings, so that treason or even disobedience were not just offences but sins. Shorn of some of its religious overtones the notion persists amongst the Chinese to this day, but in its practical applications it can give rise to a circular problem: it is a great sin to resist authority that is properly exercised under 'Divine Mandate', but how is it possible to tell who has the 'Divine Mandate' and who has not? The answer is that if someone is exercising effective power, it is prudent to suppose that they do it with divine support. Pragmatically, then, it means waiting to see who ends up as King of the Castle, and then being slavishly obedient to them; and until then, make no commitment, at least not publicly. Before the Chinese in Malaya could see who was going to win, it was always the case that they were going to stay firmly impaled. That was not just a problem for Chin Peng, it was a crucial difficulty for Gurney and the British administration as well.

Observers, looking at the progress being made by Government and MCP alike in these early months of 1949, might thus have concluded that both sides were floundering, but that, if anything, the Communists had the edge. However, although the picture was apparently one of confusion, by the middle of the year nearly all the elements of the plan that was eventually to defeat the Communists were already falling into place. The legal framework had been established, the powers to control the movement of people and goods were developing, National Registration had been imposed more or less successfully (and with it, the possibility of food rationing), and the long and weary task of resettling the squatters had been embarked on, however tentatively. Local security had been significantly strengthened by the recruitment of a Special Constabulary and some rather halfhearted attempts to form a Home Guard, and some thought had been given to the problem of concentrating the hearts, if not the minds, of the uncommitted by directing the Media somewhat shiftily more into the paths of righteousness.

One problem that had still to be solved was the problem of how to defeat the MRLA militarily.

CHAPTER TWELVE

LEARNING HOW TO WIN

At this point, in mid-1949, a year after the start of the Emergency, General Boucher believed that his tactics were working, and that he only needed more troops to finish the job completely. If he could be given the reinforcements he craved now, he was even prepared to talk in terms of troop reductions later in the year, and he was persuasive enough for these pleas to be listened to, if not sympathetically, at least with some effect.[1] 26 Gurkha Brigade was posted in, and 3 RM Commando Brigade had been promised, together with 12th Lancers, whose armoured cars were badly needed to help keep roads open for convoys of troops and food. Another battalion of the Malay Regiment was being formed, although shortage of suitable British officers and training difficulties meant that this 4th Battalion would not eventually become operational until as late as June 1950. On paper at least then, the Army was moving towards the establishment that by the end of 1950 would be deemed enough: 17 infantry battalions, six squadrons of armoured cars and one field regiment, Royal Artillery, that could be deployed as artillery or infantry as the need might dictate. As reinforcements flowed in, and the pins on HQ maps became more thickly clustered, Boucher was encouraged to find that, although many of the units under command were still seriously below strength, he now had just about enough troops at his disposal to fight the kind of war that he wanted to fight. Organised 'sweeps' on a large scale set whole brigades crashing through the jungle to remarkably little effect, with few contacts with the CTs and fewer still killed. Operations with code names such as RAMILLIES, BLENHEIM, SPITFIRE and SARONG were mounted against 5th Regt, MRLA, in North Pahang and Kelantan, and similar forays were made against 3rd and 4th Regts in South Johore (these two areas being seen as particular strongholds for the guerrillas), which achieved little more than harrying the CTs and moving them for the time being into the areas which had been denuded of troops to allow these operations to be mounted in the first place.[2] It was all really an illusion of gainful activity.

Meanwhile, however, something was happening that went almost unnoticed by Boucher and his subordinate senior officers, but was already having a most disturbing impact on the MRLA. The soldiers on the ground were learning how to fight and defeat the insurgents.

It was a slow process sometimes, and grew from the bottom up rather than being ordained by the brass hats. Some formations were better at it than others – well led and well motivated units tried harder, while others did little more than go through the motions. While some units were turning themselves into determined and lethal guerrilla hunters, others clung to the newly-rediscovered attitudes of peacetime soldiering, and even cancelled operations so that all officers could attend dinner nights.

In fact, what was happening was not so much the invention of something blindingly new, but the recovery of skills and experience drawn by the British and Indian Armies from campaigns in the 'bush' throughout the Empire, going back to the middle of the nineteenth century. The effectiveness of small, lightly-armed and fast-moving squads, the need to rely on junior leaders, the supreme importance of discipline, the development of specialised tactics and drills, the need for high standards of field-craft and weapon-handling in close country where engagements took place at point blank range; all these had been well understood by officers and NCOs who had fought in Africa, Northern India, Burma and countless other colonies, in low intensity wars from the Third Burma War of 1885 down to the major campaigns of the Second World War against the Japanese. In the strange, rather informal way that the British Army so often goes about its professional business this expertise had never been formalised as doctrine,[3] and officers had to rely on 'tribal memory' handed down from their seniors to supplement their own initiative. Sadly, much of this golden knowledge was lost when the end of the Raj severed the close links between the British Army and the Indian Army in 1947, but some units were able to draw on the experience of officers and senior NCOs who had served in the Burma campaign during the War, and there was still pre-war experience going back to colonial policing if it could only be tapped. For the most part, though, it was a case of reinventing the wheel, and regimental officers had to find out the hard way.

There were really only two ways to kill CTs, they found. The first was by waiting for them to come to you, acting on Intelligence (or guesswork) and ambushing routes that they might use, either to come into the *kampong*s or *kongsi*s to collect food, or as they moved between their base camps and their operational areas. Ambushes, however, were often time-consuming and frustrating in the extreme, and they demanded great patience and crucifying self-discipline. It was extremely hard to wait for up to 48 hours, perhaps even longer, concealed and wet, sweaty and cold by turns, being bitten by insects, unable to cook or smoke or even move more than a few feet, if you were lucky, to improvise a latrine, and yet remain alert and ready to fight at a split second's notice. All too often it was time totally wasted, the intelligence was faulty or the guess was wrong, and nobody fell into the trap. Even tiny, seemingly inconsequential things, like the smell of a soldier's hair oil, could be enough to give the game away, and alert the target CTs. Even if there was contact, bad discipline or inexperience or nerves could ruin everything by getting the first shots off too early, and then if you were lucky you might be left with a cap on the ground and enough blood to justify a claim that at least one of the enemy had been badly wounded.[4] Ambushes could be successful, and some units became expert at them, but success really depended on good Intelligence, and that was not easy to come by. One lesson that was learnt very quickly was that units that were allowed to settle in one place and build up contacts that would provide Intelligence had a much better chance of killing terrorists than units that were moved about.

That was not a particularly welcome thought to those in higher command, who were faced with the problems of withdrawing units periodically for rest and retraining, and of covering demands by the Police and civil authorities for support in other areas that seemed to be under threat. Sometimes units had to be moved, to reinforce other units that were in trouble or to replace those that were just not up to it, but often the moves seemed to regimental officers to be capricious and to have more to do with justifying some staff officer's existence than with any military necessity. Either way, a unit that was moved to fresh ground usually lost the local knowledge and trust that had been painfully built up over literally months of hard work, and what little information might have been forthcoming dried up. Success in killing CTs depended on direct, high-grade information and it took a while for the penny to drop that good Intelligence was a very tender plant.

The second way to kill Communists was to go and look for them – not in big battalions, but in small groups, perhaps a platoon, perhaps even just a dozen men. For a lot of operations the smaller the squad, in effect, the more chance it had of being successful. More and more, as the campaign continued, the terrorists followed Mao's precept, 'if you are attacked, withdraw', and an MRLA squad surprised in its jungle camp rarely stayed to count the numbers in the assault group: it was the sentry's job to fire and try to get the attackers to go to ground, while the rest would usually disappear along prepared paths to a prearranged rendezvous.[5] In dense undergrowth that meant that nine times out of ten only the first two or three men of an attacking force actually managed to get shots off, and there was little sense in trying to bring larger numbers into action. Big squads made big targets, and they meant noise and problems of control. Increasingly, junior commanders – subalterns, sergeants and even corporals – found themselves in independent commands, fighting the battle virtually on their own once they were in the jungle. That, again, was something that higher command was slow to learn. Not just generals and brigadiers, but even some colonels and majors whose experience had hitherto been gained in North Africa or Europe found it difficult to let go, and junior officers still had to cope with what they saw as 'interference' from higher up quite late into the campaign.[6]

Aggressive patrolling, to be successful, meant learning other skills. It meant learning to move quietly in an environment where everything under foot was capable of producing an explosive noise that could be heard hundreds of yards away.[7] It meant developing battle drills that would bring fire to bear in split seconds if contact was made, and it meant experimenting with techniques and modifying them, and then experimenting again, only to discard them ruthlessly if they did not work, and start again from the beginning. The Green Howards, one of the most successful units to fight in the Malaya campaign, watched slightly bemused as an expert in explosives tried to develop a technique for booby-trapping tracks and paths with anti-personnel mines and other such devices, and, when he admitted failure, continued their own experiments with homemade Bangalore torpedoes.[8] These failed, too, mainly because of a shortage of Cortex instantaneous fuse.

One experiment that did succeed remarkably well, all things considered, was the enlistment of Dyak trackers from Sarawak. The most successful were recruited from the clans in the remoter Divisions, inland near the headwaters of the Rajang river, whose jungle-craft was superb, and whose head-hunting past was sufficiently recent to make them adapt easily to the 'kill or be killed' culture of guerrilla warfare. A patrol commander who could call on an expert Dyak tracker had a great advantage, and many officers and NCOs in the Security forces learned enough of the skills of 'reading sign' from their Dyaks to become expert in their own right.[9] Sadly, however, not all the Dyaks were first rate. For political reasons, it was felt necessary to offer the chance of enlistment evenhandedly in each Division, so that for every recruit from a remote Division up country, a recruit had to be accepted from a more urbanised coastal area to balance the books. In the early days this tidy policy led to some rather odd appointments, and rumour has it that at least one 'tracker' who turned out to be useless had been a taxi driver in Kuching for most of his adult life.[10]

The great debate, though, was in the matter of weaponry. From behind a desk in Bluff Road, Kuala Lumpur,[11] an analysis of the comparative strengths and weaknesses of the MRLA and the Security forces might have led to the logical conclusion that the Security forces should capitalise on some unique advantages. For example, the Communists had no aircraft, so the logical military mind might conclude that air power might surely be used to give the Government forces an edge. Already, at Gua Musang and elsewhere, the RAF had shown that rocket-firing *Spitfires* could work in close support of ground troops, and inflict casualties on terrorists trying to operate in formed bodies in relatively open country. The arrival of *Lincoln* bombers meant that raids could be mounted, and damage done, off the beaten track, in the jungle, where the MRLA felt most secure, and in fact attempts were made to use the bombers in this way, with the RAF's enthusiastic support. There is even a story of an instance where a District Officer (a civilian administrator, be it remembered) tried to bypass the Police and the Army and call down a bombing raid on his own authority. Some air raids were rated as successful and casualties among the CTs were claimed, although these claims could never be more than estimates.[12]

However, as the MRLA changed its tactics, the opportunities for close ground support disappeared, and when the obsolete *Spitfires* were withdrawn there was no suggestion that they should be replaced. It was recognised, too, that bombing was suspect, since targets were almost impossible to identify and even harder to find with any degree of accuracy, and the risk of what later became known, euphemistically, as 'collateral damage' (casualties among innocent non-combatants) was usually too high to be acceptable. Prophylactic raids, as they were called, did continue from time to time and much expensive high explosive was decanted over trees, but it was soon realised that the only major damage being done was to the trees, and that air power was not going to win this war, not in any traditional way at any event.[13] The great danger in the deployment of specialised forces or 'high-tech' weaponry in any campaign is that they become their own imperative: 'we have this capability, therefore we must use it. If need be we must invent a problem it can solve.' It is probably true that experiments in the use of aircraft against the MRLA were tarred with that brush to some extent during the first two years or so of the Emergency. It was not long, though, before the air-minded began to turn their thoughts to other ways of using aircraft to help, and in particular to the really sterling service that the RAF was to provide, that of air supply.[14]

The same coldly critical look was being turned, at company and platoon level, on the arms and equipment that the foot soldiers carried into the jungle. In 1948 the standard infantry weapon was the Number 4 rifle, a cheap mass-produced variant of the excellent SMLE Mark 3. It had been perfectly satisfactory in Europe, but was totally unsuitable for the job of bandit-hunting in the jungle – it was too heavy and cumbersome, there was no need for the accuracy that it was designed to provide, at ranges of as much as 500 yards or more, and its bolt action severely limited its rate of fire. It was soon replaced by the Number 5 rifle, which had been introduced in the later stages of the Burma campaign, and was essentially a redesigned Number 4, cut down in length, stripped of much of its heavy woodwork and equipped with a rubber padded butt and a flash eliminator. (It was also accompanied by a knife bayonet, which was useful for opening tins). The Number 5 was an improvement on the Number 4, and remained in use until the end of the Emergency, but it still did not answer all the needs. It, too, was a bolt-action weapon, and what was needed was something automatic, or at least semi-automatic, that was light and could be relied on to produce rapid fire in the close-quarter, snap shooting conditions that were presented by most contacts with CTs. American carbines provided some of the answers, as did the Owen gun. The Owen was a re-engineered version of the cheap and cheerful Sten, which was dreaded by most soldiers as being desperately unreliable – its propensity for jamming was only equalled by the ease with which it went off spontaneously, at the most embarrassing moments. The Owen was not much of an improvement, since its greater reliability was bought at the cost of an unwelcome increase in weight, and the search for the right sub-machine-gun went on.

One weapon that usually had to be left in the barracks was the platoon commander's private artillery, the 2in mortar. Not only were the bombs it fired too heavy and bulky, but with its high trajectory, under trees it was not just useless but actively dangerous, since the high-explosive bombs were designed to detonate on contact and tended to explode on the way up as they hit the canopy above the baseplate position. In its place were issued EY grenade launchers, strange beasts that had originally been developed for the trenches in the First World War. The EY consisted of a cup, screwed to the muzzle of a rifle, into which a 36 grenade (Mills bomb) was inserted in such a way that the sprung lever was held down. The pin was then pulled, a ballistite cartridge blasted the grenade off, the lever flew off when the grenade left the cup, allowing the striker to start the seven-second fuse, and the grenade sailed off in a graceful parabola to explode who knew where. The rumour that the EY had been designed by Heath Robinson was generally discounted, and some conventionally-minded patrol commanders did take one out occasionally, but most gave them up as being just so much more useless weight.[15] The problem of platoon artillery remained unsolved, but as things turned out that did not matter too much.

One excellent weapon was kept in service, despite its weight and bulk. The Bren was not improved on then, nor has it been since. However, a high standard of training was needed to avoid an inexperienced gunner blasting off needlessly: its ammunition was carried pre-loaded into magazines, two of which were usually carried by each member of a patrol in addition to his own already heavy load, so waste was not encouraged. The Bren could be fired from the hip (by those sub-clinically insane), and a second pistol grip was available to help its use in this role, but it was most useful in ambush situations, and was retained as the heaviest weapon routinely carried into the jungle because of its high rate of fire and complete reliability. The Bren apart, the great endeavour was to try to develop and use lighter weapons that could produce a lot of shots in a very short time, with only the limited accuracy that would be needed at the short ranges at which actions were almost always fought.

The need to reduce weight did not stop at weaponry – everything the soldier carried was put under close scrutiny. The standard webbing was the '44 pattern equipment originally used in the Burma campaign, and was much better adapted to the climate and the jungle than the stiff and heavy '37 pattern that had been in general use throughout the war in Africa and Europe. Modern or not, however, most soldiers felt the need to 'modify' it considerably to meet their own ideas of what worked best. Basic pouches, for example, were slit so that they could be threaded onto the belt, dangling below it rather than in the brassière-like 'up-lift' position on the chest. Packs were worn low on the back, and not hooked on to anything, so that they could be shrugged off in a hurry if there was a need for rapid movement. Each soldier was allowed considerable freedom to come up with his own solution to the problem of making load-carrying a little easier, but weight remained the big bugbear. Everything had to be carried: weapons, ammunition, radio batteries, spare clothes, poncho, medical kits and mess tins.

Above all, there was the question of food, a question to which no-one ever really found a satisfactory answer. The standard issue in the field was 'compo', complete rations to provide in one pack all that was necessary for 12 men for one day, or one man for 12 days. Apart from the oddments needed for day-to-day life on active service, such as cigarettes and lavatory paper and disposable hexamine cookers, the contents of these packs comprised, for the most part, tins: processed cheese, meat and veg, bully beef, and a strange compound that claimed to be bacon and egg, and technically probably was. (This consisted of brownish-red fragments of something mercifully unidentifiable, suspended in a yellowish-white putty. It tasted a great deal better than it looked, but sat on the stomach like lead.) There were also slabs of compressed oatmeal that were meant to be turned into a parody of porridge but were much better eaten as oatcakes, smothered with butter and jam, when they could be sent to join the egg and bacon as a more or less permanent cure for diarrhoea. The only way to use compo on active service was to share the tins round the patrol, spreading the misery of a considerable weight as evenly as possible.

One alternative was to take 24-hour ration packs. These were flat tins that fitted tidily into the side pockets of a pack, and contained, miraculously, everything that was needed to keep one man going for one day. Once the tins were opened, however, what was inside was no great improvement on compo: more compressed oatmeal, egg and bacon and the like, together with a tiny gimcrack hexamine burner, matches in a watertight tube and ten sheets of lavatory paper. The quality of the food was usually rather better than compo, but the 24-hour packs did little to solve the problem of weight.[16] Some units managed to adapt to rice and dried fish, which were often obtained by complicated swap deals with the Police, but some clung desperately to their 'all-in' stew. Scottish battalions were notoriously hard to wean from the 'meat and two veg' school of catering.

All this preoccupation with weight might seem finicking, but winning in the jungle depended on getting right a mass of what often seemed small details, of doing everything just a little bit better than the enemy. The weight that each man carried dictated not just mobility and speed across the ground, but also the length of time that a formation could remain operational in the jungle, and that was often a decisive factor. As time went by, the RAF became very adept at resupply by parachute, but these air drops were not always a solution to the problem. They could only be made into dropping zones that were reasonably clear, so if there were no *padi* fields or natural clearings suitably close to a patrol's line of march, time and energy had to be spent felling trees and clearing scrub, which it is impossible to do quietly. In any event, parachutes floating down from *Dakotas* indicated to even the dimmest CT that something was afoot, and a unit that had taken an air drop often found that their time after that was largely wasted.[17] Hardbitten units solved the problem, at least in part, by simply going without. The four- or five-day rations which formed the optimum load could be made to stretch to ten days if need be, and any symptoms of malnutrition could be cured fairly quickly back in base camp.

Difficulties with weight and noise that were occasioned by the radio set were eventually solved in much the same way. Both the 68 and the 62 set were bulky and heavy, and in the days before transistors, got through batteries at a devastating rate.[18] Radio operators who had to carry all this weight were regarded with great sympathy (although without receiving many offers of actual help), and it is doubtful whether they contributed much to the success of any individual operations. In the jungle the sets needed long directional wire aerials to have any chance of sending or receiving recognisable signals, which meant that the patrol had to stop while the aerials were rigged up and the interminable procedures of getting on air were gone through. What that meant in practice was that the radio was virtually useless in an emergency and only came into its own at last light, when the patrol had stopped for the night. Then the noise of loud netting calls and mush sounded far worse than they probably really were, and the suspicion had to be that every CT within miles now knew that there were troops in the offing. Junior officers, who were becoming expert at jungle fighting, and were more than happy to be left to get on with it, resented having to use radios anyway, since they often did little more than provide vehicles for senior officers who wanted to be overly involved in the detail of operations, demanding 'sitreps' and issuing revised orders at awkward times. Wise patrol commanders usually ensured that the set went 'dis' at the beginning of the operation, and many eventually refused to take radios with them at all.

Success in hunting down the CTs in the jungle depended on exactly the same level of discipline and meticulous professionalism as laying a successful ambush. As much as anything it was the work done in training, and in preparation for operations, that made the difference between kill or be killed. Ambush and immediate action drills had to be rehearsed again and again so that no commands were needed and men reacted instinctively to any given situation. In musketry, the accent was on snap shooting at short ranges, and wherever possible each soldier fired a practice on the range every day, even when he was supposed to be resting after an operation.[19] More than anything else, though, it was the quality of leadership that could lift a performance from the merely adequate to the excellent. What was needed was a degree of ruthlessness in never settling for the soft option, in pressing on with a patrol when there seemed to be no point, in staying in ambush for the extra few hours when there seemed to be little chance of a kill. Determined leadership could drive tired men on to maintain their self-reliance and adrenaline when all they wanted to do was to go home, leadership could push hungry men into eating cold, uncooked food, or into going without food altogether, rather than cook and risk giving the position away, leadership could keep an injured man marching with the patrol, rather than prejudice the operation by detaching a party to take him out of the jungle. 'A patrol which is not alert is walking with death' was the saying, and the level of discipline and determination needed to maintain that vigilance which was the only true insurance could only come from the patrol commander. What the Army was doing, while the GOC was struggling with the problems of manoeuvring brigades, was developing a corps of tough-minded junior leaders who were fast becoming better guerrillas than their opponents. Spencer Chapman always maintained that, at his best, the Briton makes the best irregular soldier in the world, and certainly the skill being developed in Malaya seemed to bear him out. However, it was not just the British, of course, but Malays and Gurkhas and, later on, troops from many countries in the Commonwealth as well that were achieving this peak of excellence.

War and Peace. An armoured car of 15th/19th Hussars takes post beside a Chinese temple. *(Soldier Magazine)*.

Searching an abandoned squatter *kongsi* on the edge of some rather scruffy rubber. (IWM)

Planter at work, complete with police escort and assorted guns and dogs. (The author, Sungei Kahang, Johore, 1953)

Derailed trains were easy to arrange. (IWM)

Burnt buses were a most gratifying contribution to meeting quotas. (IWM)

Templer gets results - the road into Tanjong Malim, resplendent with guard post and barbed wire. (IWM)

Ambush country. With *belukar* as close to the track as this, ambushes could be set within a few feet of the target. (IWM)

A resettlement village under construction - no barbed wire yet! (IWM)

A soldier of 1st Bn Suffolk Regiment inspecting a Chinese tapper's ID Card - just the sort of police work the troops hated doing. (IWM)

Identity Card. By some sleight of hand Chinese village photographers made all their sitters look Chinese, whatever their ethnic origins.

Air drops often prejudiced operations, however expertly they were carried out. (Wilmot)

Bandit camp, 1955/56. Earlier camps could be much bigger and more sophisticated. (Wilmot)

Bandit camps were always burnt after being cleared. (Wilmot)

Straight rows of crops in jungle *ladangs* were easily identifiable from the air. (Wilmot)

Higgledy-piggledy planting was much harder to see clearly. (Wilmot)

CHAPTER THIRTEEN

TRYING HARD TO LOSE

Thus as 1949 wore on the underlying military situation was improving considerably, although not, perhaps, exactly in a way that the generals appreciated. What was apparent to everyone else, however, was that in other ways things were still not going at all well. For many excellent reasons, political, legal and psychological, it was vital that the conduct of operations against the Communists should be seen as a matter for the civil authority with the Armed Services acting in aid, and that there should be no hint of Martial Law being applied. This principle, of civil primacy, was accepted at least notionally by everyone involved, but at all levels of command there were many who found it difficult to grasp or apply in practice. Even someone as senior and close to the making of policy as General Sir John Harding, GOC in C, FARELF, for example, could go into print on the need for the Army's role to be carefully positioned as part of a larger, civil campaign, and justify his decision to bring in more and more troops by claiming that they were only there as a temporary expedient until such time as the civil administration and the Police were confident that full control had been regained, and yet he could demonstrate in virtually the same breath that he did not understand that rebuilding the civil machinery of government was a more complicated matter than merely issuing an order that it should be so. Like many others, he was totally baffled by the intricacies of the constitutional situation and the limitations, both legal and practical, on what Gurney could achieve in a few months.[1] Things were not helped by the fact that Harding disliked Gurney (whom he referred to as 'a cold fish'), and it was not long before he started conspiring with MacDonald to have Gurney removed. Far lower down the hierarchies, at company and even platoon level, this same lack of understanding of the niceties of 'acting in aid of the Civil Power' led to strained relations in Police stations and headquarters throughout the country. Junior officers who were beginning to get a grasp on the principles of their job found it frustrating to have to subject their plans to scrutiny in the interests of 'co-ordination', although there had already been enough cases of ghastly confusion where military patrols had fired on Police and *vice versa* for the good sense of such a procedure to have been apparent even at that mundane level, let alone in the interests of developing an effective campaign. Police and Army officers all too often saw the matter in terms of a trial of strength, and each were heard to talk darkly of their unwillingness to 'be told what to do' by the other – there was little mutual respect.

Such feelings aside, however, it has to be recognised that there were plenty of good reasons for the military mind to contemplate the scene with frustration and some considerable degree of dismay. The Civil administration, and particularly the Police, *were* failing. Senior officials, comfortable and reasonably safe in their cool offices in Kuala Lumpur, shared *stengahs* at the Lake Club or in the Long Bar at the 'Dog' with their opposite numbers in the big trading houses and agreed that it was a terrible shame that so-and-so had been murdered by the 'Bandits', but carried with them little sense of urgency when they went back in to work the following morning.[2] The attitude of the Chinese community made it extremely difficult to recruit able and trustworthy Chinese, and those who did come forward were regarded with great suspicion and resentment by their Malay colleagues. Finding Europeans who could speak any dialect of Chinese was next to impossible – there was a small corps of Chinese Affairs Officers who had become fluent in Hokkien or other Chinese dialects by dint of undergoing the MCS's 'immersion' course, living *en famille* in Amoy for three years, but with Mao Tse Tung's success this tiny source had entirely dried up.

In local Government offices throughout the country the same lack of urgency that pervaded the Departmental bureaucracy of Kuala Lumpur slowed the movement of those masses of paper so beloved of low-grade clerks almost to a standstill, and all too often gains that were won in the field were thrown away by incompetence or bumbledom or sheer bloody-mindedness under the lazy ceiling fans of officialdom.

It was amongst the Police, however, that the greatest shortcomings were still to be found. It was the Police that were supposed to provide the drive, to be the main source of Intelligence and to co-ordinate the planning and action on the ground, and they were just not delivering. A tremendous amount had been done in the year since the deaths of Walker, Allison and Christian, by Gray and his immediate subordinates, to transform the Police into something more like a competent force, but in the short term many of the reforms had generated as many difficulties as they had resolved. The rapid expansion of the Regular Police force and the Special Constabulary had brought enormous problems in its wake, problems of equipment, as well as of training and administration, but above all, of leadership and command. It was to be expected that there should be acute shortages of competent inspectors and NCOs which only time could make good, but Gray was making very heavy weather of restoring morale and drive amongst his senior officers. No amount of banging heads together was solving the problem of men who would not co-operate with others for personal reasons, or who refused to allow the comfortable habits of peacetime to be disturbed by a little local difficulty, and these attitudes naturally flowed down through the ranks so that morale in the local Police stations was appalling.[3] They might not now close down for the weekend, but if the OSPC was unlikely to be around after midday on Saturday there was not much point in carrying out duties conscientiously, and especially not if those duties involved taking part in a shooting war.

Unfortunately, a major part of the problem centred on Gray himself – on his background and his personality. Amongst the older Malaya hands there was still deep resentment that someone from Palestine had been brought in over the heads of long-serving officers, a man, as they saw it, with no understanding of the culture of the country or its peoples, and a man whose methods and tactical abilities were subject to acerbic criticism from many quarters. He seemed to be able to set himself at loggerheads with everyone he dealt with. He was fiercely protective of the Police prerogative to play the leading role in the campaign, and was involved in constant niggling rows with the Army chiefs, particularly about intelligence. In fact, although he knew that good Intelligence was the key, he failed to make any significant improvements in the areas that were so urgently needed. At junior level, Police officers were very inclined to keep 'hot' Intelligence to themselves, excluding their opposite numbers in the Army, and then to try to make names for themselves by committing ill-equipped and undertrained Police to actions for which they were totally inadequate.[4] Reprehensible though it may have been, the soldiers' reaction to this situation is understandable: they did exactly the same. Local commanders spent much time and effort setting up what was in effect a rival security system, developing their own informants and intelligence service and keeping the proceeds very close to their chests, on the grounds that they did not trust the Police not to breach security.[5] Not surprisingly, Police officers resented this attitude and the vicious circle was complete. Gray himself tried to bring Military Intelligence under his direct control, but given the failings in his own organisation it was a forlorn hope, and it was years before anyone finally gave shape to an effective joint intelligence operation.

Gray's determination to have his own way in all things and his obstinacy in refusing to listen to the views of others found their greatest expression in the bitter conflict about the Police use of armoured vehicles – or, rather, their non-use of armoured vehicles. Despite all the evidence and all views to the contrary, Gray remained adamant that the Police were to rely solely on soft-skinned vehicles. There was reason behind his policy, beyond making a merit of a necessity, since he was only too acutely aware of the dreadful lack of any offensive spirit amongst his constables. Desperate measures were needed to put things right, but his idea that men ambushed in unprotected trucks would be more likely to debus and assail the enemy than those whom he pictured cowering behind armour plate had some inbuilt fallacies, to say the least. He made little secret of the fact that he was drawing on his experience in Palestine (which did little to sell the theory to those subordinates who had criticised his appointment in the first place), but circumstances there had been totally different. It may well have been that in the desert places and open countryside where most actions took place there, ambushes were set sometimes as much as 100 yards or more from the road, initial casualties were often light, and there was usually an opportunity for well trained and experienced Police to organise an effective counter-attack.

Conditions in Malaya called for a rather more subtle approach. Ambushes could be from as little as four or five yards, on slow-moving trucks grinding their way up narrow roads through hairpin bends.[6] The only chance of reacting offensively was to drive *through* the ambush as quickly as possible, and then debus. Since in unarmoured vehicles the first casualty was usually the driver, the truck tended to get stuck right in the middle of the killing ground, and any idea of a counter-attack became impossible. The losses in the attack on the Police convoy at the Jelebu Pass stemmed precisely from this, and resulted not only in the pointless and avoidable deaths of 17 policemen, but the loss of very valuable Bren and Sten guns, together with their ammunition.[7] Nonetheless, unarmoured vehicles became an article of faith for Gray, and his defence of the policy became ever more desperate. He refused to consider ordering the armoured cars that were on offer,[8] and when armour plate became available he would not allow any trucks to be modified. When a couple of trucks had their cabs reinforced with locally bought steel plate (by courtesy of some planters), he had it removed. Eventually, under acute pressure, he relented and some armoured cars were bought, but he never retracted and his attitude was a contributory factor to the generally low esteem in which he came to be held. Most dangerously, he forfeited the respect of the junior ranks on whom he relied to fight the battle, never a wise thing for any leader to do in war.

Underlying the stress between the Police, the civil authorities and the Army was the sense that things were stagnating. The number of incidents was lower than at the beginning of the Emergency, but remained high enough to show that the MRLA was still very much in business, and although MacDonald may have been right in saying that Chin Peng had lost the initiative he had by no means lost the war yet. In fact, however confident the generals might sound, the truth was that the Communists' military capability had not even been dented, and although the capability of the Army's jungle squads was being honed to a sharper edge every day, killing CTs was still far too much a matter of luck. As far as expansion was concerned the Police could go no further without first consolidating, selecting and training officers, and, most importantly, giving them experience in operational conditions.

Then, looming over this whole situation there was still the problem of the Chinese. Gurney and his officials complained constantly about the refusal of even the most prosperous Chinese to 'rally round', and the phrase 'sitting on the fence' became a continual refrain in his reports. He was deceiving himself, however: the Chinese may not have been rallying round the Government but were by no means so reluctant to co-operate with the Min Yuen, and 'sitting on the fence' was a hopelessly optimistic description of their position. In February 1949 Tan Cheng Lok, with the support of the Government, had formed the Malayan Chinese Association (MCA), in an attempt to provide a political focus for all those Chinese who had supported the Kuomintang in the past, as well as those who it was hoped would be prepared to take a stand against Communism if only a lead were offered. So far, however, it did not seem to be making any impact and Gurney, particularly, was frustrated and baffled by the way in which even the most prosperous Chinese were prepared to act, as he saw it, against their own interests. The less well off did not even make much attempt to hide the comfort that they gave to the CTs – rich and poor preferred the evidence of the reports of Mao Tse Tung's success in mainland China, as well as the compelling arguments of the terrorists who came to their doors late at night, to the wavering pleas for loyalty from a Colonial Government that they had always tried to keep at arm's length. How much the support given to the MCP was voluntary and how much was exacted by fear will never be clear. Certainly no-one who was prosecuted for paying protection money or 'dues' to the Communists ever admitted doing it except in terror for his life, but with the Security forces unable to protect any but a tiny proportion of those vulnerable to CT threats there was really very little point in Gurney waxing indignant about Chinese reluctance to support the Government.[9] Once again, it was proving impossible to break the vicious circle. Until the Security forces could demonstrate convincingly that they were going to win, then the Chinese would at best keep their options open, and would certainly not support the Government in any active way. But without the active support of the Chinese then there was little hope of the Security forces notching up any victory that would affect the situation significantly. Winning the hearts and minds of the uncommitted Chinese was emerging as a major concern for Gurney and his administration.

In these rather unpromising circumstances it may seem a little odd that anyone might have felt confident enough to suggest offering terms for surrender, and no doubt the flawed military appreciations that were being bandied about did lead to some unrealistic hopes. However, the notion had been canvassed for two or three months and had some merit in retrospect. No one remotely thought that any of the high-ranking Politburo members or committed Party idealogues were going to come sheepishly out of the jungle, asking that all might be forgiven, but it was widely believed (and not without foundation) that many of the MRLA recruits in 1948 had been inadequate social misfits who had been gulled into joining up for all sorts of reasons and might now be becoming disillusioned. Even without guarantee of amnesty, upwards of 100 rank-and-file CTs had surrendered during the first few months of 1949, and those who understood the Chinese mentality believed that this tiny trickle could be turned into a healthy and worthwhile stream if the right terms were offered.[10] Surrender terms were promulgated on 6 September 1949. Some slight results were obtained; between 6 September and the end of 1949 just over 150 CTs surrendered.

However, perhaps a more cogent response to the Government's offer was delivered by the 26th Independent Company, MRLA, commanded by Chin Nam, on 11 September when it attacked the small township of Kuala Krau, in Pahang, just north of Mentakab. This was the second time that the CTs had fallen on Kuala Krau: just ten days into the Emergency, on 28 June 1948, 40 or more had opened fire in a rather slapdash assault on the Police station, but had withdrawn after an inconclusive engagement, leaving the wife of one of the Malay policemen dead. This time things were better managed. Around 300 CTs burnt the railway station, the stationmaster's house and the house of one of the rail inspectors. They also succeeded in burning what was described as the 'water hose', a feat which, if true, demonstrates technical ingenuity of a remarkable kind. The attack on the Police station was pressed home with greater skill and determination but with no greater success, the Police holding out with great courage for several hours until the Communists withdrew. In the meantime, the CTs had been able virtually to take over the town in a way reminiscent of Batu Arang and Gua Musang. Two British railway engineers were killed, an armoured train coming to investigate was derailed, and by the time the attackers finally withdrew they had killed, besides the two Britons, four Malay Policemen and two Malay women.

A fortnight later, on 25 September, a similar attack was made on another village in Pahang, by a squad estimated at about 150, and then, on 4 October, a group of 200 terrorists attacked Kamayang Estate, burning down the manager's bungalow, the labour lines and the factory. There was an attempt at a follow up by a detachment of 1st Devons, but the guerrillas had disappeared. While some thought that these attacks showed that Chin Peng had not yet entirely given up hope of establishing liberated areas, no-one could ignore the implications of the numbers that had been involved. Far from being defeated, the MRLA was still capable of concentrating significant forces against worthwhile targets and had learnt a great deal about command and control. At the same time, the number of relatively minor incidents shot up, to something like four times the level that had been noted by the generals only a month before as evidence that the situation was coming under control. By the early weeks of 1950 it was clear that the MRLA had made good use of the time spent on reorganisation and retraining, and had returned to the war with new confidence, determined to subject the Security forces to such pressure that they must eventually crumble. It began to dawn on Gurney and Boucher that they were in grave danger of defeat.[11]

In January 1950, the Labour Government in London loaded yet another problem onto Gurney's plate. Mao Tse Tung's campaign in China had achieved total victory, Chiang Kai Shek being forced into embattled isolation on the island of Formosa. Accepting reality, the British probably had no alternative but to offer the new Chinese Communist Government full diplomatic recognition, but the offer as part of the deal to reinstate Chinese Consuls in Malaya was a disaster. MacDonald backed Gurney in his scream of rage and eventually the idea was scrapped, but not before untold damage had been done, especially to all the efforts that were being made to bring at least the majority of the uncommitted Chinese in Malaya behind the Government. More than ever the Chinese in the towns and villages had reason to believe that it would only be a matter of time before the British gave the MRLA best, while in the jungle the guerrilla foot soldiers were buoyed up by the thought that they would soon be fighting alongside regular troops of the Chinese Red Army.[12]

Gurney might well have felt that he stood alone. The Foreign Office, intent on establishing a working relationship with the new regime in China, seemed not to care that they were undoing what little good Gurney had been able to do with the Chinese community. Although they had supported him in the matter of the appointment of Chinese consuls, MacDonald and Harding were doing their best to undermine Gurney's standing with the Colonial Office, Gray seemed quite unable to work with anyone to sort out the Police force, and while the soldiers were having some success in killing CTs for the most part they were failing to break up the MRLA units that Boucher had promised so confidently he would harry in the jungle and bring to action on ground of his own choosing. Civil administration was still totally inadequate for the tasks that were looming up, and his colleagues and subordinates were gripped with gloom. It was becoming clear to Gurney that, although he was responsible for making sure that the Army, the Police and all the agencies involved in combatting the CTs worked smoothly with each other, there was little chance of his providing the expert and firm direction of operations that such troublesome subordinates as Gray required, especially while there were so many other calls on his time. His mind turned to the possibility of appointing a professional who might take over the detailed security work from him – a Director of Operations to run the whole shooting match. He needed help – another white knight to ride at his right hand.

CHAPTER FOURTEEN

BRIGGS – THE NEW WHITE KNIGHT

Lieutenant-General Sir Harold Briggs, KCIE, CB, CBE, DSO, had retired recently at the age of 55 after a military career of quiet achievement that had reached its peak of success in Burma in 1944 and 1945. He had fought bravely and most effectively as a battalion and brigade commander during the Arakan campaign and at Kohima/Imphal, and had so impressed the commander of 14th Army, Bill Slim, that Slim had given him 5th Indian Division, in which command he had continued to lead with imperturbability and efficiency, even in the most difficult of situations.[1] When Gurney asked for a Director of Operations to be appointed, it was Slim, now Field Marshal and CIGS, who persuaded Briggs that it was his duty to return to service, and it was Slim who ensured that he got the job – an inspired intervention that history will record with gratitude.

What Slim could not do was to give Briggs the clear-cut authority that he needed if he was to pull things in Malaya together successfully, and Briggs himself knew right from the beginning that to some extent he would be in an anomalous position. Crucially, he could not really give orders to anyone, since although he was charged with bringing Police and armed forces together in one unified command, Gray retained the right to appeal to Gurney, and both GOC and AOC could go over his head to their own higher commanders. He would have to exercise influence by force of personality and by right of whatever relationship he was able to build up with Gurney and Harding, and would surely have to draw heavily on his friendship with Slim if things did not go well. It is very much to the credit of his GOC, Malaya, and even of the much-maligned and reluctant Gray, that in the event Briggs was able to achieve so much, although throughout the appointment he was to complain that he had never been given the powers that he had been both promised and needed.

Nevertheless, like a good soldier Briggs did what he was told and went where he was sent. He arrived in Kuala Lumpur on 3 April 1950, for what was meant to be a tour of a year (although he later agreed to an extension to 20 months), and immediately set about his duties with a drive and enthusiasm that blew like a fresh breeze across the turbid waters of Government. On 10 April, exactly a week after his arrival, he produced the appreciation of the situation together with an outline plan of action that was later to be expanded into the detailed and seminal 'Briggs Plan', since recognised as the turning-point in the campaign. Unfortunately, in that crowded week he also found time to give a press conference before he had really come to grips with all the political nuances of the situation, and blotted his copybook by blurting out some truths that were welcomed by some but cordially resented by others for whom he was too right for comfort.

Briggs was not the only new broom to be brought to the Augean stables of Malaya. The GOC, General Boucher, had been suffering increasingly poor health, particularly with an ulcerated leg, and in February 1950 he had to be invalided home, it was hoped only temporarily. His replacement was Major General Roy Urquhart, who had commanded the 1st Airborne Division at Arnhem and who brought to the Malayan battlefield a firm Scottish toughness in place of Boucher's more flamboyant style. Urquhart had not expected to get the job, and was told it would probably only be for six months or so, until Boucher could return to duty, and then he was earmarked to move to the Sudan to take up duties as GOC, British Troops and Sirdar of the Sudanese Defence Force.[2] When Briggs arrived in Kuala Lumpur, therefore, he found that his Army commander had been in post rather less than a month, and was still trying to find his way round a command that he thought was his only as a stopgap measure. Being the man he was, however, Urquhart was not one to sit on his hands and he proved a great strength as part of Briggs' team, staying in Malaya as GOC until June 1952.

In London, too, things were changing, and not before time. In some quarters at least the realisation had finally struck home that matters in Malaya were serious, that there was a strong chance of defeat, and that it was no longer possible to treat the Emergency as an irritating local problem that was to be solved by the people on the ground without discommoding those in Whitehall with their minds on higher things. On 19 April 1950, at 10.30 am, in Conference Room E at the Ministry of Defence building in Great George St, London SW1, a meeting of the senior ministers and officials most concerned with the Emergency convened under the chairmanship of the Rt. Hon. Emmanuel Shinwell, Minister of Defence, to establish a new Cabinet Committee – the Malaya Committee (MAL.COM.). Besides Shinwell, that first meeting included the Rt. Hon. James Griffiths, Secretary of State for the Colonies, the Rt. Hon. John Strachey, Secretary of State for War, and the Rt. Hon. Patrick Gordon Walker, Secretary of State for Commonwealth Relations. The Chief of the Imperial General Staff, Field Marshal Sir William Slim, was co-opted, as was Air Marshal Sir William Eliot, the Chief of Air Staff.

Although Briggs' initial appreciation was in front of the Committee, it is obvious from the minutes of that first meeting that no one had really had time to give it any very deep thought, understandably. Much of the discussion was superficial and cast in clichés, with lip service being paid to the need for tightening up the civil administration 'behind the advance of the military forces' *(sic)*[3], to dealing resolutely with the squatters, and with strengthening the Army on the ground. Slim agreed that the Chinese Red Army seemed to be preoccupied with preparations for an assault on

Formosa (Taiwan),[4] and that it was probably an acceptable risk to transfer 3 Royal Marine Commando Brigade from Hong Kong for at least a short time to give the Malayan Police a breathing space. He also agreed to send more armoured cars from MELF, but suggested that an approach be made to the Australian and New Zealand governments for help – a first sign of the 'overstretch' that was to become so serious later as the Korean War syphoned off still more troops.

The overconfidence of 1949 and the shock of the MRLA's renewed attacks were explained by reference to the Communist success in China, which had encouraged the CT's 'outrages', rather than by any failure of British intelligence or command. Throughout the proceedings there was stress given to the hope that everyone was pinning on Briggs – he was to be the cavalry riding over the hill in the nick of time to save the settlers from the Indians, the wizard with the magic wand who was going to make everyone live happily ever after. All the greater, therefore, was the dismay at the news of his press conference, when he had called a spade a spade in a way that had horrified the professional civil servants. In particular, there was concern about his use of the phrase 'war cabinet': as the powers that be were not prepared to admit that they were fighting a war, then there could not be a war cabinet. And when Briggs had gone on to describe Communist China as 'one of the roots of terrorism', Shinwell had become very worried indeed. Briggs was to be instructed that, in the light of His Majesty's Government's recognition of Mao Tse Tung's China, it was to be policy to describe the troubles as being due to 'banditry', not an organised Communist uprising. On no account was any reference to be made to 'fighting a war'. The troubles in the Federation of Malaya constituted a Police action, aimed at restoring 'law and order'. So that was that!

Having received various detailed reports about the squatters and the resettlement programme, the terms of service for British officers serving with the Gurkhas and the Malay Regiment, and the judicial implications of proposed changes to the rules of evidence, the meeting adjourned for one week, significantly having not touched in any way on the political future for the Federation when once the Emergency might be at an end.

Meanwhile, back in Malaya, Briggs was getting to grips with his job. In truth, there was little that was original about his first appreciation, and it is unreasonable to expect that within a week he might have discovered that magic wand that the Malaya Committee was looking for him to wave. It is clear that in the time available to him all he could possibly do was to collect the views of the very able officers who had been struggling with the problems for close to two years, subjecting them to his own analysis and presenting his conclusions in a clear-cut and professional manner. That was his way – to use what time he might have to work carefully and calmly through the problem, listening to those who seemed *au fait* with the situation, and then making his own decision about what should be done. He produced not one final prescriptive plan, but a series of appreciations and proposals, each building on the last and refining what had already been proposed as he came to a better understanding of the situation.

He was never one to stand on a plan after it was shown to be wrong, but rather would go back to the beginning and set things right. It is ironic that history records the 'Briggs Plan' as being the keystone of the British success in Malaya (which it was), but picks out as the most important element in the plan the programme of resettlement, that Briggs did not conceive and for which he had less responsibility than many others – Gurney for one. That is not to say that he did not recognise its importance and he repeatedly stressed the need for it to be carried out with vigour and urgency, putting constant pressure on the civil authorities, especially at State level, to solve all the legal and logistical problems. In his plan for the Security forces, too, he placed a high priority on the need for military and police back up, and laid down that whether resettlement had been effected or not (or was in prospect), it was a military imperative that the Chinese-populated and squatter areas must be dominated in such a way as to deny the MRLA food, money and information. Drawing on his experience in Burma he emphasised the vital need to make the more loyal elements of the Chinese community feel secure, 'inducing them to provide us with information and a means of putting out our own propaganda'.

There was far more to the Briggs Plan, though, than an endorsement of the resettlement policy. He touched on many factors: Intelligence (always the problem), Communist and British propaganda, village responsibility and the potential of the Home Guards, weaknesses in Police organisation and equipment. There were, however, two key elements in his plan that overrode the other considerations.

The first was the need to get detailed co-ordination and co-operation right, from the top at Federal level right down to platoon commanders working with the local Police. What he instituted was a Federal War Council, with himself as Chairman, and comprising the Chief Secretary, the GOC, the AOC, the Commissioner of Police and the Federal Secretary for Defence: a small and it was hoped, flexible tool for devising policy and allocating resources. Executive responsibility was to lie with similarly constituted State War Executive Committees, which in turn were underpinned by Circle and District War Executive Committees, as far as possible working to the boundaries of Police circles and civil districts. What Shinwell thought about the word 'war' in these designations is not recorded, but it was important to emphasise the thrust of these bodies, which might so easily become bureaucratic and cumbersome: they were to meet daily when necessary, the meetings were to be brief, minutes were to be vestigial and decisions were to be translated into action without delay. It did not always work quite like that; the inertia of Malayan officialdom was not to be defeated quite so easily, and Briggs was to be driven nearly to despair by his failure, as he saw it, to get things on to a 'war footing'. However, at the local level the improvement was immense as the philosophy worked down through the echelons of command, so that in practically all locations Army and Police set up joint ops rooms, usually in the local Police station, and gradually the officers involved learnt the need to share Intelligence first and fast at this level.[5] The root causes of the dearth of sound Intelligence remained, but at least there was now a chance of what there was being put to better use. The true success for which Briggs deserves to be remembered is that under his direction Malaya for the first time had a properly co-ordinated and effective command structure that would carry the load for the rest of the campaign.

The second element in Briggs' proposals was a plan to 'roll up' the MRLA regiments from the south to the north, using the reinforcements that were coming in to allow a large troop concentration in Johore and to mount a 'sweep and clear' style operation behind which the civil administration might restore law and order and sound government. Once more, the 'big battalion' mentality was in the ascendant, and the plan in consequence was deeply flawed. The operation started in June and July 1950, and was an almost complete failure. With his experience in Burma it is surprising that in those very early days of his command Briggs did not seem to understand that in the jungle it is just not possible to grip a small mobile force that is intent on avoiding battle.

Once again, and by no means for the last time, thousands of sweaty, weary troops plunged through the undergrowth, wasting hundreds of hours, killing a handful of Communists but otherwise achieving very little but to move the CTs away from their usual camps for a time, forcing them to go to ground until the hoo-ha was over. Meanwhile, this concentration in Johore (and later in Negri Sembilan) had dangerously weakened the Security forces in other States, where the number of incidents actually rose.[6] Even so, senior officers continued for years to plan and mount large scale operations in defiance of the evidence of their ineffectiveness.[7] The lesson of real value from this phase of operations was that the civil and Police administration that had been expected to move in behind the troops to re-establish authority over the cleared areas was as inadequate as the Jeremiahs had predicted, and Briggs' reports and submissions to Gurney and the Malaya Committee became increasingly urgent in pressing for improvement. From HQ, FARELF in Singapore, General Harding joined in the complaints with some gusto, which did nothing to help his relationship with Gurney, nor did it help that in essence he was right, even if he did seem to believe that all that was needed was for someone to issue an order and, magically, competent young Chinese Liaison Officers and Police Inspectors would leap like dragons' teeth from the ground. Harding's views were not unexpected: he did not think highly of Gurney.

In London, Briggs' appreciation of the situation and his plan to put things right were met with some enthusiasm. In itself, the formation of a Cabinet Committee to deal specifically with Malaya says a great deal about the confusion in the minds of the politicians and soldiers who had to try to cope with events that were taking place 8,000 miles away. On the one hand, the awful possibility that the MRLA might actually win had been enough to bring together some very senior people indeed, (although it was not long before the novelty wore off and deputies and assistants started to attend as substitutes), but at least Malaya was being taken seriously, albeit nearly two years after the start of the Emergency. On the other hand, although all these high-powered people felt that something must be done, it is clear that nobody had any very cogent ideas about what that something should be, so enthusiasm for Briggs' proposals was laced with a good deal of relief – here at last was someone who seemed to know the answers. Minutes show that meetings soon became concerned with a mixture of broad and rather vacuous expressions of confidence in Briggs and Gurney, as well as with a nit-picking preoccupation with matters of detail that it really made no sense to try to control from such a distance.[8]

There was one important issue that Gurney, Briggs and the top brass in London had to face up to, and that was the reality of Chinese attitudes. At every stage of the Emergency this was one consideration that was to loom over all others, and time and again was to baffle those involved. In his earliest reports Briggs talked about the preference of the Chinese for a quiet life, even if that meant subsidising the MRLA, and made clear his view that part of the problem lay in the weakness of the Government propaganda apparatus, a belief that caused near-apoplexy when relayed to London. How could he possibly claim that British propaganda was 'nearly non-existent' when, since the beginning of 1949, 50 million leaflets had been distributed, there had been continuous radio transmissions, radio sets had been issued free to communities throughout the country, four million copies of Government-sponsored vernacular newspapers had been circulated, and mobile public address systems were reaching a quarter of a million people every month? How could British propaganda be 'nearly non-existent' when the Department of Public Relations in Kuala Lumpur employed 200 people? Never mind the quality, look at the width! Briggs was not to be deflected by such arguments and continued to demand improvement. What was needed was an expert in psychological warfare, and in particular someone who could grasp the need to communicate with the rural Chinese in terms they could understand, and in ways that they found compelling. Bureaucratic phrases and Civil Service jargon sometimes did not mean a great deal even to native English speakers, and they lost something in translation when put into Hokkien for the edification of the pig farmer scrabbling for a living on the jungle fringe, in daily fear for his life from both the Security forces and the Min Yuen.

One propaganda measure that had been taken just before Briggs arrived must have been much in his mind when he voiced his criticism. At the end of 1949 Gurney had announced 'Anti-Bandit Month' to the Legislative Council. It was to start in February, and everyone was to be encouraged to commit themselves on a voluntary basis to helping the Security forces in an 'intensified combined operation' for a period of a month or so – a conscious effort to get people to commit themselves publicly to defeating the MCP. Those who came forward were largely unskilled in anything that might really help the conduct of operations, since by definition virtually anyone who had anything of value to offer had either already been co-opted in one way or another, or had no intention of volunteering at all. The result was that the projects that were tackled were either cosmetic, or were aimed at such unspectacular if worthwhile ends as clearing roadsides of *lalang* and *belukar* to reduce the scope for ambushes.

Heavy work like this was not undertaken by senior officials, of course, but to show willing they closed their departments for a time and helped to man roadblocks and the like. Gray was justifiably unhappy about the need to divert Police resources to guarding and supervising this sort of activity and made no secret of his view that the whole exercise was a waste of time, while the *Straits Times* poured ridicule on the idea, before, during and after the event, claiming that all it achieved was to make the authorities look fatuous. Whatever the truth of that, the attitude of most of the Chinese remained totally unaffected, unless it be to confirm them in their view that the British were incompetent and likely to lose, while the Europeans and Malays, military and civilian, became more sure than ever that it would be necessary to come down on the Chinese roughly if they were to be discouraged from siding with the Communists. 'Anti-Bandit Month' cannot be counted as a propaganda triumph for the Government and its most interesting outcome ought probably have been to have raised the question of how it was possible for Civil Service Departments to be virtually closed down without noticeable effect. There is no record of that question being asked.

CHAPTER FIFTEEN

THE WORST IS YET TO COME

While the Malaya Committee were expecting great things from Briggs, the course that he and Gurney had embarked on was necessarily one of unspectacular development. There was to be no magic wand, but a coherent plan, to be applied with a painstaking eye for detail, with hard work, application and professionalism taking the place of grand gestures and sweeping strategic manoeuvres. However, while they were setting out to build anew the foundations of victory, in the field the Communists had retaken the iniative. Kuala Krau had been the beginning of a reinvigorated campaign which saw the number of incidents rise from an average of 50 a month to more than 400, ranging from major attacks by relatively large numbers of CTs on targets such as Police stations, to the murder of individuals by small groups of Min Yuen. The Army suffered, too, from increasingly competent MRLA ambushes of road convoys where there was a chance of achieving surprise and local superiority of numbers, and success would be rewarded by a haul of arms and priceless new, reliable, ammunition. This renewed aggressiveness came as an unpleasant shock to those who only a month or so earlier had been speaking with growing confidence of a foreseeable end to the Emergency – Harding, who had looked upon the reinforcements that he had authorised as being only a temporary measure, had even joined MacDonald in looking forward to troop reductions within the year. Now he had to accept that the wish had been very much father to the thought.

In fact, although in tactical terms many units of the Security forces were becoming expert at killing Communists when they could get near them, the military situation was probably as rife with problems as it had been at any time since the start of the Emergency. As ever, one major difficulty was manpower: despite drafts and reinforcements, units remained obstinately under strength and it was not unusual for a battalion to be expected to operate at as little as two thirds of paper establishment, while those troops that could be made available were often the least experienced. One reason for the shortage of well-trained, experienced men lay in a scheme called 'Python', which was designed to ensure that no individual could be required to serve more than three years overseas, whatever his battalion might be doing. Any man who was 'Python protected' must be offered the option of being posted back to the

UK, to be rebadged temporarily into another regiment in the same brigade and serve at home for at least a year. Many refused to accept reposting and insisted on continuing to serve with their own regiment despite their 'Python' rights, but for most British battalions it meant a continuing trickle of losses, mostly amongst their most experienced NCOs and men. In terms of numbers National Service could be of some help, but at the start of the Emergency men were only conscripted for eighteen months, so that after four months of basic and continuation training and a month on a troopship they were only available in theatre for some 12 months before they had to be put back on the boat. That was a very short time to turn them into skilled jungle fighters and then to make effective use of them against the MRLA. When the National Service commitment was extended to two years in 1949 matters improved considerably and the way was opened for National Servicemen to play a vital role in the campaign in later years.

In London, the Malaya Committee saw another aspect of National Service. It was true that conscription provided a steady flow of recruits, and there were decided benefits in the availability of specialists such as doctors, surveyors and such like whom the Army might otherwise have found it difficult to attract into service, but there were worrying adverse effects as well. It was recognised that there would be no possibility of meeting military commitments worldwide without National Service but the business of training thousands of new intakes each year soaked up just those skilled and experienced regular NCOs that might otherwise have been stiffening the active service battalions. Debates about this problem came to no very fruitful conclusions but illustrate well a degree of ambivalence in the minds of many senior officers at the time, who knew that they could not carry on the campaign without National Servicemen but found it hard to believe that a conscript could turn in a professional performance that would be up to their standards. Many found it unpalatable to discover that the quality of National Service intakes was on average as high if not higher than that of regular recruitment and it is interesting that personal accounts of the campaign written by serving officers of the time are often at pains to distinguish between actions where regular officers took part and the 'surprising' success of NS officers on similar occasions. When Briggs had analysed the results of his early operations to 'roll up' the MRLA, he told Harry Miller, the *Straits Times* journalist, that in future the brunt of the fighting and the decision-making was going to have to fall on the subalterns and the corporals, which effectively meant National Servicemen; knowing the military mind he added that that would make uncomfortable hearing for some brigadiers and colonels.[1] That was not an attitude that he ever succeeded in eradicating entirely.

Within only a few weeks of Briggs' appointment the euphoria surrounding his takeover was starting to evaporate, particularly in London where hopes had been so high. In the third week of June 1950, John Strachey, the Secretary of State for War, reported to the Malaya Committee on a visit he had just paid to Malaya, a visit that had given him a great deal to think about. Maybe his despondency was conditioned to some extent by the rough ride he had been given at planters' meetings up and down the country, where his status as a Cabinet Minister was not enough to shelter him from some fairly pungent opinions about the effectiveness of the Government's anti-terrorist campaign in general and his own abilities as an organiser of military activity in particular. Being confronted by reality had given him some acute anxieties. For the first time it is possible to read into the Committee's minutes a note of real apprehension that things might take a long time to get right and that there might be hard times still to come. (One person he had talked to, of course, was Briggs, who had emphasised that there was no overnight transformation possible.)

Some aspects of the situation seemed to be reasonably under control. At a pinch overall troop numbers were probably just about enough and equipment and weaponry were adequate, subject to getting the Police into armoured cars more rapidly, but while the CTs had not been able to inflict any telling number of casualties, they had been able to lock Britain and the Colonial administration into an enormous commitment which could not be sustained *ad infinitum*. Once again, the point had to be made that the police, administrative and political effort was not nearly good enough, and Strachey talked of the need for 'administrative reinforcements' – quite what he meant was not clear, but possibly he had been influenced by his conversations with Harding, who saw Gurney as a major part of the problem and lost no chance in saying so. Strachey's comment, that the civil administration was 'too weak and liberal in using its powers' and at the same time 'not liberal enough in that they are not nearly active enough in forging ahead with the political development of the country' sounds very like an amalgam of a soldier's views and his own instincts as a senior Labour politician. One thing that Strachey had brought home with him was a major preoccupation about Malaya's place in the Communist plans for South East Asia as a whole. 'In the long run we can suppress the rising,' he reported, but added, tellingly, 'if we are left alone to do it.' Gurney and Briggs had shared with him their fears that the MCP might soon be able to draw on active assistance from Red China, and Strachey himself found the rapidly deteriorating situation in Burma, French Indo-China, the Philippines and Indonesia far from reassuring. He was forced to an unpalatable conclusion: 'In South East Asia as a whole the absolute condition of success seems to me to be that each western nation concerned must come to terms with the genuine local nationalist movement even if this means the granting of full independence prematurely'. This conclusion can be seen as a watershed – the first evidence of any member of the Attlee Government taking seriously the need for a political dispensation that paid more than lip service to independence for Malaya at some time that was not still unimaginably distant.[2]

Hard on the heels of Strachey's report came further bad news from the Far East. At 4 a.m. on Sunday, 25 June (2 a.m. on 24 June in Washington DC) North Korean forces crossed the 38th Parallel into South Korea and pushed the Republic of Korea (ROK) forces back in a two-pronged advance converging on Seoul. On 26 June the USA convened a meeting of the UN Security Council, which called for a ceasefire and the withdrawal of North Korean forces,[3] and on 29 June President Truman gave effect to the UN Resolution calling for members to 'furnish such assistance to the Republic of Korea as may be necessary to repel the armed attack and to restore international peace and security in the area' by authorising General MacArthur, US Supreme Commander in Tokyo, to commit whatever troops he thought appropriate in support of the ROK forces, drawing initially on the US garrison in Japan. On 1 July 1950, 406 men of 1st Battalion, 21st Infantry Regiment, US Army, landed by air at Pusan, the first of many thousand American troops that would be deployed, and a month later the British 27th Infantry Brigade arrived to form part of the Commonwealth Division. Even the commitment of so small a British contingent to the UN force added immeasurably to the manpower problems of the CIGS, and the chances of further significant reinforcements for Malaya virtually vanished. The world view shifted to bring Korea to the centre of public attention and even in the United Kingdom Malaya took second place to the rapidly shifting developments in this new and infinitely more threatening war.

And rapid the developments certainly were. By the middle of October, less than four months after the North Korean Army had crashed over the 38th Parallel into the poorly equipped ROK forces, Seoul had been retaken and the invaders driven back far beyond their original positions by rallying ROK forces and second-rate American garrison formations that had handled the change from a sedentary life in Japan to active service conditions far better than might have been expected. Then the scene changed again – on 16 October 1950, regular Chinese troops started to cross the border at the Yalu River, by Christmas they were fully engaged all along the line, and the UN forces that had driven the North Korean Army from the field had in turn been pushed back below the 38th Parallel in disarray. Once again, the world contemplated a victorious Chinese Red Army, and drew its own conclusions.

In fact, for Malaya, Korea was both bad news and good news. The most obvious bad news was that troops were needed for the Commonwealth Division, and commanders everywhere else (but in Malaya in particular), were put under pressure to cut back below what they saw as being the minimum to meet their immediate commitments. The hope that Australia and New Zealand might provide for Malaya was dashed, while everywhere there was the expectation that World War III was about to begin, and morale in the Malayan Government and Security forces took a turn for the worse.

The good news, however, was that world demand for tin and rubber went up by leaps and bounds, the Malayan economy boomed and suddenly the country was wealthy. Individual planters received huge bonuses as rubber prices went up from less than 75 cents a pound to over $2.50, workers on rubber estates and in the tin mines were able to negotiate greatly improved wages and conditions, standards of living rose and increased tax revenue made the Briggs Plan and resettlement nearly affordable.[4] These benefits took some months to become apparent, of course, and from the point of view of Gurney and Briggs as well as the Government in London, the start of the Korean War merely made the outlook for Malaya more depressing. It was Gurney's job to try to maintain confidence, so it is not surprising in his reports to the Colonial Office and to the Legislative Council to find him forecasting a successful end to the Emergency by December 1951, but if he really believed that it is hard to see where his optimism came from. 1950 and 1951 were to be the worst years of the Emergency, a time when anything that could go sour did its very best to do so, and a glance at some of the key statistics for that period fully justifies the underlying feeling of despondency that gripped both London and Kuala Lumpur.

In 1950 the total number of terrorist incidents was just under 5,000, compared with 1,442 in 1949: an increase of over 250 per cent, and very clear evidence, if any were needed, of the CTs' renewed aggressiveness. During the course of these incidents the CTs inflicted 889 casualties on the Security forces, and a further 1,161 on civilians, at a cost of just under 1,000 casualties to their own forces.[5] On the face of it, the Security forces might have taken the view that the exchange had not been too unequal until it is realised that, in spite of casualties, the number of CTs in the jungle actually *grew*. The MRLA had found no difficulty in replacing losses (although recruiting methods often owed more to blackmail and intimidation than to any convincing appeal to idealism), and the major limitation on recruitment was not lack of 'volunteers', but the chronic shortage of weapons to arm them. (This shortage dictated that the MRLA was forced to confront the Security forces more often than might be advisable, attacking escorted convoys and progressively better defended Police stations.) Even with this limitation, however, Intelligence estimates put the total number of MRLA guerrillas at the end of 1950 at between 5,000 and 6,000, an increase of nearly 1,000 over 1949.

Then there was the resettlement programme. By the end of 1950, barely 120,000 squatters had been moved into 'New Villages', less than a quarter of those who had to be moved, and the whole venture was bedevilled by the continued failure of the Malay Rulers to release land, as well as by ridiculous shortages of even the most basic raw materials – for instance, it apparently proved impossible to get hold of barbed wire, so that many of the resettlement villages that had been established were virtually unfenced. Such New Villages as there were (just over 80 by December 1950) were nothing like working communities yet – they were not economically viable, had not yet become socially cohesive, were usually politically unstable and were often subject to the civil authority in name only. It was a pity about the barbed wire, since security tended to be vestigial at best, and at worst was in the hands of unreliable Home Guards whose loyalty was shaky, and who all too often saw the slender issue of shot guns with which they were armed as a useful contribution to the success of the MRLA.

However, all was not black, and there were some successes. Long before the phrase, 'hearts and minds' became fashionable in Government offices, the soldiers who were charged with closing down the *kongsis* and moving their inhabitants to the New Villages often managed to handle what was a difficult and thankless task with such understanding and good humour that they did much to build those bridges of trust that were to prove so important in later years.[6] In some cases what was being offered was clearly so much better than the squatters' present meagre homes and worked-out plots that the move was made voluntarily, with an enthusiasm that only a cynic would have said was in any way due to the generous subsidies available. In most cases, however, it was observed that, far from being a step forward in the campaign to cut off the CTs from their logistical bases, the resettlement programme so far had only succeeded in concentrating the Min Yuen's sources together in a series of convenient 'one stop' shops.

To add to Gurney's gloom, relationships with the Malays were proving more strained and nervous than he could be happy with. For the *kampong* Malays – the rural Malays, those working or living on the rubber estates or in relatively low skilled jobs in the towns and cities – the Emergency, if they thought about it at all, was a threatening but not too serious irritant that usually happened to someone else, and had at least the merit that it offered congenial employment in the Police and Special Constabulary with the satisfaction of being able to take up arms against the Chinese adversary. Amongst the educated Malays, however, those in Government or in the professions, as well as the Rulers and their officials, there was beginning to be resentment at the privileges and resources that seemed to be flowing towards the Chinese, apparently as a reward for their lack of commitment.

Then, in 1950, came the 'Maria Hertogh' crisis in Singapore, to disturb Malays of all classes throughout the Federation with its religious and racial overtones. Maria Hertogh was a child of Dutch Eurasian origins, who had been adopted as a five-year-old into a Malay family when she had become separated from her parents by the Japanese invasion, and she had been lovingly brought up as a Malay and a Muslim. Her parents did not discover where she was until late in 1949, when, in accordance with custom, a marriage had been arranged for her with a suitable Malay man. While her parents struggled through the Singapore courts to get her returned to their custody, the marriage took place, perfectly legal under Muslim law, but anything but legal under either Dutch or British colonial law. A court order was made, assigning her to safe keeping in a Roman Catholic convent, her husband lodged an appeal, the hearing ruled against him and gangs of Malay youths went rioting through the streets of Singapore in protest. Europeans and Eurasians were dragged from cars, buses were overturned and set on fire, and in the first 24 hours the rioters killed nine people and injured 26. Troops had to be withdrawn from the campaign against the MRLA to be put into Singapore to aid the Police, and eventually these troops had to fire on the mob, killing a symmetrical nine. Besides the 18 deaths there were 173 injured, 72 vehicles burned and 119 damaged.[7] Within a few days things were back to normal with little long-lasting harm apparently done. For the Malays in Singapore and in the Federation, however, it seemed another example of heavy-footed colonial government trampling on their culture and religion, and Gurney found himself with yet another problem of morale and mistrust, a problem he would have been happy to do without.

To some extent this distrust found its expression in the growing strength of UMNO – the United Malay Nationalist Organisation – a political party that had started life as a pressure group in 1946, aimed at reversing the MacMichael treaties, and had since come to represent the nationalist aspirations of the Malay community. Under the erratic and cantankerous leadership of Dato Onn bin Jafar (the *Mentri Besar* of Johore and a member of the Legislative Council) UMNO had gained standing as a not always helpful partner of the British administration in the fight against insurrection, and Gurney could not be happy that the Maria Hertogh affair had driven its members into perceiving themselves as vulnerable to British neglect. Ironically, although he could not have known this, this drawing together of Malays in support of UMNO would eventually make possible many of the policies that would result in a successful ending to the Emergency, but in the short term it was just another thing to cast a cloud.

Contemplating the situation in the Police gave neither Gurney nor Briggs much cause for comfort either. Gray's acceptance of Briggs' appointment was grudging, the deep-seated problems of leadership and training were being eradicated only slowly and painfully, and attempts to improve the intelligence situation were foundering on a typical personality clash between Gray and one of his associates. In May, 1950, Sir William Jenkin, a retired officer of the Indian Police Service, had been appointed with Gray's agreement to advise on the reorganisation of the CID and Special Branch. Under his direction things did get better and there was a notable improvement in the quantity and quality of information flowing to the Army and Police units in the field. Gray being Gray, however, the two men were soon at odds and as their relationship deteriorated so it seemed that the whole Intelligence-gathering set-up would soon be back virtually to where it had been a year ago. The dispiriting row rumbled on through 1950 and into 1951, with Jenkin doing his best to prise the Intelligence function away from Gray's detailed day-to-day control, and Gray determined to lose no part of his empire, however much sense the change might make in organisational terms.

What must also have been particularly galling for Gurney was to know that he did not have the whole-hearted backing of his masters in London, or of the senior military figures to whom he might expect to look for support and counsel. Increasingly, the tone of correspondence and minutes began to betray the feeling that Briggs was doing a good job, but being let down by the 'civil' – perhaps Gurney was not the right man? That was certainly the view that Harding continued to promote. In a letter dated 24 October 1950 to the CIGS,[8] he damned Gurney with faint praise for his ability as 'an official administrator', complained that he had a 'legalistic training', and then took a sideswipe at MacDonald for having 'too many political inhibitions and local ties'. His solution was to replace both of them with an 'S.E. Asia Supremo', and proposed Mountbatten for the job. Slim wrote back on 21 November, dealing with other matters that Harding had raised, such as the poor French performance in Indo-China and the effect that the Korean War might have on Red China's ability to influence things elsewhere in South East Asia, but largely ignoring the 'Supremo' suggestion – perhaps having served under Mountbatten he had his own views about his suitability.

Understandably, this correspondence was not marked to be copied to Gurney, but it is unlikely that he did not have at least an inkling of what was passing. All in all, though, there was little he could do but grit his teeth and get on with it. He was not the sort to resign, so the alternative was to dig in for a long, unrelenting battle where ground would be gained slowly, and unremitting hard work would be all that could be offered.

Perhaps 1951 might bring better prospects.

CHAPTER SIXTEEN

DISSENT, DECEIT AND DEFECTION

1951 was to be even worse. There was no slacking off in the number of terrorist attacks, which continued the trends of 1950 in a brutal crescendo. Official records showed a total for the year of 6,082 incidents against 4,739 in 1950,[1] with July 1951 reaching a peak for the entire Emergency. As some consolation the number of contacts between the CTs and Security forces was also a record, just under 2,000,[2] and those who were looking for straws to grasp could claim that these figures showed the growing effect of some of the Government measures. Food rationing and controls, escorted road convoys and the consolidation of squatters and estate workers into New Villages and line-sites were beginning to draw the MRLA and Min Yuen onto the Security forces' chosen battleground, the fringes of the jungle and the areas around the new settlements. In effect, the insurgents were being forced to fight for supply, although that was not the way many observers interpreted what was going on at the time.

As the battle intensified, the casualties on each side mounted, too. The CTs lost 1,077 killed, 121 captured and an estimated 650 wounded, and 201 MRLA and Min Yuen supporters surrendered. Against these successes the Security forces had to set 504 of their own troops and Police killed, and 691 wounded, besides 533 civilians murdered, 356 wounded and 135 missing. For Briggs the losses inflicted on the Communists were a welcome sign that something was going right, but all was not entirely as it seemed. In the exchanges, although the CTs were losing a significant number of men (and women), the MRLA's renewed aggressiveness was not being dented in any way, nor was their effective strength being significantly reduced. Not only were the Security forces suffering more than was acceptable, but they were losing far too many weapons, and captured weapons meant that the MRLA and Min Yuen could arm more recruits to make good their losses. Intelligence estimates of MRLA strength in the jungle at the end 1951 were slightly higher than at the beginning: the Communists were certainly not being defeated, and, like the White Queen, the British were having to run as hard as they could just to stay where they were.

This stagnation did not stem from any lack of effort by the Security forces, although the Intelligence diet was still meagre enough to dictate that a lot of the effort was wasted. Operations such as CARP, CLEAVER and JACKAL involved large numbers of troops over several days and weeks, and at best resulted in a handful of kills and claims that CT formations had been broken up and moved on – it is hard to disprove a claim that the enemy has been 'disrupted'. Sadly, not all these operations were by any means one-sided, however. The days had not yet come when the CTs would be reluctant to challenge any but the softest targets, and many actions resulted in painful reminders that the MRLA were able and skilled fighters who were perfectly capable of taking advantage of lapses in discipline or training amongst their enemies. In October 1951, for instance, a patrol of the Royal West Kents lost 11 men in an ambush at a cost to the CTs of six, a nasty shock when seen against the dribble of casualties that had been taken in the previous months. Despite heavier and heavier investments in troops and activity, there seemed no end in sight.

In the high places of King's House and Bluff Road the atmosphere became ever thicker with complaint and recrimination, and disagreements and bickering continued, usually with Nicol Gray involved in some way or other. His relationship with Jenkin went from bad to worse, and was not helped when, while he was on leave, Jenkin tried to suborn the Deputy Commissioner of Police into hiving off the Intelligence function as a completely separate unit reporting to the Director of Operations, Briggs. When he returned to duty Gray lost no time in putting a stop to that little ploy, and it soon became apparent to his colleagues in London and Kuala Lumpur that Jenkin was heading for a nervous breakdown, and that he could not last long. In September he finally broke down and resigned, and it was thought advisable to accept his resignation, although he was asked to remain in post pending the appointment of a successor.

Faced with problems that would have overwhelmed a lesser man far sooner, Gray, too, was fast coming to the end of his tether, and increasingly took refuge in a negative defensive stance that left him more and more isolated from his colleagues. He became embattled in a minority of one about the resettlement programme, claiming that it was going ahead too fast, there was no way he could police perhaps half a million squatters in what might be as many as 400 New Villages, and everything must be put on hold until he could reorganise the Police and Special Constabulary, train officers and rebuild morale. Gurney overruled him, pointing out that if the squatters were not resettled then he would have even less chance of policing them, and even while Gray was struggling to resist the overstretching of his resources, Briggs and Urquhart were putting him under pressure to accept new burdens.

Once again, the problem was rooted in the shortage of troops: Briggs' overall strategy involved the Police being responsible for conducting the campaign up to the jungle edge while the Army penetrated into the interior, hunting the MRLA on its own ground. However, because of Police inadequacies troops were having to be used far too much in a Police role, doing cordon and search work in the squatter *kongsis* and New Villages, implementing food denial programmes, and, in particular, patrolling and ambushing the jungle edge in the hope of killing CTs as they moved between their jungle bases and supply sources. Gray was by no means clear that these tasks *were* Police work, and indeed much of the tension between him and Briggs reflected the view that he shared with many of his senior officers, that the

Police were 'degenerating' into a paramilitary force that would soon have no time for proper police work at all. The soldiers were equally clear that, whoever did undertake these tasks, it must not be the Army.

The result of this muddled quarrel about aims and roles was a compromise that was implemented with so many reservations that in the end nothing was really affected at all. The idea was that the Police should effectively split into two operating parts. The larger should revert, as far was possible, to conventional policing (although given the Min Yuen's penetration of so great a part of the community, the distinction between 'conventional' and 'counter-insurgent' work was artificial); and the remainder, organised and equipped as 'jungle squads' on the same basis as an infantry platoon, should assume the paramilitary role. It might have worked – some jungle squads had already been formed on an *ad hoc* basis, and had shown that when they were well equipped and trained, and well led, they could be effective. Therein, though, lay the problem: it proved impossible to find enough good officers to allow the formation of more than a handful of efficient squads, and the right quality of constables could only be obtained by milking the regular Police and Special Constabulary of good men who could ill be spared. Jungle squads were deployed but it was not until much later in the Emergency that they could provide such significant force as to offer any real solution to the difficulties of the Police or the Army.[3]

While the would-be Olympians in Kuala Lumpur were firing paper thunderbolts at each other, planters and miners were still suffering in the forefront of terrorism. The European estate and mine managers stuck doggedly to their tasks, although they were ever more vociferous in their demands for greater Government activity and determination, but their morale took a bad knock when it seemed as though the CTs were adopting a new tactic of deliberately targeting their wives and children. Two-year-old Susan Thompson was shot dead while she was being driven in an unarmoured estate Landrover, without an escort or any vestige of what might have been deemed a 'legitimate' excuse for the murder, even by the warped standards of the MRLA. Mary Burne, the wife of a tin miner, was ambushed on the Taiping–Selama road, near Ipoh, in a favourite MRLA set-up, trees felled across the road, and then the vehicle surrounded when it stopped. Her husband got out and was left totally unharmed, while she was shot in the passenger seat of his Ford V8 car. One or two planters did pack up and go, but still the majority refused to be shifted, and in truth they were not really in much more danger now than their workers. They were still easy targets, and attractive ones too, since if a planter and his SC escorts could be killed there would be a welcome small haul of arms and ammunition as a bonus to the psychological effect on other vulnerable Europeans. But the workers were even easier targets and amongst them the benefits to the terrorists of a few exemplary murders were even greater. If the Revolution were to thrive, then it was these workers who must underwrite it, with money, food, medicines and information, and if they were not going to provide what was needed willingly then they must be made to suffer until they did produce the goods. So tappers were abducted from their tasks and left mutilated in their own blood in the monsoon drain at the side of the road, overseers were nailed to trees to have their throats cut, and women and children were 'executed' in front of their families, often being quite literally hacked to pieces, so that the enthusiasm and zeal of the masses might be encouraged.

One small thorn in Gurney's side was removed when Harding came to the end of his tour as C-in-C, FARELF, and handed over to General Sir Charles Keightly, departing on a road that would lead him eventually to the Governorship of Cyprus (where he was to learn the hard way that it is a great deal easier to criticise the way others do the job than to have the direct responsibility oneself). The pressure from the brass hats to get rid of Gurney was not eased, however: in a minute dated 16 February 1951, Brownjohn, the VCIGS, wrote again to Slim canvassing the need to appoint a 'Supremo' who should bring together the Direction of Operations and the conduct of Civil Government under one hat, but stressed that it was vital that whoever was appointed must be a civilian with good knowledge of the Far East and especially of the Chinese. (In a pencilled note attached to the minute, without any apparent sense of the ridiculous, he went on to suggest as candidates Montgomery, Alanbrooke, Auchinleck, Mountbatten or Slim himself). It is perhaps not surprising that his thoughts do not seem to have excited much interest, but the correspondence rumbled on through the War Office and Malaya Committee files for some months longer, a needless worry to Gurney and Briggs who had more pressing concerns than watching their own backs.

Amongst these concerns continued to be the anxiety that, if the Emergency was not brought to a favourable conclusion very quickly, matters might be taken out of British hands by decisive intervention from outside Malaya. Contemplating the runaway success of the Chinese in Korea, and the situation in French Indo-China where Giap's forces had ridden out De Lattre de Tassigny's offensive and were now in the process of bundling Salan out of Hoa Binh, Gurney and Briggs had every reason to be worried. The telling phrase had not yet become current, but South East Asia's dominoes were falling fast, and it looked very much as though Malaya's turn might be next.

Bulking larger than all these apprehensions, however, Gurney's failure to extract any kind of commitment from the Chinese community began to dominate his thinking – he was fast losing patience. When he had first come to Malaya one difficulty that he had faced was that there was really nothing that he could call a 'Chinese Community', no overarching representative structure, nobody that he could talk to or make demands upon or turn to for guidance and support. There were Chinese Chambers of Commerce with some kind of central co-ordinating function, and there were friendly societies and such like associations, but no tradition of political co-operation that might bind together the different dialect groups, trades and professions in a 'movement' that could be steered away from Communism into more righteous paths. Above all, there were none who might truthfully be described as leaders, just some rich and powerful men who had already contrived to give Gurney the impression that they were interested in nothing but their own well-being and advancement – men such as Khoo Tek Ee, Yong Shook Lin and H S Lee. Virtually as soon as he took up office Gurney had started to try to address this problem and turned to one of the most prominent of the *towkays*, Tan Cheng Lok, with every encouragement to take positive action.

The result was the formation of the Malayan Chinese Association (MCA), in February 1949. Some observers say that this was an entirely spontaneous surge of Chinese chauvinism, others that the whole affair was Gurney's brainchild, and only happened because he was prepared to put Tan Cheng Lok under a degree of unscrupulous, but very effective, pressure. MacDonald was happy to give Gurney most of the credit (which might tell us no more than that he thought it might all go wrong), but if the MCA was to play a useful part in the political battle against Communism Gurney must not take any credit, nor even hint that it might be a Trojan Horse that he could use to penetrate the defences of a suspicious Chinese population, and he merely contented himself with reporting that the formation of the MCA was 'being undertaken'. Right from the start things did begin to go wrong. Tan Cheng Lok was a member of the Legislative Council, a hard-bitten survivor of the Malayan Union debacle, embittered by the way in which Chinese interests seemed always to be subordinated to those of the Malays. Rather than seeing the MCA as a tool that the High Commissioner could use to prise the Chinese out of their studied lack of commitment to counter-insurgency, he and his colleagues very soon constituted themselves as the Chinese voice of opposition, and, it seemed to Gurney, not always a very loyal opposition at that. In the Legislative Council and the Chinese-language press they made their views known, sometimes so stridently that Gurney's forbearance can only be wondered at, and throughout 1949 and 1950 the atmosphere can best be described as one of mutual mistrust and antagonism. The major flaw in Gurney's plan to use the MCA as a way of countering the MCP's influence was that Tan Cheng Lok and his colleagues had so little in common with the peasants who were in the firing line, either by way of interests or understanding, that there was no chance of them bringing the Chinese en masse behind the Government. There was no more reason for the Chinese to come off the fence for Tan Chen Lok than for the Government, and for the time being he was in that most impotent and unenviable of positions, a leader who has no party to follow him. In later years, the MCA was to become one of the most potent forces in Malayan politics, one of the pillars upon which Independence would be built, but at this stage its weakness and reluctance to do anything but carp filled Gurney with dismay.

In the first week of October 1951, Gurney committed to paper a frank *aide-mémoire*, unable to hide his bitterness and despondency. How could the Chinese not realise that their only hope of survival, let alone prosperity, lay in defeating the Communists? And yet these wealthy, self-styled leaders were only interested in their own short-term material gain, 'living in luxury and *** criticising the security forces'.[4] Like a country parson in a rich parish who can yet not rally enough enthusiasm from his congregation to get the roof mended, Gurney looked with frustration at the way these wealthy men lived in comfort, devoting themselves to making money, forever calling on others to protect them, and apparently not caring one jot that their smug demands were causing resentment amongst the rest of the community. As far as Gurney was concerned the battle was probably being lost and he did not have far to look for someone to blame.

While Gurney sat on his veranda trying to maintain his resolve, yet finding every prospect increasingly depressing, Chin Peng was looking out over the jungle from his hill top in Pahang and finding himself in a very similar frame of mind. His army's performance had improved, local leadership was more aggressive, tactics and junglecraft were more professional, and it had certainly been possible to achieve some notable successes. However, there were some worrying trends developing again: casualties had been higher than expected, and although there was no fundamental difficulty in recruiting replacements, the failure of attacks on the Security forces to seize any significant number of weapons meant that the MRLA platoons could not expand. The force of 20,000 or so that Chin Peng had hoped for in 1948 was still no more than that, a hope for the future.

What really concerned him was that he stood alone. In Korea, when the North Korean Army was driven from the field by the UN and ROK forces, Chinese regular troops could be brought in to reverse the defeat without any problem. A decade later, in Vietnam, the Vietcong were able to bring masses of war material of all kinds into South Vietnam, and to move divisions of North Vietnamese regular troops in when they were needed to confront the Americans. Chin Peng could call on nothing of the sort, as there was no open border with a friendly power. The mountainous country of the Thai border could have been ideal for smuggling in arms and infiltrating reinforcements, even though the border was short and not impossible patrol, but the Thais to the north were no sympathisers to the Communist cause, and were co-operating with the British to ensure that overt movements across the border were controlled. The sandy beaches of the long east coast were open to smuggling arms in small boats, but this was never possible on a scale large enough make a significant difference, and the Royal Navy became very good at intercepting most of those who tried. Effectively, Chin Peng was limited to the resources that he could find in Malaya, and that meant fighting for them.

It was not just against the Government that he must contend. Looking behind the bald statistics of incidents and contacts it is possible see how the nature of the Communists' campaign was being forced into change. The number of incidents was up very considerably on the period before Kuala Krau, but a high proportion of the increase was focused on the civilian Chinese population rather than on the Security forces. Police stations were being attacked, but not now with the success of the early months of the campaign. Police and Army convoys were being ambushed, but as the Security forces deployed more armoured vehicles and as response tactics became more sophisticated and aggressive, so these ambushes became less successful and more painful for the MRLA squads involved. At the same time, the squatters were beginning to appreciate that the penalties for lending comfort to the enemy were harsh, and, in any case, as the people grew more prosperous so doubts began to grow as to whether it was really sensible to sacrifice well-being now for the sake of some sketchily-drawn Communist heaven that might or might not materialise in the future. It became harder to squeeze rice and medicines out of reluctant workers, and the Communist campaign degenerated still further into pure terrorism.

Behind the façade of renewed aggressiveness Chin Peng was in fact finding it hard to maintain the morale of his fighting troops. As many inexperienced commanders have found to their cost it was not enough to issue directives from the relative safety of a headquarters deep in the jungle; he had to lead and encourage his men by example, and, given the way the MRLA units were dispersed and the slow and erratic communications system that was the best the insurgents had been able to devise, it was just not possible for him to provide that sort leadership. A charismatic leader might have been able to find a way to overcome the difficulties and lift the spirits of his men by sheer force of personality, but Chin Peng was no Mao Tse Tung – he was an organiser, an administrator who was largely out of contact with his army, and rarely saw his rank and file.

For the rank and file, the problem of poor morale was rooted as much as anything in the mundane fact that they were having to live in growing discomfort and privation. Moreover, there was increasing resentment of the way that the senior Party 'cadres' seemed to be able to enjoy, not just better food and luxuries such as toiletries and radios, but wives and mistresses too. About ten per cent of all CTs in the jungle at any one time were women, but for the ordinary guerrilla these women were strictly out of bounds. For the leaders and political commissars, however, there was a different rule book. Many had brought their wives with them when they went into the jungle, and some did not hesitate to take mistresses from among the women in their platoons. Once again, the Chinese tendency to think the worst of their superiors did its insidious work and the resentment was by no means always misplaced. To start with, the Central Committee's response to low morale was to issue edifying pamphlets with titles such as 'Let us fight together against the phenomenon of wavering confidence', and 'Maintain a serious attitude to Party resolutions', but judging by the growing number of surrenders the CTs in the jungle were not terribly impressed, and 'wavering confidence' continued to be a serious problem.

When this increasing disaffection began to infect some of the senior military and political officers it was time to do rather more than issue pamphlets. Isolated from colleagues by the conditions under which they were operating, and from their own subordinates by intellect and the responsibilities of command, some of these officials had started to think – and disliked what they thought. The trouble started in Johore, where the 4th Regt MRLA was as remote as any from the authority of the Central Committee, and had furthermore been on the receiving end of a great deal of bruising activity from the Security forces. Even if this activity had not resulted in exceptionally high casualties amongst the CTs, the even tenor of camp life had been disrupted to a most disheartening extent, so much so that many of the 4th Regt CTs had been forced to make a gruelling trek to the area of the Tasek Berak swamp in south-west Pahang, in a rather pallid but conscious effort to emulate Mao Tse Tung's 'Long March'. In Tasek Berak the survivors of the march were reasonably secure, but largely isolated from supply and a long way from the kind of targets that might have provided even the semblance of successful guerrilla activity. 'The devil makes work for idle hands to do', and the work of denouncing the Party soon started. To the complaints about material discomfort and the privileges taken by the leaders were added charges of military incompetence and a lack of accountability amongst the members of the Central Committee. One fairly accurate accusation was that members were unelected, and were even afraid to let anyone know their names. Worse, these Olympians were sometimes described as politically unsound – 'bourgeois' was the ominous word that began to be heard at mutual criticism sessions.

One prominent critic was Lam Swee, a Hokkien who had been head of the Barbers' Union in Singapore and then Vice President of the Pan-Malayan Federation of Trades Unions. When the MRLA went into the jungle in 1948 he had become Political Commissar of the 4th Regt, while retaining his position on the South Johore Regional Committee with a reputation as both a thinker and an effective activist. Investigations of the general despondency pervading 4th Regt platoons in Johore and southern Pahang yielded the shocking truth that not only had Lam Swee been an accessory to attacks on the leadership by the rank and file, but that he had in fact instigated many of them. One of his platoon commanders was summarily shot in consequence, while Lam Swee was disarmed and placed under a form of open arrest, so that he might face up to his 'mistakes'. Realising that he could no longer look forward to a flourishing career in the MCP he gave himself up to the Police in Bentong on 27 June 1950.

The surrender of so prominent and senior a member of the MCP and MRLA hierarchy was a triumph for the Security forces, and caused a considerable stir. Desmond Neill, the Chinese Affairs Officer in Bentong, was in the Police station when Lam Swee was brought in, and remembers the effect of the report to the Special Branch Kuala Lumpur:

> The result was explosive. The OCPD was told to hold him and look after him until someone could come over and interview him. As a European officer I was asked to stay with him as an assurance that he would be well looked after and I supplied him with piles of Hokkien noodles and hot drinks. We spoke in Hokkien and he told me that he was physically unable to stand up to the rigours of jungle life. He was sallow and looked as if he was a malaria case, and was covered in sores and scratches.[5]

At first, Lam Swee's defection was concealed while he was interrogated, in the hope that the MRLA might be put at a disadvantage. Then, after some weeks, his sores and scratches healed and his malaria cured, he was paraded for the benefit of the press, now sleek and well covered (no doubt due to further supplies of Hokkien noodles). Much play was made with the notion that here was a senior idealogue of the MCP who had defected because he had come to see the flaws in Marxist-Leninist doctrines, and it is true that he later became an effective contributor to the psychological campaign that the Government was beginning put together.[6] However, Desmond Neill, who had questioned Lam Swee in his own language before he had had the chance to rationalise his situation, was not wholly convinced of his conversion to rectitude and still believes that it was mostly the privation of guerrilla life that had broken him. 'The softer life that he had led in Singapore did not equip him for the rigours of the Malayan jungle as much as it did for some of his Malayan counterparts'.[7]

As it transpired, there was no need for the Police to have tried to conceal Lam Swee's defection. For once, the MCP's courier system worked, and the Central Committee knew of his surrender almost as soon as he had walked out onto the Mentakab road and flagged down the local driver who took him into Bentong. Chin Peng reacted as explosively as the Special Branch. His response took the form of a violent diatribe, a tract called 'The incident of Lam Swee going over to the enemy and betraying the Party', and he clearly resolved that nothing like this must ever be allowed to happen again. Lam Swee's pessimistic view of the prospects for his survival if he had stayed with the MRLA was well founded. He had before him the example of Siew Lau.

Siew Lau had been a schoolmaster until the mobilisation in 1948 when, like Lam Swee, he had become a political commissar, operating in the north Johore and Malacca areas. Amongst the second echelon of MCP leaders he was probably the finest academic, having a good enough understanding of the theories of Marxism-Leninism and of the 'new democracy' of Mao Tse Tung to be able to produce a flow of critical pamphlets condemning the Central Committee for being undemocratic, and Chin Peng and the Politburo for deciding to wage war at the wrong time and in the wrong way. He was bitterly scornful of the MCP's published manifesto, which he believed showed no understanding of Mao's principles, and he was especially critical of the Party's proposal to reform the ownership and management of estates and mines in a way that could only antagonise the masses. He went on to condemn the slashing of rubber trees that destroyed the peasants' livelihoods, the burning of identity cards, the murders and brutality, the whole slide into terrorism that was alienating the Movement from the very people whose support was so desperately needed. Early in 1950 Chin Peng moved to put a stop to this blatant apostasy. Siew Lau was arrested and given the option of execution or confessing his 'errors' but he refused to recant, and on 15 May 1950 he paid the penalty, along with his wife and three associates. There seems little doubt that the order for his execution came directly from Chin Peng.

Despite the draconian way in which Chin Peng dealt with dissidents the rumblings of discontent within the MCP and MRLA were not silenced. Lam Swee and Siew Lau were only two among many dissatisfied senior members of the Party and Chin Peng was once again forced to reconsider his position. The galling fact was that much of the criticism was well aimed, and a great deal of what Siew Lau had died to maintain was true. Despite the optimistic tone of the orders and exhortations from Central, whatever local tactical successes the MRLA and Min Yuen might achieve, it was apparent that the Revolution was failing in its overriding objective, to mobilise the masses. Both Gurney and Chin Peng faced the same problem, how to gain the active support of the Chinese community, and both were baffled. It seemed to each of them that he was losing the war: if that were possible, each was right.

CHAPTER SEVENTEEN

THE UNKINDEST CUT OF ALL – GURNEY'S DEATH

Fraser's Hill was a little mountain resort, some 60 miles north of Kuala Lumpur on the borders of Selangor and Pahang, in the main west Malayan mountain range, about 5,000 feet above sea level north of the road from Kuala Kubu Bahru to Raub. Like Rome, it was built on seven hills,[1] but there the resemblance ended, for Fraser's Hill was no neoclassical city but a self-conscious re-creation of suburban English nostalgia, an estate of 'stockbroker Tudor' bungalows standing each in its own tree-clad compound, loosely gathered round a nine-hole golf course. Here, refugees from the heat and stress of Kuala Lumpur could enjoy cool evenings and log fires, could walk in the morning through swirling mist on grass that was only a shade too coarse to be the idyllic parkland it was meant to call to mind, and could drink beer in a fake British pub. Never mind that when you looked closely the trees that shaded the driveways and the walks were not elms or oaks, or that the colours in the gardens were more likely to come from the familiar cannas and morning glory than from hybrid tea roses: for a time you could pretend.

On the morning of 6 October 1951, sick at heart, Sir Henry Gurney set off to spend the weekend at the Lodge, the High Commissioner's bungalow on the Hill, anxious for just a couple of days to get the Emergency and all its foetid problems out of his mind. With him went Lady Gurney and his Private Secretary, D J Staples, and as was his custom, they travelled in the official unarmoured Rolls Royce with the new Federation flag fluttering on the little jackstaff on the bonnet. Gurney sat behind the driver, with Lady Gurney beside him on his left, and Staples beside the driver. Presumably someone had telephoned through to the Lodge warning the servants that the High Commissioner was on his way, and arrangements had also had to be made to pick up a Police escort on the way out of Kuala Lumpur. On the main road north the little convoy was able to make reasonably good time, but at Kuala Kubu Bahru they had to turn off onto the narrow, winding road that leads upwards towards Raub and then on to Kuala Lipis, and it was nearly one o'clock when they reached the Gap – the start point of the rough, single-track road that wound perilously up the side of the mountain to Fraser's Hill. This road was difficult at the best of times, steep jungle-covered slopes rising on one side, the ground falling away precipitously on the other to ravines several hundred feet below, and the road itself, sometimes little more than a track, so narrow that only one-way traffic could use it in a tidal-flow system, alternating hourly, up and down. It was an ideal set-up for an ambush.

Just after one, the little convoy started to grind slowly up the hill, first a Police Landrover carrying six policemen armed with rifles and carbines, then the High Commissioner's Rolls Royce and finally an armoured Police scout car bringing up the rear. Presently the scout car overheated, and was left behind.

About half way up the hill the two vehicles were ambushed. Even today it is not entirely clear what happened. The ambush was apparently set by Siu Mah (who had commanded the raid on the coal mine at Batu Arang in 1948), with a squad of 30 or 40 CTs from 11th Regt MRLA. As might have been expected, Siu Mah's organisation was expert: the ambush position extended for about 200 yards along a curving stretch of the road where the bamboo and *belukar* hung close from the steeply sloping hillside above. Carefully prepared positions for three fire sections had been hacked out and concealed, access had been cut for the usual charging squad to collect ammunition and weapons, escape routes had been cleared and a simple but efficient system of communication with flags had been installed.[2] From examination of the scene afterwards it appeared that the CTs were armed with two Bren guns, a Sten and rifles.

The first burst of fire hit and stopped the Landrover, putting it out of action so as to block the track, and wounding all six constables. Although some of them were able to debus and return fire there was very little that they could do and the terrorists were soon able to concentrate on the Rolls Royce which had been brought to a halt some 40 yards back down the hill, its tyres shot to pieces. After a short time, during which the car was hit several times, the offside rear door opened and Sir Henry Gurney got out. Without seeming to be in any way hurried, he closed the door and walked to the side of the road, towards the terrorist ambush. Before he got there he was shot dead, falling into the foothill ditch at the bottom of the slope. No-one can say what was in his mind on that last, almost leisurely walk: Harry Miller[3] believes that he deliberately tried to draw the fire away from his wife, and that would surely be in tune with all we know of him. Gurney lived quietly and gallantly doing his duty, and he died as he had lived.

The firing continued for what seemed an age but was probably only a few minutes, then a bugle sounded, the terrorists withdrew and everything fell silent. Lady Gurney and Staples were miraculously unhurt, but the driver who had managed to get out of the car into cover had been wounded. It was 45 minutes before reinforcements came and Lady Gurney could be persuaded to leave her husband's body.

In the appalling shock that rippled through the Government and Security forces that dreadful evening when the news broke, the first thought was that there had been a terrible breach of security, that the ambush had been laid with the High Commissioner as its specific target, and that Siu Mah had been acting on information about Gurney's movements given by a traitor amongst the staff at the Lodge or at

King's House,[4] or at the Police station that had provided the escort. Every Special Branch officer was called back to duty, and Army units were mobilised all over the country. Virtually the entire 1st Battalion, Royal West Kents, besides Gurkhas and anyone else who could be co-opted, were put into the jungle to follow up Siu Mah's gang, RAF *Lincolns* dropped tons of bombs on what were hoped might be the terrorists' escape routes, batteries of 25 pounders and medium artillery laid down prophylactic fire from gun positions on the Raub road, and with a hint of desperation units everywhere were turned out and set to flogging the jungle no matter how far away from Fraser's Hill they might be. The jungle, rather than the terrorists, defied all these efforts. One or two CTs were killed, the rest followed standard practice and split up into small groups to re-form later, and after a month the monsoon broke, washing away any chance of catching Siu Mah.

To this day it is not clear whether Siu Mah planned to kill the High Commissioner, or even whether he fully understood what he had done, at least at the time.[5] A log of the ambush party's activity which had unaccountably been kept since it moved into position, and just as unaccountably been left behind for the Police to find, showed that the ambush had been in place for over 36 hours before Gurney had driven into it. During that time there had been many vehicle movements up and down the road, some of them military convoys where the pickings in terms of arms and ammunition would have been well worth the costs, and many of them 'soft' targets that must have looked very tempting at the time if Siu Mah did not want to risk taking casualties. General Poett, for example, the Chief of Staff, FARELF, had driven through the ambush unknowingly on the Friday, and only ten minutes before Gurney was killed. Rear-Admiral Faulkner, Flag Officer, Malayan Area, had come down the Hill in a convoy of three vehicles, flying his pennant from the bonnet of his car for all see. Other documents captured soon afterwards seemed to show that Siu Mah had set the ambush as a training exercise as much as anything, with no specific target in mind, and nothing that fell into the Security forces' hands then or later gave any indication that he was acting on the basis of a security leak – for some weeks he did not even seem to be sure who it was that he had killed, thinking it was the Commissioner of Police. And yet why wait so long? Why ignore so many excellent and rewarding targets? And why did the log itself peter out on the morning of the Saturday, long before the Gurneys drove into the trap, as though the writer had lost interest in an academic exercise and was now preparing for what he knew was the real business of the day? The official verdict, after study of the site and the captured documents and the testimony of the survivors, was that Siu Mah had brought off a fluke, that he had set a speculative ambush which had proved tragically but unexpectedly successful, and that there had been no culpable breach of security. That may have been right, and probably was, but it must be borne in mind that any other conclusion would have been an admission of ghastly failure, a gift to the morale of the insurgents beyond anything they had already achieved by Gurney's death, and it would moreover have had a most harmful effect on the careers of several officers and officials at all levels:

there has to be a question mark even today over the whole affair.

Frustrated by the failure of the Security forces catch Siu Mah, the authorities turned in cold fury on the little town of Tras, a few miles away from the murder scene. Tras had had a bad reputation as a hotbed of Communist sympathy since the beginning of the Emergency three years before. In that time, 15 actions had been fought between the CTs and the Security forces in or near the town, 20 people had been killed, and time and time again camps and dumps had been found in the nearby jungle. It was as certain as could be that the Communists were getting very active support from the 2,000 or so townsfolk, and any lingering doubts about their disloyalty were finally dispelled when a terrorist who was shot trying to get into the town to collect food and medicines was found to be carrying letters and documents that were totally incriminating.

Early on the morning of 7 November 1951, troops and police sealed off Tras and removed the entire population under 17 D regulations. The town was destroyed – it simply disappeared from the maps.[6] Not long afterwards, in the War Office in London, someone intercepted the file containing the correspondence in which Gurney's replacement had been so assiduously canvassed, and returned it to Registry with a simple note: 'NFA. Overtaken by events'.

CHAPTER EIGHTEEN

TWO MANIFESTOS OF FAILURE

Only a few days before Gurney met his death on the Fraser's Hill road, Chin Peng put the finishing touches to what was to become known as the 'October Manifesto'. Some reports say that, faced with the apparent failure of his campaign so far, he had convened another top-level conference at his jungle HQ near Mentakab in Pahang, at which this completely new statement of policy and strategy was drafted. If so, who attended the conference and contributed to the new thinking is not recorded,[1] but one major contributor was surely Siew Lau, whose voice, only slightly muffled by the mould of his jungle grave, can be heard in every important passage. The policy towards the masses had been mistaken, the use of terrorism to extort support had only fomented hatred and opposition rather than cooperation, sabotage at the mines and in the rubber estates had attacked workers' livelihoods, and attitudes to the 'bourgeoisie' had been too rigidly doctrinaire. It was recognised that some of the richer Chinese (such those who led the MCA) were irredeemable, but the less wealthy, the smaller businessmen and estate owners, were surely exploitable provided they were handled in such a way as to win them over rather than antagonise them. (The unspoken thought behind this shift in policy was that these minor bourgeois must not allowed to realise that their usefulness to the cause would be shortlived and that in time they would be purged.)

All those involved in the struggle must from now on ensure that any action taken was 'broadly acceptable to the masses', methods were be 'regulated and moderate', and only 'legitimate' means were to be used. That meant that taking and destroying identity cards must stop, rubber trees (especially on the smaller Chinese-owned estates) must not be slashed, buses must not be burned, and 'executions' must be confined to proven traitors, and not used as a means of extortion. Tin miners and planters were still legitimate targets (the question of their wives and children was not addressed), but attacks on the Army and Police were to be made more discriminatingly, where propaganda results might be significant, or where there was a good chance of a worthwhile pay-off in seized arms and ammunition.

Most importantly, political activity would from now on rank on equal terms with military activity – that is to say, trade unions were to be infiltrated and manipulated, strikes were to be fomented, New Village committees were to be suborned and the effort to indoctrinate in the schools was to be stepped up. To anyone who had been a Party activist before 1948 this was all familiar stuff: the only problem in trying to turn the clock back in this way was that most of those who were expert in this kind subversion had been drawn into the jungle when the MRLA mobilised and could not now used. Chin Peng was rather in the position of someone who has been trying to hammer a screw into a piece of wood only to find, when he finally understood that there was a more effective way of going about things, that he had already improvidently thrown away the screwdriver. By contrast, the Government's control over the unions, the press and the levers civil power was now far more sophisticated than it had been three years previously, and the chances of stirring up strife were that much the less. For the first time, the wisdom of the decision to risk all on armed struggle began to look questionable, and Siew Lau's view that it had been taken at the wrong time and in the wrong circumstances appeared more logical than at first scrutiny.

Rather forlornly, the Manifesto also faced up to one of the MCP's fundamental defects. Right from the beginning, there had never been any real possibility that the MRLA might have made common cause with any but a handful of Malays, the history of the war years militated against that, but now, far too late, it was realised that the failure to win any significant support from the Malay 'workers' was a potentially fatal flaw. There was little enough that Chin Peng could offer, but the Manifesto held out the promise of resettlement and security of land tenure as though it was in the Party's power to confer them. Even more forlornly, recognising that the new policy would make it harder to maintain supply to the MRLA squads, the Manifesto enjoined all the Comrades to start cultivating vegetables in clearings deep in the jungle. Survival had moved to the top of the agenda.

Although the Manifesto was issued at the beginning of October 1951, the MCP's courier system worked as slowly as usual, and copies of this new directive did not reach some of the remoter MRLA units or their undercover Min Yuen supporters until several weeks into 1952. Its effects were not immediately obvious in the field, and the Security forces did not lay hands on a copy until midway through 1952; Briggs never saw it. If he had known of it, he would have been able to appreciate the extent to which it tacitly admitted how successful his policies had been, and then perhaps he might have been able leave his post with a greater feeling of satisfaction at a job well done. As it was, he was coming to the end of his contract with a sense that he had still so much to do.

On 12 November 1951, General Sir Robert Lockhart, KCB, CIE, MC, was due to arrive in Kuala Lumpur with time for a short handover before taking up his post as the second Director of Operations on 27 November, and Briggs would retire, for the second time in his career, to his home in Cyprus.

In anticipation of Lockhart's takeover, Briggs sat down to compile his last report and appreciation, which was published in the first week of November. It was in effect both a briefing for Lockhart and an account of his own stewardship during 20 months in office, but it was also a chance to get off his chest many of the frustrations that he had found debilitating. There was, once again, a diatribe about the Chinese refusal to come down 'off the fence', in his appraisal of Police strengths and weaknesses he made little attempt to hide his feelings about Gray, and he was most uncomplimentary about that category of European businessman 'most of whom are in towns, are engrossed in their flourishing businesses and are almost out of touch with the Emergency', contrasting their lack of commitment with the staunchness of the rural planters and miners. He commented bitterly on the failure of Sir William Jenkin and Nicol Gray to co-operate in achieving a significant improvement in the flow of Intelligence, and he acknowledged the shortcomings of the 'big battalion' mentality in military planning, comparing it unfavourably with the growing success of locally planned and executed operations within what he called 'framework' troop dispositions.[2] After some discussion of relatively minor factors, such as the effect of antiquated leave provisions on the availability of experienced officers and administrators,[3] the success of food controls,[4] and the difficulties and advantages of setting up an efficient system of Kampong Guards, and Home Guards in the New Villages, he did feel able to report satisfactory progress in the resettlement programme, with the proviso that there was still a great deal to do to provide adequate security. This was the vital ingredient: 'security leads to confidence, confidence leads to better information, better information leads to greater Security force success, and greater Security force success leads to more security'. In that circular creed he summed up his whole philosophy: the problem 'was anything but a purely military and Police one, but one which affected in varying degrees the whole structure of Government'.

Briggs' most serious complaints, however, were reserved for the British Government in London. He despaired of getting Shinwell or Strachey or Griffiths to realise the gravity of the situation. Despite promises made at meetings in London a year earlier nothing had improved, equipment and stores were only trickling through,[5] and in no dealings with the Colonial Office did there seem to be any sense of urgency. This lack of urgency pervaded Government circles in Kuala Lumpur as well: the need to lobby so many decisions through State Governments slowed things down, approval for expenditure was still subject to peacetime procedures and paralysing bureaucratic delay, decisions were avoided while the buck was passed, and very few senior officials were seized of the need to put the Federation on a war footing. As he left Malaya for the last time, Briggs made no secret of his feeling that he had been badly let down, and that he had not received the authority or the support that had been promised when he accepted the appointment. So often it seems to be the fate of men in Briggs' and Gurney's position that they build better than they know, that they leave behind them a reputation that is high enough, yet fails to recognise in what they were truly successful, and that they are replaced by successors who are able to build on what they inherit in a way that attracts fame and praise that would be the better earned if more critically applied. Briggs himself did not recognise how far he had led the Federation down the road to victory, nor did he live to savour the triumph. Within a few months of his retirement to Cyprus he died, worn out by the weight he had been carrying.

Ironically, as Briggs was leaving Malaya, the man who would finally bring many of the answers to his complaints was setting out from London to see for himself what needed to be done. On Trafalgar Day, 21 October 1951, two weeks after Gurney's assassination, there had been a change of Government in Britain, the Conservatives taking office with a slender majority of 16. Churchill's choice for the Colonial Office was Oliver Lyttleton, a tough-minded, experienced politician and administrator who fully shared Churchill's predilection for action when difficulty loomed. 'To put out your hands and grasp the danger is surely less deadly than wringing them,'[6] had been his guiding precept throughout a successful career that had encompassed service with the Brigade of Guards in the First World War, the Chairmanship of London Tin and Anglo-Oriental (both of which had substantial mining interests in Malaya), and ministerial office in the wartime Coalition Treasury team. He had also served as Minister of State in the Middle East, during Wavell's term as GOC, and had been tough-minded enough to sack the hero of the hour, Alan Cunningham, at Auchinleck's insistence. As Lyttleton saw it, the Attlee Government had been ousted only just in time, having brought Britain to the verge of economic disaster[7] and knowing Malaya well he was appalled at the possibility that its vital contribution to the prosperity of the Sterling Area might be lost to Communism for lack of any coherent effort to save it. When James Griffiths, his Labour predecessor, came to see him by way of handover, Lyttleton was decidedly unimpressed by the jaded defeatism that he showed. He felt 'first boredom and then exasperation' at Griffiths' naïve belief that 'universal suffrage . . . with a few trades unions and co-operative wholesale societies thrown in spell immediate peace, prosperity and happiness' and was particularly struck by his spiritless admission that the Labour Government had been baffled by Malaya. Griffiths summed up the situation as 'a military problem to which we have not been able to find the answer', a comment which seemed to show that he had either not read or not understood the endless reports, appreciations and plans that had passed over his desk during the previous three years which stressed the interrelation of political, economic, social *and* military factors. It is really no wonder that Gurney and Briggs were driven to despair by the lack of understanding and educated support from London.

However, things were about to change dramatically under Lyttleton: 'doing something' about Malaya was at the top of his list of priorities, and the first step was to go there and find out what that something ought to be. He arrived in Kuala Lumpur on 29 November 1951, after a tedious and exhausting journey via Colombo and a stopover in Singapore, to get some tropical clothes made and meet MacDonald. As he stepped from the plane he was met by a phalanx of journalists with a barrage of questions, and like so many others before him, he gave some unguarded answers which seemed to him unexceptionable, but caused considerable dismay to his listeners: his visit was exploratory, he had come to see for himself, the first priority was to restore law and order, he could say nothing until he knew more, then he would give a press conference and they should know what he thought and ask whatever questions they wished. MacDonald, who knew what was in people's minds, and understood the oblique way of journalists in Singapore and Malaya, told him politely that he had put his foot it – and so he had. What the journalists had wanted to hear was that he came bearing the gift of political advancement and that Independence was not far off, but of these things he had said nothing. Headlines the following day were on these lines: 'Secretary of State denies constitutional change', and 'Continuance of police state forecast', and Lyttleton acquired that deep distrust of journalists that politicians so often develop when they find they don't know how to handle them.

After a wasted day meeting the Governors of other British dependencies in the area that fell under MacDonald's aegis as Commissioner General for South East Asia, Lyttleton was finally able to get down to the business of seeing for himself. He met del Tufo, the Chief Secretary, who had been recalled from leave to act as Officer Administering the Government, he met Gray and Urquhart and Jenkin, he was harangued by planters and miners and soldiers and policemen and civil servants and bankers and businessmen, all of whom assailed him with their complaints and nostrums, and Lyttleton was appalled by what he saw. 'I have never seen such a tangle as that presented by the Government of Malaya', he wrote later. He could see no clear dividing lines of responsibility between the Acting High Commissioner, del Tufo, and Lockhart, the Director of Operations, the Police were in chaos and a state of schism, 'intelligence – was scanty and unco-ordinated between the military and civil authorities', there was a shortage of armoured vehicles and equipment of every kind and nobody was trying to do anything about it, the Constitution was a tangle and many of the officials involved were not adequate for their tasks.

Some decisions were easily and quickly taken. He sacked Gray, who left the country immediately in a clandestine way that many found upsetting;[8] he got rid of Jenkin (in fact, he claimed to have sacked him too, but since Jenkin had already had his resignation accepted by Gurney in September, perhaps all that Lyttleton did was to ensure that no-one agreed to him withdrawing it when he found out that Gray was leaving); most controversially he decided that what was needed was a new High Commissioner who should be responsible for both the civil and military sides, the 'Supremo' for whom Harding had been canvassing for so long. This would mean direct responsibility for operations so whoever was appointed would need an experienced colonial administrator as Deputy High Commissioner to take the weight of everyday civil administration from the High Commissioner's shoulders. This last decision presented certain problems. There was no provision in the Constitution for a Deputy High Commissioner, and all the signs were that the Rulers were already disaffected enough with the way that the British were, as they saw it, perverting the Treaty relationship and giving undue favour to the Chinese, without them asking the Rulers to accept a further reduction in their status and power. Lyttleton gave the job of persuading them to del Tufo, who spoke excellent Malay and was able to use his experience to get their agreement, even though it did nothing to allay their suspicions when Lyttleton refused to appoint a Malay to the post. He also refused to appoint del

Tufo himself, although he was the obvious candidate, preferring instead Donald MacGillivray, Chief Secretary in Jamaica. MacGillivray's appointment turned out extremely well in the long run, but del Tufo was understandably piqued and rather than lose face reverting to his substantive post of Chief Secretary, chose to retire to his native Malta, taking with him a knighthood as some kind of consolation for his disappointment.

After a short trip to Hong Kong, Lyttleton went back Kuala Lumpur for a very brief stay in the Chief Secretary's house (now empty), to draft his submission to the Cabinet, finally returning to London 21 December 1951. The next day he went to lunch with Churchill at Chartwell, to find that the Prime Minister had already invited Montgomery to join them. To both of them, then, Lyttleton summed up the Malayan situation by repeating Briggs' ideology: the war could not be won without gaining the support of the whole population, in particular the Chinese, and to get that support it was necessary at least to start winning the war. Whoever took the job would have to break this circular situation – when once it was broken things should improve at an accelerating rate. When he had been in Malaya, Lyttleton had been told by many vociferous lobbyists that the man for the job was Montgomery, a view that was shared by journalists in the UK, and when the press found out that Montgomery had been at Chartwell for the critical meeting, speculation became very vocal. The day afterwards Lyttleton got a letter from Montgomery:

Dear Lyttleton,

MALAYA

We must have a plan.
Secondly, we must have a man.
When we have a plan and a man,
we shall succeed: not otherwise.

Yours sincerely,

(Signed) Montgomery, FM.

Lyttleton was less than overwhelmed by the depth of Montgomery's perception. 'I may, perhaps without undue conceit, say that this had occurred to me'.[9] If there had been any idea in Lyttleton's mind that the planters in Malaya had been right, and that Montgomery was the man for the job, it evaporated there and then. In fact, the man he did want, and whose possible appointment he had discussed with Malcolm MacDonald before flying back to London, was General Sir Brian Robertson, GOC-in-C, MELF, who had served under Alexander in Italy and shown himself to be a level-headed and efficient administrator as well as a sound tactician. At this time, in

1951, Robertson was coping sensitively and effectively with the dangerous political situation in Egypt that followed the deposition of King Farouk, as well as the growing anti-British feeling in the Suez Canal Zone. Lyttleton saw him as the ideal choice, and was distressed and surprised when he refused: he did not feel able to leave the Middle East at such a critical time and in any event did not want to take on another overseas tour, having spent 28 of the last 31 years out of Britain. When MacDonald was told by cable that Robertson had turned the job down, he infuriated Lyttleton by cabling back that he could not guarantee to keep things under control if an appointment was delayed, and that in any case he did not approve of giving the job to a General, since this would be read as the imposition of a military dictatorship – this after agreeing the approach to Robertson apparently without reservation when discussing the possibility face to face with Lyttleton only a few days earlier in Singapore. Lyttleton replied, telling him in round terms that the responsibility was not MacDonald's but his own, and MacDonald's stock with the new administration slipped several points more.

In the meantime, someone had to be found. Lyttleton went into conclave with his friend and colleague, Anthony Head, the new Secretary of State for War, with the Army List in front of them. It is not clear which of the top-ranking generals they considered, nor why some were rejected and others made their way on to the short list – even many years after the event the Ministry of Defence refuses to let the crucial documents into the public domain. Lyttleton's only published comment was that the name they finally came up with was not their first choice, although excellent in every respect. His appointment came as a surprise to nearly everyone: the new High Commissioner and Director of Operations was to be Lieutenant General Sir Gerald Templer, KBE, DSO, at that time GOC, Eastern Command, a man well known in the Army but hardly at all to the public.

CHAPTER NINETEEN

A VERY NECESSARY PURGATIVE

General Templer may have been a surprise selection and not even Lyttleton's first choice, but he brought to Malaya a mixture of experience that was uniquely fitted to the task. As a major commanding 'A' Company of the Loyals in Palestine before the Second World War he had impressed everyone with his staff analysis of what was a bafflingly complex political and military situation, and had then gone on to show that he was no desk-bound theoretician but an aggressive and inventive tactician, dealing with Arab and Jewish partisans alike with a trenchant firmness that was in later years to be recognised as one of his trademarks. Even in those days he stood out from his brother officers as original, impatient and eager, intolerant of others' shortcomings and as much a driver as a leader, characteristics that were to be intensified in later years. In those days, too, he learnt the value of good Intelligence in dealing with insurgents, and started to acquire the skills in managing and using it that would be so important to him in Malaya 15 years later.

During the Italian campaign he had commanded 56 (London) Division at the Anzio landings, driving his brigades on by sheer force of personality, smoking incessantly, carrying with him an assortment of noxious bottles clanking in the back of his jeep, always looking pale and close to exhaustion, living on his nerves and exuding such a vibrant energy that he became known to his rueful subordinates as 'the scalded cat'. When his jeep was blown up on a mine, presumably dissipating his stock of alcohol, he was invalided home with serious back injuries,[1] and was given temporary command of the German section of SOE while he convalesced – not perhaps his first exposure to the nefarious ways of covert warfare, but again experience that would prove helpful to him in later years.

In 1945 he was appointed Director of Military Government in the British Zone of Germany, and found himself having to cope with a starving population and the vindictive intransigence of a pettifogging bureaucracy that appeared bent on frustrating rather than helping the business of getting the totally fractured German economy moving again. Many of his views about civil administrators were formed at this time. One of his biggest problems lay in getting the Germans to help themselves: defeat seemed to have induced a bovine apathy that was unexpected in a nation that, until now, had been distinguished by its disciplined and industrious approach even in the worst causes. It was not just that he was expected to get the local administrative system working well enough again to deal with problems of rationing, hygiene and all the myriad small matters that might make life liveable once more, but he was also charged with fostering active democratic institutions in a community which had known and accepted dictatorship not altogether reluctantly for 14 years. To do all this he must draw on only a meagre pool of able people who were not too obviously contaminated by Nazism.

He tackled these tasks with the same nervous passion that he had shown in the Anzio beachhead, respecting neither person nor regulation if they stood in his way. One of his appointments, as *Bürgermeister* of Cologne, failed to meet his demanding standards and was peremptorily sacked. It is revealing of Templer's mindset that when that failed *Bürgermeister*, Konrad Adenauer, became Chancellor of West Germany, Templer expressed neither regret nor approval for what he had done – the decision was in the past, it had been right at the time, and anyone who didn't like it was free do the other thing. There was little room in Templer's make-up for self-doubt.

From Germany Templer went to the War Office, firstly as Director of Military Intelligence, and then as VCIGS – it was clear to everyone who could read the runes that he was already marked as a possible future CIGS. Lyttleton, convinced, proposed his appointment as High Commissioner to Churchill, who made some small to-do about agreeing and made Templer fly to Canada (where Churchill was in the middle of intergovernmental meetings), so that he could receive approval and some rather maudlin good wishes. All was set fair for Templer to go, except that Templer himself now started to make difficulties. With the example of Briggs' miseries in front of him, and unimpressed by the defeatism and political temporising of the principal players in the previous administration, he was not prepared to rely on good wishes; he refused to move until he had been given a crystal-clear directive that laid out simply and unambiguously what his aim was to be and what authority he had in setting out to achieve it.

He got what he wanted from Lyttleton, who understood such matters. For the first time since 1946, a High Commissioner was to go to Malaya with an unequivocal mandate to bring the country to Independence and with a statement of the steps that must be taken before that Independence could be achieved. With authority as Director of Operations over all the Security Forces, Army, Police, Air Force and even the Royal Navy operating in coastal waters, he could grip the military situation as it had not been gripped up until now. As High Commissioner he could restructure the civil administration virtually as he pleased, hiring and firing officials, committing expenditure, modifying the Law, and tearing down old institutions as he saw fit, replacing them with new. He was to all intents and purposes a dictator, untrammelled except in his responsibility to defeat the Communists and create the democratic foundations of Independence.

He arrived in Kuala Lumpur on the afternoon of 7 February 1952, the day after the death of King George VI, and profiting from the sorry experiences of his predecessors he held a carefully prepared press conference in a tent at the airstrip. Del Tufo had not yet left for Malta and was at his side. In an anodyne statement Templer promised no easy solutions, and called for commitment from all the peoples of Malaya to solving the problems that faced the Federation. Then, in a gesture not entirely sensitive to someone who had already shown that he was going to be careful for his own safety, he was driven to King's House in Gurney's Rolls Royce, the bullet holes roughly patched but still very visible. Early that evening he was sworn in by the Chief Justice, and within a few more hours his first statement of policy was in the hands of the printers, with his Directive from the British Government appended.

His appointment was not universally welcomed. There were the ritual complaints about his background in Palestine, his draconian powers were loudly resented (most often by those very people who had called just as loudly upon Government to take firm action), to anyone who cared to listen MacDonald bemoaned the appointment of a soldier and made no secret of his resentment at being snubbed by Lyttleton, and there were the usual threats of boycotts. The Army generally greeted his arrival with relief (although some idle and incompetent officers were to regret their enthusiasm before long), but for the civil servants the pleasure was decidedly muted. Many were still convinced that the Emergency was a horrible dream from which they might soon awake, meanwhile clinging to the peacetime ways of years gone by as if nothing had happened. Urgency and haste were to be avoided, bucks were for passing, systems were to ensure that things were done in the right way rather than that the right things were done, and orders were the basis for discussion, not action. Gurney's murder had frightened some out of their complacency for a moment, but four months had gone by and the heavens had not yet fallen in. As Harry Miller of the *Straits Times* put it, 'The public of Malaya pondered, paid tribute to the memory of Sir Henry Gurney, mentally hitched up its trousers and sarongs with an oath of determination, and did nothing all'.[2]

Four days after he had taken office, Templer called some 200 senior civil servants and policemen together and read them the riot act. He started by establishing his credentials. Although he was a soldier, he was not inexperienced in the business of civil administration – as Military Governor of the British Zone of Germany he had dealt with Russians, Americans and French at the highest levels, as Vice Chief of the Imperial General Staff he had frequently attended Cabinet meetings, and his appointment had been made by Churchill, who had told him to write personally if he had any problems. The inference was clear: he would be master, and would brook no obstruction from subordinates. He would listen and take advice, he said, then make his decision. Once the plan was made and the orders were given there was be no further discussion. In the same way, each one of them was there to take decisions in his own sphere, and anyone who failed to take decisions would be sacked. Then, after a pause, he told them that anyone who took the wrong decision would be sacked as well. It was a chastened and quiet group of civil servants and policemen who left the Council Chamber, determined to do better in future; some of them even meant it.

For the European commercial community his arrival was hardly less distasteful, and Templer in his turn made little attempt to hide his feelings about what he saw as the silken ease and privilege of the boardrooms of Kuala Lumpur. Unfortunately, in his cocksure way of judging others, he started off by lumping the rural Europeans in with these nabobs, and many planters who had welcomed his coming and whose support he would have done well to nurture soon turned to suspicion and resentment. To be a planter at that time in Malaya was to live a life of almost constant strain, a life of work and fear and loneliness, with only the illusion of comfort to provide any relief. Except in the larger townships, European foods were difficult to get,[3] in the best British tradition alcohol was heavily taxed, and getting out to the club or to see friends was often hazardous. Some planters were well off but most were not, and many estate bungalows were dilapidated mouldy relics or gimcrack post-war contraptions, with vestigial plumbing; if electricity was available it depended on erratic generators that were frequently targeted by CTs as easy demolition exercises. Married planters left for work before first light, knowing that their wives would spend the morning wondering if they would come back for lunch, and those with children worried that the nearest doctor was often many miles away, at the end of a telephone line that worked only spasmodically. Running a rubber estate was a demanding business, with responsibility for everything from personnel management and welfare to arboriculture, roadmending, drains, hygiene, building, transport, engineering, schooling, marketing and profitability eventually ending up on the shoulders of one man. When, on top of this, he did duty as an Auxiliary Police Inspector, tried to keep a watchful eye on security and the performance of his Special Constables, acted as Registration Officer and supervised a host of other small but irritating functions that the Emergency and the Kuala Lumpur bureaucracy occasioned, a planter could perhaps be forgiven for feeling aggrieved when the new High Commissioner snarled at him that he was not doing enough to help win the war. In time, Templer was largely to mend his fences with the planters and miners – success excuses many things – but even to the end of his tour there were many who acknowledged and respected what he had done, but found little in him to admire or warm to.

In the aftermath of Gurney's murder the Chinese looked upon this new man with apprehension, nervously speculating what he might be planning to visit upon them. Seven weeks after he had taken office they found out. Late on the night of Monday, 24 March 1952, CTs believed to be from 36th Independent Platoon, MRLA, breached the pipeline supplying water to the town of Tanjong Malim, 52 miles north of Kuala Lumpur on the borders of Selangor and Perak. It was the kind of attack specifically condemned in the 'October Manifesto', and was really more of a nuisance than a serious incident. It had happened five times before, and each time the break had been repaired without too much difficulty, things being restored to normal until the next time 36th Platoon needed to fill its quota. The District Officer in Tanjong

Malim was Michael Codner, best know as one of the three men who had got out of Stalag Luft III during the War in the 'Wooden Horse' escape, and who had joined the Malayan Civil Service when he had been demobilised. He had been at Tanjong Malim virtually throughout the Emergency. At dawn on the morning of 25 March Codner collected a PWD repair gang together with a police escort of 15 men, and set off with the local PWD Engineer, W H Fourniss, for the sixth time, up the pipeline to find the breach and restore the water supply.

Unfortunately, this time it was not just a nuisance attack: following the best guerrilla precepts the CTs had laid an ambush at the breach, waiting for the repair gang to arrive, and Codner and his men walked into the middle of it. Codner and Fourniss, with several of the police, were killed in the first burst. Most of the rest of the party were wounded, but fought back, suffering more casualties, until Police reinforcements from Tanjong Malim arrived and charged the terrorist position. Including Codner and Fourniss, 12 men had been killed and eight wounded, only one, a Malay overseer, being unharmed. The CTs had lost two out of an estimated 40, and escaped with priceless weapons, including a Bren gun and several sub-machine guns.

With calculation and intent, Templer went apoplectic. Urquhart, his Army commander, was not best pleased to be required to deploy an entire brigade to cordon off Tanjong Malim, but Templer wanted a show of force, besides an insurance of his own security, as he went in person to the town to stage one of the most celebrated dramas of the entire Emergency. Community leaders from the town and the surrounding countryside, Chinese, Malay and Indian, 350 in all, were mustered in the hall of the Training College and subjected to one of his most pyrotechnic and spectacular tirades. He told them that he was sure that the ambush could only have happened with the connivance of some at least of Tanjong Malim's 5,000 inhabitants, that they knew who these people were, and only cowardice explained why they were keeping silent. There were active terrorists in the jungle near the town who were able to operate only because the people of the town were giving them support, information, food and comfort. In the first three months of the year there had been five ambushes, ten attacks on Army and Police patrols, lorries had been burnt, rubber slashed, trains derailed, buses destroyed, and eight policemen and seven civilians had been murdered;[4] yet through all this the citizens of Tanjong Malim had remained virtually silent. Since they were not prepared to assume the responsibilities of citizenship, Templer would use his powers under Regulation 17D to punish them all, innocent and guilty alike. They would all be confined by a house curfew for 22 hours each day, no-one might leave Tanjong Malim for any reason, the rice ration, already a calculated minimum, was reduced by half, shops might only open for two hours each day and the schools would be shut. Other towns that might be similarly inclined to offer succour to the Communists should take note. Meanwhile, each household was issued with a form on which information about Communists in the town was to be given, and these forms, unsigned, complete or blank, were to be collected in sealed boxes, which he himself would open – confidentiality was assured. In the event, along with the expected malicious rumour, some useable information was gleaned from this exercise, about 40 relatively unimportant fellow-travellers being arrested, while the big fry were left to carry on, perhaps a little more cautiously than before. Tanjong Malim was further shamed by losing its status as the centre of the administrative District, a disgrace that may or may not have been keenly felt by its inhabitants, and Templer decreed the setting up of a new District based on Slim River, 15 miles further north. (This decision reinforced his doubts about the quality of many of the MCS officials: when he asked the British Adviser to Perak how long it would take to get the new District up and running he was told, 'four to six months'. Templer wanted it in 48 hours, and got it.)

The restrictions on Tanjong Malim lasted in full for two weeks and were then progressively lifted. In time, the township settled down to be a secure and law-abiding community, and it seemed that Templer's brutalist approach must have shaken its inhabitants into a positive acceptance of their duty. Perhaps it did play a part in the town's redemption, but more probably the process was given impetus by the investment in security that followed. Enough barbed wire, for instance, was found to build a double fence with floodlighting and guard posts around the perimeter, and a well armed and supervised Home Guard was formed which did much to restore a sense of belonging. Templer had got what he wanted, though. His reputation as a hard man went before him now, and those who were still uncommitted in the conflict began to suspect that the 'Mandate of Heaven' might now have been transferred to the Government.

In Britain, 8,000 miles from the reality of the bitter conflict in Malaya, reaction was mixed. Those who approved saw in Templer's severity a welcome firmness, while a minority who disapproved cried 'brutality'. Listowel, who as Minister of State for the Colonies had so misled Parliament by his complacency at the start of the Emergency, inveighed against Templer's harshness but got short shrift from Lyttleton, who was determined that his man should not lack full backing as Gent and Gurney had done. In the Federation the reaction was almost wholly favourable, even amongst the Chinese, who instinctively respected firmness, and Templer was able to move on, focusing his restless energy on the many pressing tasks that faced him.

He sacked two British Advisers, and told Lyttleton that he would have liked to have got rid of more, but felt that dismissing all the doubtful starters at one go would undermine the standing of those few he valued. He travelled incessantly, appearing where he was least expected and harrying inefficient and lazy policemen and District Officers and PWD officials – anyone who seemed to him to be incompetent or idle. He withdrew one unsuccessful battalion from operations, sacking the CO and putting the troops back into training. Dismayed by the variability of performance between units, he set up the Jungle Warfare School at Kota Tinggi in Johore, which was to train the advance parties of all units arriving in the theatre on a cadre basis, besides appraising weapons and equipment, and developing new tactics and operational methods. Finding that there was no standardised course of instruction in jungle warfare he deputed one of his staff officers to gather from every successful unit the experience that each had derived of how to operate and defeat the MRLA, and put it all together in a comprehensive instruction manual, which was to become the sacred book of every soldier and policeman Malaya.[5] Drawing on his personal knowledge of the 'old boy net' in Whitehall, he badgered the War Office and the Ministry of Supply for shot guns and radios and armoured cars[6] – and he turned his blistering energy towards the problem of Intelligence.

If the vicious circle – poor security, no Intelligence, unsuccessful operations, poor security – was to be broken, it was in the field of Intelligence that the greatest opportunities lay. Any change was almost bound to be for the better. Templer poached an MI5 officer, J Morton, from MacDonald's staff in Singapore, where he was serving as Head of Security (Intelligence) for South East Asia, and appointed him to the new post of Director of Intelligence, ranking alongside the Deputy Director of Operations, the GOC and the Commissioner of Police. Morton had briefed Lyttleton's PPS, Hugh Fraser, when they were in Singapore before Christmas, Fraser had briefed Lyttleton, and Lyttleton had briefed Templer, so it was not overwhelmingly surprising that Templer's analysis of what needed to be done was very similar to Morton's own. In any case, both were Intelligence professionals and were at one on the principles that should be followed. There had never, since the start of the Emergency in 1948, been expert professional management of the whole Intelligence function, nor had there been effective co-ordination of Special Branch and Army Intelligence at any level. The need and the opportunity was to set up an integrated Intelligence operation, giving clear-cut responsibility for collecting Intelligence on the one hand, and interpreting and disseminating it on the other in such a timely way as to allow it to define Security forces' activity. While Morton was not line responsible for what the Special Branch or Military IOs did, he was functionally able to lay down policy and operating methods in some detail, and, more importantly, he had Templer's ear: if he found the old jealousies and inefficiencies persisting he could arrange for heads to be banged together with the maximum amount of cranial grief.

The structure that he imposed was essentially simple. From now on Special Branch was totally responsible for *all* Intelligence collection and reporting; at every level down to battalions and companies operating joint HQs with the Police, military IOs were to work alongside the Special Branch interpreting and presenting information so that it could be used to bring soldiers into action against the MRLA. There were to be no more 'private' informants, and Intelligence must no longer be seen as the 'property' of Police or Army, to be used as often to score points off one another as to kill Communists. One thing that both Templer and Morton were adamant about was that if the use of information by the Army might prejudice the Special Branch's penetration of MRLA or Min Yuen cells, then the Special Branch's needs must take priority.[7] In the matter of setting up an effective Intelligence function, as in so much else that he tackled, Templer characteristically wanted everything done yesterday, yet was also able to take the long view. The Emergency was *not* going to be over in a few weeks or months (whatever he might himself have said in an unguarded moment), and there was both the time and the need to build the careful accumulation of data that alone would lift the campaign out of its short-term, fire-fighting mode. It was worth while, for instance, setting up an Intelligence (Special Branch) School, which not only trained Special Branch operatives, but could also be used to open the eyes of senior officers to some of the arcane methods and uses of the world of Intelligence – a very necessary function!

In his book derived from his own experiences on the Staff in Malaya,[8] Richard Clutterbuck describes the way in which the Intelligence battle was fought on the ground. It was not always fought to Queensbury rules, and it is sadly true that in Malaya, as in so many campaigns, much had to be done in ways that, from this remove, may seem unsavoury and unscrupulous. What Clutterbuck and others describe, however, is the way in which dedicated, expert and often very brave men and women painstakingly gained the ascendancy over an enemy who was himself perfectly ready to use all the techniques of blackmail and terror that he could devise. In one field in particular the Intelligence services were already becoming expert and successful: increasingly good use could be made of information that seemed to flow freely from that best of sources, the surrendered terrorist. From 'Surrendered Enemy Personnel' (SEPs) it was possible to develop an increasingly detailed picture of the MRLA's order of battle, who its important leaders were, what their strengths and weaknesses were, and which units they commanded and where they operated. This kind of information was to make it possible to devise much more effective strategies, especially in concerting Police activity in the New Villages with targeted patrolling in the jungle against the MRLA.

However, the role of SEPs went considerably further than just providing information. The great majority saw what they had done not as surrendering, but as changing sides, and many became even more ardent in the Government cause than they had been in the cause of the Revolution. It was an extraordinary phenomenon: men (and women) who had served in the jungle for months and years alongside comrades they had depended upon, and with whom they had often formed close friendships, were perfectly prepared to go back into the jungle after only a few hours' rest, and lead Security forces to their camps, even taking part enthusiastically in the assault that followed. Their motives were a puzzle. Rewards for obtaining the surrender or capture of CTs had already been established, but, although Templer increased them very substantially,[9] and it was possible for lucky or brave informants to become quite wealthy, money was rarely the most important motivation. Professor Lucian Pye of Princeton University conducted a series of psychological studies of SEPs[10] and broadly confirmed Spencer Chapman's view that matters of face and self-esteem could make many Chinese CTs go to extraordinary lengths to revenge themselves for some slight or perceived injustice. Their motives for going into the jungle in the first place were often muddled and complex, a mixture of factors such as desire for status, ambition, a search for education, an impulse to conform to what was seen as 'Chinese' behaviour, and the need for comradeship – very rarely were the reasons ideological. When the MRLA failed to deliver, it was easy for them to feel that they had been misled and made to look naïve, so that face could only be regained doing something drastic.

Whatever the motives, inducing surrenders and their use for both Intelligence purposes and the psychological war were becoming very important factors in the conduct of the campaign. From the very beginning of the Emergency there had been a thin trickle of these surrenders each month, and Templer found in the embryo propaganda machine that he had inherited a tool that, with improvement, could be used to turn this trickle into something like a flood. Late in 1950 Gurney had appointed Hugh Carleton Greene (later to be Director General of the BBC), as Head of Emergency Information Services, with the intention of developing propaganda and what would nowadays be called psychological operations that went hand-in-hand. Things had got better than they were when Briggs complained and called such ire down upon himself; under Greene's direction people such as C C Too and the defector Lam Swee mounted an increasingly sophisticated campaign aimed at persuading the wavering terrorist to give up. The national media – English language and vernacular press, Radio Malaya, films – were fed material that was subtly aimed at New Village and *kampong* dwellers, while 'voice' planes flew low over the jungle and *padi* fields broadcasting similar seductive messages. An increasingly effective ploy involved dropping leaflets, purporting to have been written by SEPs who were known to the MRLA units in a particular area, explaining how they had seen through the fraud that was Communism, and offering safe conduct to any of their erstwhile comrades who would join them. There was usually a photograph of the SEP, looking sleek and well turned out, as evidence that he had been well treated, and the safe conduct was printed out in full on the back, offering immunity to anyone who carried it. These safe conducts were carefully honoured: apart from the fact that a dead terrorist will give little useful information, 'personal appearances' by SEPs in or near their old stamping grounds were a most effective way of building a climate of surrender that could permeate the Min Yuen's undercover organisation and in time seep back to the rank and file, giving the lie to the Politburo's claim that the Security forces routinely tortured and killed their prisoners.

With memories, perhaps, of his time with SOE, Templer took hold of the propaganda operation with some relish. He recruited Alec Peterson, an ex-Force 136 officer who had later served on Mountbatten's staff doing nefarious things under the heading of 'Political Warfare', and appointed him to the new post of Director General of Information Services; the Federal Information Department, the Emergency Information Service, the Malayan Film Unit and all the various radio and press offices were brought into one organisation, and even Radio Malaya which, based in Singapore, was outside Templer's direct control, was pressured into accepting 'policy guidance'.[11] Slowly but surely the impetus began to build up and the number of surrenders grew. By the end of the Emergency surrenders were to outnumber kills in the 'elimination' statistics.

The need to do something about the Police had impressed Lyttleton so much that even as he went through the process of selecting a new High Commissioner he felt it necessary to appoint a replacement for Nicol Gray, without waiting for Templer to take up his post, or giving him a voice in specifying the type of man who could best fit in with his idiosyncratic style of command. In effect, Templer had to accept Lyttleton's appointment of Arthur Young whether he liked it or not, and it is a reflection of the Colonial Secretary's happy knack of finding just the right man that on the whole things worked out much better than the pessimists might have expected. Young was the Commissioner of the City of London Police, a traditional bobby who brought to the job an analytical and careful mind that was yet capable of working quickly when circumstances required. He arrived in Kuala Lumpur two weeks after Templer himself, having made it clear that he would stay for one year, no more, and after some acrid moments soon after his arrival when Templer tried to bully him and was firmly put in his place, the partnership developed reasonably amicably and constructively.

In fact, it did not need any great intellect to see what was wrong: the whole Police operation was just too big and unwieldy. It lacked any sense of direction, had no clear idea whether it ought to be a paramilitary gendarmerie or a traditional colonial Police force concerned to maintain law and order (or both), it was poorly led and trained and in consequence suffered, not surprisingly, from low self-esteem and morale. Leaving aside the Auxiliaries and Special Constabulary, the regular force was over seven times larger than it had been in 1948, which meant that not only had there been an appalling dilution of command at all levels, but that by far the greatest number of policemen, officers and constables had had no experience of practical policing other than in the unique circumstances of an insurgent war. Relations with the bulk of the civil population were largely conditioned by fear, on both sides. Thus far, the analysis was not too difficult to make. The solutions were not going to be so easy to find.

What Young did was effectively to split the force in two – the plan that Gray had toyed with, but failed to implement. The one part was to be truly paramilitary, organised as a fighting force into Area Security Units which would complement the Army in operations against the Min Yuen and MRLA in and around the towns and villages, up to the fringes of the jungle. The other part was to revert, as far as possible, to the traditional police role. This entailed a *reduction* in numbers, reorganisation into functional Divisions – CID, Traffic, Signals, Training, and so on, each under its Assistant Commissioner – and the whole was to be subjected to an urgent programme of retraining at all levels. Young was able to bring experienced officers from the United Kingdom to carry out this programme. Men and women leaving the force were given substantial resettlement packages, and serving Police were brought within the ambit of the armed services welfare organisations (SSAFA, for example) and were admitted to military hospitals when necessary; morale began to improve dramatically.

Young's biggest step, though, was to try to change the whole cultural relationship between constable and citizen. 'Operation Service' was designed to teach the Police that the public were there to be served and protected, not dominated or bullied, while the public had be persuaded that the *mata mata* could a trustworthy friend who could be relied on in times of trouble, not a dangerous foe to be avoided. Subtle ploys were used. The word 'Force' was dropped, so that Young now led the Malayan Police 'Service', constables in the larger towns no longer carried rifles or SMGs, just holstered automatic pistols, the uniform cap badge was changed to show two hands clasped in friendship, and the Police building in each town or village was now to be known as the *Balai Polis* (Police Station), rather than the traditional *Rumah Passung* (Handcuff House).[12]

While Young had set himself a monstrous hill to climb, and in the short time he was in Malaya he was not able to do much more than make a start, 'Operation Service' is usually rated as having been something of a triumph – certainly by the time he left, the changes in the Police Service were already marked. However, perhaps it was never realistic to believe that the public attitude could be radically altered, and, if the touchstone of Chinese recruitment is applied, the effort to make the public love and trust their local 'copper' was not a great success. Nevertheless, it is to Young that the credit must go for turning the ramshackle, overblown structure that he inherited into the efficient, responsible service that would later underwrite orderly progress towards democracy and Independence.

CHAPTER TWENTY

BREAKING THE CIRCLE
– THE SUBALTERNS' WAR

In the early afternoon of 6 July 1952, a patrol drawn from 5 Platoon, B Company, 1 Suffolks, under the command of a National Service subaltern, Second Lieutenant L R Hands, found and attacked a CT camp in the South Selangor Swamp, about a dozen miles from Kajang. Three CTs were killed, the patrol suffered no casualties and, although the area was then ambushed over several days by units of 22 SAS equipped for a long stay, any remaining CTs who had been flushed from the camp were not caught. On the face of it, it was a fairly typical and unremarkable action of its kind, but in many ways that contact and kill provide a classic illustration of the emerging pattern of the campaign at that time. It undoubtedly had a significant effect on the situation in the Kajang area for the remainder of the Emergency.

Even after Bill Stafford had killed Lau Yew in 1948, Kajang and the Kuala Langat district had remained a stronghold of the MRLA, in particular of a notoriously unpleasant and brutal squad led by one Liew Kon Kim, who rejoiced in the rather unusual ability for a Chinese to grow a half-way decent beard. With rare imagination the press took to calling this squad 'the Kajang Gang' and with equal inventiveness gave Liew Kon Kim the nickname 'the Bearded Terror of Kajang'. Liew did all that he could to foster his reputation for brutality and relished the belief of many of the estate workers and villagers that he was a warlock, who could only be killed by a silver bullet. His grip on his sources of supply was firm, and the Security forces had found it almost impossible to break the cycle of fear that prevented informants from coming forward with good intelligence about him. However, now that the flow of intelligence was improving, and the controls on food and movement could be tightened up enough to become really effective, it was possible to close down the whole Min Yuen operation in the area for a short period so that Liew Kon Kim could be isolated and a systematic operation could be mounted to get rid of him once and for all. Curfews, road blocks and random searches were stepped up, food denial measures were rigorously enforced, and Special Branch put ever greater pressure on double agents and undercover informants for information to narrow down the area which troops would have to beat. The target could be specified: Liew Kon Kim himself, even though in the event there was no really solid Intelligence about his precise location.[1]

The patrol from 1 Suffolks went into the swamp on 5 July. The going was appalling, the soldiers frequently wading waist-deep in nauseating brown slime, and at some time in the past such solid ground as there was had been heavily bombed and shelled, resulting in large craters which by this time had become covered in dense *belukar* and secondary jungle. During that day Hands' patrol passed very close to Liew Kon Kim's camp without knowing it, and without disturbing Liew either – an interesting sidelight on the difficulties of operating in such conditions. On 6 July Hands went on with the same pattern of search, marching on a compass bearing for 1,000 yards or so, then turning through a right angle and marching for what he hoped was another 1,000 yards, or perhaps 2,000, before again turning through a right angle and setting off once more. It sounds a rough and ready way of going about things, and would not have been used if the ground had been better, but experience had taught that it was the only technique that had any chance of being effective in featureless, largely unmapped terrain where visibility over ten yards was 'good', and progress at 1,000 yards in an hour was fast moving. Early in the afternoon Hands made his last turn, which he hoped would take him back towards the road, and almost immediately found an unoccupied *atap* hut in a clearing. The hut was set on fire with a phosphorus grenade, an activity which for some reason was not noticed by Liew Kon Kim or his gang. Hands' account goes on:

> It was only a few paces more to another larger clearing, which had a raised sleeping area with two people clearly visible, plus another walking on the other side, maybe 50 metres away. It was this target I fired at first, more in hope than anger, because the range was excessive in jungle terms. I missed, I think, but may have wounded because my section corporal subsequently accounted for him. All this had taken me forward into the clearing and towards the sleeping area, from which two people ran across my front and away from me. The range was now about 20 or 30 metres. I dropped the first [a girl with a 410 shotgun] and fired at the sound of movement in front of me, finally catching up with Liew Kon Kim who was draped over a large tree trunk and clearly in extremis. It was a typical action, in that it happened very quickly and probably only one or two of the section actually saw and engaged a target.

The action was also typical in that it demonstrated the very high degree of alertness and skill-at-arms that troops were required to show, especially when contact was made at the end of a gruelling and tedious patrol which up until then had been uneventful. Raymond Hands was awarded the MC; it is not clear whether Liew Kon Kim had time to realise that he had been shot with an ordinary copper-coated round.[2] At the time no-one may have realised what the reverberations of Liew Kon Kim's death in and around Kajang would be.[3] An outstandingly successful action had effectively broken the Intelligence logjam, and all operations could from now on be based on timely information and focused on sensible, achievable objectives. Terrorist activity continued, of course, but within a relatively short time the atmosphere had totally changed, and the Security forces were able to seize the initiative and dominate the remaining CTs in the area. Kajang lost its reputation as being one of Malaya's blackest spots, and by 1954 Ulu Langat was being used by the SAS as a virtually safe area for helicopter and parachute training.

It was at this time, and in consequence, at least in part, of new thinking and new technology, that it became possible to tackle one strategic problem that had seemed insoluble up until now. The withdrawal of the main MCP committees and major MRLA units into the deep jungles of north Johore, Pahang and the Perak/Kelantan borders had effectively put them out of the reach of the Security forces, not least because they were able to shelter behind a screen of aborigines who were too isolated, childlike and nervous to have any chance of standing up to the pressures engendered by lies and terrorism. Continuing the relationship which many of the tribes had had with the MPAJA during the war, the aborigines were cajoled and coerced into feeding the CTs and also acting as an early-warning system in depth, watching the movements of Security units that attempted to 'go deep' and giving the MRLA units so much advance notice of danger that that kind of operation was almost always a waste of time.

Early in the campaign, in 1949, 1 Seaforths had tried find some sort of an answer to the problem in their district of Johore by setting up a Police post, to be supplied by air, in the Tasek Berak area, on the border between Johore and Pahang. Tasek Berak was a sprawling region of swamp and lake which was so inaccessible that the MRLA were able to use it virtually at will as a safe enclave for rest and retraining as well as a posting house on the courier route to and from Johore and Pahang. Spencer Chapman had said that the journey into Tasek Berak was quite impossible for a European, but, notwithstanding, the Seaforths managed to get a company into the area after a horrifying 16-mile march that took three days. With enormous effort over a period of 15 weeks a clearing was hacked out, a Police post built out of local materials, and a landing strip was cleared on which an *Auster* could just about make a landing if there was a reasonable headwind. In a forerunner of the 'hearts and minds' campaign of later years, doctors and dressers were flown in to set up a clinic to treat the local Semelai tribesmen for the ills and disabilities that a life of malnutrition and endemic disease made rife, and the Seaforths withdrew, leaving the Police to get on with the lonely business of defending the fort and trying to curtail Communist activity in the neighbourhood. It was a good idea, and if the move had been more successful it might have formed the model for other forts in other places, but it came before its time – it was too big a task for the numbers that could be deployed and the logistics of air supply and troop movements with the aircraft available were too stretched. After a few months the project was abandoned.[4]

Not long after the Seaforths abortive foray into the Tasek Berak swamp, 'Mad Mike' Calvert appeared in the corridors of GHQ, SE Asia, in Tanglin, Singapore, hawking another solution to the problem. Under David Stirling, Calvert had been a founder member of the SAS during the War and had eventually commanded 1st SAS

Brigade until it was disbanded in 1945. He was one of those peculiarly British eccentrics who revelled in the derring-do of irregular warfare, and he sold Harding the idea that it ought to be possible for a special force to be maintained in the jungle for several weeks at a time, supplied by air, instead of for just the six or seven days it was believed were the optimum for European troops. Harding gave the go-ahead for Calvert to raise a force to be called the Malayan Scouts (SAS), which was destined eventually to provide the basis of that crack formation, 22nd SAS, whose reputation would reverberate around the world. Unfortunately, in the early days during 1949 and 1950 this newly re-formed unit failed to live up either to the standards of its predecessors during the War or to the attainments of its successors in later years. Recruitment was hurried and uncritical, too many 'hard cases' and professional café-gangsters being accepted. Alcoholism was rife, discipline was allowed to founder, and too much time was spent 'swanning' in Landrovers with the windscreens folded flat, flexing suntanned pectoral muscles at what it was fondly thought were suitably awe-inspired lesser units.

By the time Templer came to Malaya, however, the SAS had settled down, most of the cowboys had been weeded out, and the troopers had learnt a great deal about how to move and fight in the jungle. A nerve-racking technique for parachuting into jungle had been developed and SAS squadrons had taken part in several worthwhile operations, although there was still a question mark over a military philosophy that was inclined to see 'staying in' as an end in itself. Some were also worried about the diversion of a disproportionate amount of logistic support that might have been more cost-effectively used in other ways. As always, the problem was the air: parachuting in was possible but dangerous; resupply meant clearing DZs and prejudicing the security of the operation by delivering *Dakota*-loads from hundreds of feet up in a clear sky; casualties several days in from base meant the end of the operation (and very often of the casualty as well). The truth is that in recreating the instrument that had been so effective in the deserts of Cyrenaica, Calvert had presented Templer with yet another solution in search of a problem.

It was the introduction of the helicopter that gave a real role to the SAS and at the same time provided an answer to the question of how to harry the enemy deep in the jungle just where he thought he was safe. In the early 1950s helicopters were brand-new gadgets, and any idea that they might achieve battlefield dominance on the apocalyptic scale of American operations in Vietnam or later wars was pure speculation. At the end of 1951, senior air officers admitted that they saw helicopters as having reached much the same stage of development and use as fixed-wing aircraft in 1910 – they were definitely useful, but nobody was quite sure what for.[5] However, late in 1949 a joint bid had been put forward by GOC Malaya, and the AOC for a small casualty evacuation unit to be set up, and in May 1951 a flight of three *Dragonflies* was formed, on an experimental basis, operating out of Tengah in Singapore. There had been the predictable unforeseen difficulties: the only aircraft that were deemed vaguely suitable were just going into production at Westland, but were earmarked for the Navy, which was reluctant to release them. The Ministry of Supply could not understand why any period of experimentation was needed, since it was understood that the aircraft were only to operate in Malaya, where to the best of the Ministry's knowledge atmospheric conditions were *not* tropical, 'and the reduction in performance compared with that in an English summer would be only slight'.[6] After this peculiar misconception had been laid to rest, it was discovered that there were only four RAF pilots with suitable helicopter experience, one of whom was due for demobilisation and another had a hearing defect that prevented his flying operationally. Once in Malaya it was realised, of course, that doubts about the *Dragonfly's* performance in the tropics were well founded, and that the problems of flying 'hot' and in humidity approaching one hundred per cent meant that range and performance were badly affected. Most importantly, payloads were greatly reduced, so that in most operational circumstances only one person apart from the pilot could be carried. In the first six months, the three *Dragonflies* successfully evacuated 29 casualties, a boon to troops who would otherwise have had to march for days carrying their sick or wounded, but not really a cost-effective way of deploying this new form of air power. As the techniques and requirements of clearing jungle LZs became better understood and troops and pilots learned to co-ordinate their casualty evacuation missions more professionally the productivity of the flight improved, and in its second six months of operations 42 casualties were uplifted.

As might be expected, however, it was not long before devious minds were finding other ways of using up the *Dragonflies'* flying hours. Senior officers discovered in them a pleasing alternative to their usual personal transport, and MacDonald enjoyed frequent trips from Bukit Serene to his office in Singapore, a journey of only a few miles by perfectly secure roads for which his official car would have been quite adequate. During the Maria Hertogh riots a *Dragonfly* was used to monitor crowd movement and to help with directing troops and Police to crucial points, and this aircraft was also loaded with grenades. However, this embryonic attempt to turn it into a helicopter gunship was never put to the test, since whenever it appeared all the rioters stopped rioting so that they could stare at it. More prosaically, a *Dragonfly* was modified to spray out ticks on the 15-acre pasturage in Singapore on which Cold Storage ran a dairy herd, a seemingly frivolous application which ironically would lead to an effective military use later on (and eventually to the American defoliation programme in Vietnam). There were some tentative trials of troop movements, severely restricted by the limited payload: early in 1952, for example, 17 exhausted men from 1 Cameronians, who had been on patrol for nearly three weeks, were airlifted one at a time from a swamp whose waters were rising rapidly and would shortly have cut them off entirely. Helicopters proved invaluable, too, during Operation HELSBY, a resettlement operation which entailed moving elderly and sick *orang asli*, besides getting doctors and medical supplies into a particularly difficult area of northern Pahang. There remained, though, limits to which the *Dragonfly* could be used for resupply and for load-carrying. One pilot had to refuse to carry a consignment of eight severed heads being forwarded to Police HQ for identification, not out of any squeamish sensitivity, but because they were too heavy.

However, the penny was beginning to drop, that if a better workhorse than the *Dragonfly* could be found, helicopters could open up a complete new dimension, literally, in the battlefield. Under Templer's urging a bid was put to the Combined Chiefs of Staff in London for the establishment to be increased to a squadron of 18, of which six at least should be capable of undertaking tactical troop movements.[7] By October 1952, the Americans had been persuaded to overcome their initial reluctance and supply Sikorsky S-55s,[8] and at the beginning of 1953 No 848 Squadron, RN, equipped with ten S-55s, started operations based on the Royal Naval Air Station at Sembawang. It now came as little surprise to find that the capability of the S-55 was severely reduced in the tropical conditions and an effective lift was limited to four men with their kit. Nevertheless, by May 1953, during Operation COMMODORE, eight S-55s of 848 Squadron were able show what could be done by lifting 564 troops into the jungle in a movement that lasted seven hours – a considerable improvement on the two to three days it would have taken by foot. By the end of the operation a total of 623 men and 35,000 pounds of stores had been lifted, in 415 sorties, over a period of two weeks. The reliability of the S-55 was proved.

The importance and worth of the helicopter during the Malayan campaign should not be overstated. From the time of its introduction early in 1950 it played an increasingly valuable role, not least in opening the eyes of the planners and strategists to its potential and the complexities of using and maintaining it, but it had nothing like the impact that it was to have when the Americans used it in Vietnam a decade later; it was not decisive and it did not win the war. One thing it did do, however, was to allow Templer to tackle the problem of denying the MRLA the safety of the deep jungle and preventing them from using the aborigines as a source of supply and as a security screen. It also gave the SAS the tool they needed to turn doctrine into worthwhile operations.[9] About the same time that the bid was going forward for more helicopters, including S-55s, the planners in Kuala Lumpur submitted a proposal for the establishment of jungle forts, to be sited close to centres of aborigine habitation, from which patrols could operate against MRLA units known to be near, and which could provide a military shield for the aboriginal tribesmen themselves. The proposal arose because earlier attempts to resettle the aborigines, on the same lines as the squatter programme, had been a dismal failure: the few aborigines who had been cajoled into these new settlements had found the whole way of life uncongenial and within a short time most of them had wandered off, or given up and died.

What was proposed now was a rehash of the Tasek Berak scheme, with the difference that helicopters could be guaranteed to maintain supply and movement, in and out.[10] These forts were not to be flimsy outposts of the Civil administration, but extensive, well-defended garrisons, manned by 100 or more policemen or soldiers, and each offering a clinic, primary school and trading post. Apart from providing bases for military action against the MRLA, it was hoped that by offering medical treatment, schooling and some, at least, of the modern amenities that the *orang asli* had done without up until now, the clans would be wooed away from their adherence to the CTs and effectively resettle themselves. The equipment needed to underwrite this proposal was coming to hand, the SAS could provide the skill and the long-range endurance to implement it, and it offered Templer the chance of a new outflanking movement against the MRLA that would lift the tempo of a campaign that always ran the risk of becoming pedestrian and predictable. By the end of 1955, ten forts, set up by the SAS and now manned by a specialist Police Field Force, had been established in the three regions that Intelligence had identified as the main safe stronghold areas for the MCP's leadership – Perak/Kelantan, Pahang, and Johore (Tasek Berak). Slowly but surely the battle was being brought nearer to the MRLA's most secure bases, the aborigines were being won over and their co-operation with the guerrillas was being broken down.

Where they dominated the surrounding area, these jungle forts were also able to make a contribution to the food denial programme. When major MRLA units and Party cadres pulled back to the remoter jungle areas in accordance with the October Manifesto's new policy, the problem of food supplies left no alternative but to return to the growing of basic foods – vegetables, tapioca and hill rice – in clearings slashed and burnt out of the *belukar*. Unfortunately for the guerrillas, these *ladangs* were usually clearly visible from the air and soon became targets for the Security forces, who put much effort into destroying them. At first, it was relatively easy to tell which were the CT *ladangs* that could be legitimately bombed by the RAF, since the orderly-minded Chinese insisted on planting everything in straight rows which showed up clearly on air photographs. However, the CTs realised what they were doing wrong and started imitating the higgledy-piggledy chaos of the typical aborigine plot, so that Intelligence had to try to guess which plots were fair targets by estimating from very suspect evidence how many people a *ladang* was designed to support in comparison with the number of aborigines thought to be legitimately in the area. Bombing on this basis undoubtedly ruined a lot tapioca but unfortunately an unknown number of *orang asli* were killed or maimed in the raids, and other methods had to be tried. *Dragonflies* fitted with spraying booms like the ones developed for the benefit of Cold Storage's ticks were used to spray the *ladangs* out with sodium arsenite, but that is a difficult and dangerous chemical to handle, very effective as a herbicide but highly toxic to men and animals,[11] and again, innocent aborigines suffered to an unacceptable extent. The only really effective way to deal with these vegetable plots, where they were anywhere within reach of foot patrols, was to put troops or policemen in to ambush them in the hopes of killing the gardeners, before setting fire to the crops. With jungle forts established this became a realistic proposition over a much wider area, and for the Communists the jungle became a still less friendly place.

When Templer left Malaya on the last day May 1954, he could look with some satisfaction at the scene he was leaving behind. The resettlement programme was virtually complete and the New Villages were developing fast into successful and prosperous communities where the Min Yuen were finding it harder and harder to maintain any kind of psychological dominance. Food controls were tight and ever more effective, the Police were increasingly efficient and the propaganda battle for 'hearts and minds'[12] was swaying feeling markedly towards the Government. Chin Peng and the MCP Central Committee had been forced to withdraw from their relatively accessible HQ in the Mentakab area of Pahang up to the Thai border near Betong, and as the MRLA 'Regiments' had been broken up into independent platoons, often only a handful strong and operating from bases further and further away from the critical ground of the New Villages and jungle fringes, so cohesion had been almost totally lost and the insurgent effort had degenerated still more into directionless terrorism. The war in the jungle was going well, with inspired amateurism replaced by a hard-bitten professionalism in training, tactics and skill-at-arms, and with the best modern technology harnessed in support of the men on the ground. Perhaps because senior officers could play so little part in the detail of operations, junior leaders uninhibited by inappropriate experience and traditions were able to turn themselves into true guerrillas, and this largely National Service Army was outdoing the CTs at what was supposed to be their own speciality. The number of kills was growing, and from the evidence of SEPs it was clear that morale amongst the CTs was eroding. The Intelligence machine was beginning to pay real dividends, the flow of information was steadily improving in quality and it was proving less and less necessary to bring pressure to bear on antagonistic villagers by using the 17D Regulations. Perhaps not as much of this progress is due to Templer as has since been claimed, but there is no doubt that it was his driving energy that breathed life into what had seemed a fast-dying body politic, and he had completely reversed the accidie that had infected so many when he had first come to Malaya 28 months before. When Templer had made his famous comment, 'I'll shoot the blighter who says this Emergency is over', he had good cause to make a stand against the creeping complacency that he saw seeping back into attitudes in Kuala Lumpur, but in truth the military battle *was* all but won.[13]

On this score alone Templer earned the accolades that were showered upon him. It was in the political development of the Federation of Malaya, however, that the greatest and most significant changes had been brought about.

CHAPTER TWENTY-ONE

THE BIRTH PANGS OF A NEW NATION

Lyttleton's directive to Templer before he took up office in February 1952 made it clear that his overriding objective was political, not military. He was to prepare the Federation of Malaya to become a fully self-governing nation. It was his duty to 'guide the peoples of Malaya towards the attainment of this objective and to promote such political progress in the country as will without prejudice to the campaign against the terrorists further our democratic aims for Malaya'. The newly independent nation was to be for all its inhabitants, not for any one ethnic community in particular: 'To achieve a United Malayan Nation there must be a common form of citizenship for all who regard the Federation or any part of it as their real home and the object of their loyalty'. Independence could only follow the defeat of the MCP, but it *would* follow.

So Templer found himself in a familiar situation: as in Germany after the War, he was a military governor charged with building stable political structures in a society that really did not understand democratic institutions and was emerging from a period of such violence and rancour as to make bitterness a way of life. Somehow, out of what was virtually a political void, he had to construct an effective mechanism of government which could take over when it was time for him to go, and this government must be one of national unity. There could be no question of handing over to some chauvinistic Malay cabal that might well return to the bad old days of 'burn and deport' as soon as the way was clear to deal with opposition, nor was it possible to envisage some kind of Malayan Union Mark II, in which the commercial power and concentration of the Chinese must eventually overwhelm the Malays and subjugate them to a new form of colonialism. An academic proposal for the country to be partitioned, with those States where there was a Chinese majority being federated in one union and the traditional Malay states forming another, was rejected out of hand and Templer had to do the best he could to make bricks with some very wispy straw indeed.

The problem was that there was still no coherent political party that was representative of *all* the interests. For the ordinary *kampong* Malay there was little reason to take any interest in politics in general, since loyalty and trust were traditionally given to the Royal households while for those who sought some sort of political expression there was the United Malay Nationalist Organisation (UMNO), which had been born in 1946 at the meeting of the Pan-Malayan Congress in opposition to MacMichael. However, UMNO's presiding genius was Dato Onn bin Jaafar, a member of the Legislative Council with a reputation for fiery rhetoric and a formidable opponent of any dilution of Malay predominance, the early composition of UMNO's ruling caucus gave rise to suspicions that it was little more than a pressure group with no great strength in the country, and the prospect of UMNO providing a stable and balanced successor to the British administration did not seem good. Dato Onn himself was a volatile man, capable of being partisan and intransigent while also showing a statesmanlike breadth of vision, leaving those who were dealing with him to work out which frame of mind he was in that day. There was no other obvious Chief Minister of an independent Malaya in waiting, however, so Gurney had spent a great deal of his quiet tact cultivating him – not an easy task, in view of the growing Malay perception that in pouring cash and effort into the resettlement programme, the Colonial administration was showing a lamentable pro-Chinese bias.[1] At this stage UMNO's support of the campaign against the Communists looked grudging, given more because the terrorists were predominantly Chinese than out of any revulsion against terrorism or strong feelings of loyalty to the Federal Government.

For Templer, looking for someone to whom he could talk about independence, things were not simplified when Dato Onn fell out with UMNO[2] and formed a new group, the Independence of Malaya Party (IMP), leaving UMNO in the hands of a politician who had not made much of a mark until now, one Tunku Abdul Rahman. Abdul Rahman was the younger brother of the Sultan of Kedah, an aristocrat with a reputation as a bit of a playboy, who had had an undistinguished career as a barrister in the Government Legal Service and showed little sign of being the dominant statesman that he would turn out be. For a time, then, Templer was content to let Dato Onn carry Government support with him into the newly formed IMP, rather than backing the unpromising Abdul Rahman. When the President of the MCA, Tan Cheng Lok, aligned his party with the IMP Templer's policy decision was vindicated – at last there were signs of a political grouping that might transcend ethnic boundaries. However, it was not long before Tan Cheng Lok saw that Dato Onn had not managed to get any substantial Malay backing for his new party, and he withdrew his co-operation. The wheel had turned full circle and UMNO and MCA were left once again as the only two significant groupings, apparently locked in mutual distrust and resentment.

For the Chinese, the MCA did not appear to offer a notably more attractive vehicle for engaging their political imaginations than UMNO did for the Malays. Since its shaky beginnings as a platform for anyone with Kuomintang leanings, the MCA had been adapted into little more than a forum for a limited number of wealthy and influential *towkays* who lacked any real empathy with the Chinese workers and peasantry. It was true that under some pressure from Gurney its founder members had made an appreciable contribution to the resettlement programme, by speaking out in its favour and by raising funds for welfare in the New Villages, but the effect was rather spoilt by their frequent protestations about the effects of Government policy on the Chinese community, by which they usually meant themselves and their affairs. The Malays may have been convinced that Gurney and Templer after him were both biased against them: Tan Cheng Lok was equally convinced that the boot was on the other foot, or at least that is what he professed.

In fact, he did have quite a good case. Since the insurgency was an almost entirely Chinese affair, it was not unnatural that many of the Emergency Regulations bore most heavily on the Chinese, and there were continuing difficulties over such matters as entry to the Malayan Civil Service and seeming prejudice against potential Chinese recruits to the Police Service. These situations were never quite as clearcut as they appeared, though: it was a moot point, for instance, whether the Police had so few Chinese officers because so few offered themselves, or because the Malays refused to serve with people they did not trust.[3] Tan Cheng Lok did not do his cause much good, however, by holding forth loudly about the loyalty to the Government that had always been shown by the Chinese, and when he proposed that Kuomintang troops should be brought into Malaya from Taiwan to beef up the campaign against the MRLA, people were forced to doubt whether he really understood the situation or the sensitivities of the Malays at all. He was not an easy man to deal with,[4] and the MCA that confronted Templer was still largely a special interest group concerned to put pressure on the British and the Malays on behalf of the Chinese, rather than a mass movement aimed at bringing the Chinese community out against the Communists, as Gurney had hoped, or preparing them to play a full role in a united democratic Malaya, as Templer needed them to do. Having said that, to criticise the leadership of the MCA for failing to turn the majority of Chinese into good democrats is to impose an inappropriate Western cultural filter over the picture (a failing of many at the time and since). The average Chinese worker was totally baffled by concepts of democracy – Government simply meant power, and power moreover in which he was never likely to share. If he wanted to survive, or to exercise any influence, then traditionally he must turn to the secret societies. There was no quick answer to this, no short cut to a general franchise, and Templer could do little but set out a long-term programme that might eventually create the right culture.

He tried. He tried in the Chinese schools, where the MCP had had its greatest success, and where separatism was deliberately maintained and intensified. Subversive teachers were weeded out, money was poured into buildings, staffing and teaching materials, and on the surface at least things started to improve.[5] Taking up Gurney's 'hearts and minds' theme, Templer inaugurated a lavish public spending programme that was probably overdue but which turned the Federation's finances upside down, putting the budget into such serious deficit that the British Government came close to intervening, appalled at the notion that money might actually have to be put into Malaya, rather than extracted. Besides the improvements in schools, hospitals were built and staffed, clinics, served by travelling Red Cross nurses, were established in villages and and *kampongs* throughout the country, and the building of mosques and temples was encouraged, with generous financial support from Federal funds. There was even a project to establish Women's Institute branches in the rural areas, though whether 'jam and Jerusalem' were entirely appropriate symbols in a move to liberate the minds of the women of Malaya was a shade doubtful.

Probably more significantly, the Village Councils Ordinance was passed in May 1952, which provided for New Villages, as they reached laid down standards of maturity, to be withdrawn from the special Emergency administrative controls under which they had been set up, and put on the same local government footing as established villages and *kampongs*. In particular, District Officers were to give the highest priority to establishing elected local councils, which would have power to raise taxes to be spent on building and maintaining roads, drainage and other local amenities, the Federal Government contributing on a one-for-two basis to funds raised in this way. So the New Villagers were being given a taste of power and responsibility, in a tiny way perhaps, but a vital first lesson in the conduct of democracy that would, it was hoped, progressively lead on to much greater issues. Progress there was, although sometimes it was frustratingly slow, with fear and incompetence compounding attempts by the local Communist Party disrupt what was rightly seen as a most threatening development: here was the Government giving the people something that the MCP could talk about but never now deliver, a degree of self-rule, albeit on a microcosmic scale. At first, some of these village councils degenerated into 'cover' organisations for the local Min Yuen Committee, but by the end of 1955 most of the New Villages were administered by councils that seemed to be fairly well founded. At the same time, great effort was made to give the New Villagers secure legal title to the land that they were working, again something that the Communists could not begin to give.

This process of feeding feelings of security and well-being was given a fillip in September 1953, when the district around Malacca was declared the first 'White Area'. A delineated area was declared 'White' when the incidence of overt terrorist activity in it was negligible, when civil authority was working well with the active support of the inhabitants, and the risk in relaxing controls was thought to be justifiable. In the White Area food restrictions and curfews were lifted, movement was allowed with very little hindrance, military activity was scaled down and such irksome Regulations as 17D were put into abeyance. Life could return almost to normal. This easing of restrictions was not allowed to go too far, though: regular Police presence was maintained, the military framework was kept in place, and although Home Guard units were reduced in size, they were kept in being on a cadre basis, retaining their best men. Planters were expected to go on using their Special Constables as close escorts while they worked around their estates, to travel in armoured vehicles where possible and to carry arms whenever they were outside their bungalow compounds. The message was put across very clearly that if there was any relapse, any resumption of terrorist activity, then the whole process would be put into reverse very quickly, especially if there was the slightest hint that the CTs were getting co-operation from the public. In the event, no area that had been declared 'White' was ever returned to Emergency restrictions, and for people living in areas not yet declared 'White' the prospect that they might be able to achieve this status for themselves became one of the most attractive carrots they could be offered.

In all this business of trying to shape some coherent body politic that could carry the country into Independence Templer was once again bedevilled by lack of time; there was little realistic hope that he could achieve much in only two short years. All he could do was to try to create the climate in which the tensions might be resolved and a settled and secure nation might begin to tackle the problem for itself. If the Chinese and the Malays still distrusted and resented each other, if the Chinese still sought roots and certainty in China rather than Malaya, if the Malays refused to give any latitude to the aspirations of new generations of Chinese Malayans, then Malaya after Independence would relapse into the chaos that had so nearly overwhelmed it during the last six years. In the event, the answer to the problem had already been found, but when it came, it came not from Templer but from an act of statesmanship by Tan Cheng Lok and Tunku Abdul Rahman.

In February 1952, UMNO and MCA came together in a temporary alliance to fight the first municipal elections in the Federal capital, Kuala Lumpur, in opposition to Dato Onn (whose IMP had collapsed and who was now leading yet another new grouping, Party Negara). This alliance swept the board, winning nine out of the 11 seats contested, and the possibilities opened up by this kind of rapprochement could be considered on a Federal scale. In 1953, the Alliance Party was formally inaugurated, incorporating both the MCA and UMNO, early in 1954 it was joined by the Malayan Indian Congress (MIC), and Templer shifted support from Dato Onn, signalling that in the British view the void had been filled and that there was now a valid successor government with whom he could treat. In particular, there had emerged as leader of the Alliance a man of stature, Tunku Abdul Rahman, who was destined to lead the country forward with a great sureness of touch – cometh the hour, cometh the man.

On 31 May 1954, Templer left Kuala Lumpur on the crest of a personal wave, lauded by most and with the bitter dissent of a minority firmly suppressed for the time being. His successor was Sir Donald MacGillivray, who had been his Deputy High Commissioner, and who had held the reins of civil administration and government while Templer fought the war. There was to be no supremo, no virtual dictatorship, any more. The shooting was by no means over, but the critical phase was past and the country could return to a more constitutional way of doing things. MacGillivray was to be High Commissioner (the last), and working beside him there was to be General Sir Geoffrey Bourne, up until then GOC Malaya, in succession to Hugh Stockwell, who had replaced Roy Urquhart in 1952 in circumstances that caused some disquiet both at the time and afterwards.[6] Bourne was to combine the post of Director of Operations with continuing duty as GOC.

No sooner had MacGillivray moved into King's House than he found himself under pressure from Abdul Rahman to move things on quickly towards Independence. Ideally, there should have been deliberate progress, with each step secured before the next was taken, but the Alliance was in no mood to allow rival organisations time to achieve credibility and there was in any case a sound rationale for making progress quickly. While terrorism still continued, the back of the MCP's military campaign had been broken, and Independence would leave Chin Peng defeated politically as well. The Colonial Government, in the person of MacGillivray, was content to go along with that analysis, and in July 1955, a year after he took over from Templer, elections were held to State and Federal Councils which for the first time were constituted with a majority of elected members. Out of the 52 seats contested for the Federal Council the Alliance won 51, and Tunku Abdul Rahman became Chief Minister of an administration that already had considerable autonomy and would negotiate a new constitution to come into effect when full independence was achieved in August 1957.

Chin Peng had no difficulty in realising that he had failed. It was not just that his Army in the jungle had been broken up and reduced in detail, its sporadic viciousness no more than the last resentful actions of a lost cause. In the New Villages and towns and *kampongs*, in the Chinese schools the estate line-sites and the mines the Min Yuen were failing him, losing the support of the 'masses' and increasingly in danger of being betrayed to the Special Branch informers who could see clearly now where the Mandate of Heaven had settled. Now he could not even hold himself out as fighting against colonialism – the captains and the kings were about to depart, voluntarily and without demur, and his ostensible cause had blown away. There was one last throw that he could make, he could sue for terms and hope that he might salvage enough to make it possible to come back another day. Soon after his election as Chief Minister Tunku Abdul Rahman had offered an amnesty to all CTs, even those who had committed murder under Communist direction, and in early October 1955, Chin Peng responded by proposing a ceasefire and talks.

Inexperienced in government but not in the ways of man, Abdul Rahman was not naïve enough to take this proposal at face value. During the rest of October and throughout November careful and cautious exploratory meetings took place between a delegation from the Communist Central Committee and a Government delegation headed by Mr J S Wylie, the Deputy Commissioner of Police, who had served in Force 136 during the War and knew Chin Peng. These meetings took place at Klian Intan in the far north of Perak, hard against the Thai border near where Chin Peng and the Politburo had finally found a haven, and their only purpose was to clear the way for Chin Peng himself to emerge in safety to treat with the new Malayan regime – a prospect which, especially amongst the outgoing British officials, was viewed with some alarm, since Chin Peng was known be a devious and hard-bitten negotiator who could be expected to outmanoeuvre Abdul Rahman given the slightest chance. With some trepidation, then, it was agreed that a summit meeting should take place, and the two leaders came face to face at the end of December 1955, in conditions of tight security, at Baling in Kedah, about ten miles from Klian Intan, still close to the Thai border so that Chin Peng might not have to venture too far from safety. Apart from Abdul Rahman, the Government negotiating team comprised David Marshall, the Chief Minister of Singapore, and Tan Cheng Lok.[7]

Chin Peng was accompanied Chen Tian, the head the MCP's propaganda department, and Rashid Maidin, who was presumably there as the token Malay, to lend credence to the claim that the MCP was *not* a Chinese organisation to the exclusion all other races, and who distinguished himself throughout the proceedings by saying nothing whatsoever. During the preliminary discussions at Klian Intan, it had been agreed that the talks might last for three days. They broke up in two, there being no possibility of any agreement at all on the central issue. As Abdul Rahman himself said, there was no way in which two such opposing ideologies could work side by side – if there was to be peace then one side must give in, and he did not intend it to be him. Abdul Rahman's strength of character and sharp mind were only just beginning to be appreciated, and if anyone won the contest, it was he; the fears expressed before the meeting, that Chin Peng would prove too tough and too clever for the Tunku were completely unfounded. Chin Peng had come to the meeting with only one objective, and he failed dismally to achieve it.

He was prepared to order his men to lay down their arms and come out of the jungle, submitting to the terms of the amnesty, on the major condition that the MCP should be recognised as a legal body, fully entitled to take part in the political process as though it had never waged armed rebellion. In other words, he wanted to turn the clock back to 1948, with his followers able to return to a campaign of subversion and civil disruption, no doubt after a suitable period during which an appearance of constitutional rectitude might be painted, and the Party *apparat* could be reconstructed. Taking the long view, at least his party would still be in being, and tomorrow was another day.

The Tunku was having none of it, and the meeting broke up part way through the second day. Chin Peng was escorted back into the jungle with nothing gained and with little chance of anything except a slow decline into insignificance, and Abdul Rahman left to go to London to put the finishing touches to the agreement that would bring total independence to Malaya. On 31 August 1957, that peculiar form of British colonial rule that had grown up like Topsy in a typically haphazard and inconsistent way over 150 years finally came to an end, and Tunku Abdul Rahman became the first Prime Minister of a fully autonomous and independent Malaya within the Commonwealth.

Although the Emergency was not finally declared at an end for a further three years, in truth it had effectively petered out many months before then. With the clarity of hindsight it is possible to see that the military defeat of the MRLA was to all intents and purposes completed by the end of 1953, the contacts and incidents that happened after that being more in the nature of death throes than any coherent insurgent activity. The emergence of credible political groupings made it possible for the British to live up to pledges of an early grant of independence, and Abdul Rahman's refusal at Baling to grant the MCP legal recognition marked the political defeat of the Revolution. In 1958 the MRLA in the jungle completely disintegrated. Surrenders were at an astonishing level[8] and by the end of the year most of the country had been declared 'White'. Even in areas that had previously been notorious bandit country CT units were reduced to a handful of men and women, often only four or five, dispirited and hungry, struggling for survival and with little appetite for any aggressive action against the Security forces. These desperate little squads were being hunted down with such success that at the end of 1959 Special Branch estimates put MRLA strength at less than 700, of whom perhaps 200-300 were still operational in the Federation and the remainder, with Chin Peng himself, were over the border in Thailand. During that same time, on the Government side the Emergency command was effectively dismantled, the post of Director of Operations was abolished, War Executive Committees were put into virtual abeyance and military operations could be described as mopping up.

On 31 July 1960 – the Year of the Rat in the Chinese calendar – the State of Emergency was formally declared at an end (in the view of many, several months later than need be) and the war that 12 years previously General Boucher had said would be one of the easiest tasks he had ever had to tackle was over. During those 12 years 2,473 civilians had been killed, 1,385 had been wounded and 810 had disappeared. The Security forces had lost 1,865 killed and 2,560 wounded, a total of 4,425 casualties, and had in turn killed just under 6,700 and captured a further 1,200. In addition, 2,681 terrorists had surrendered.[9] At the end there was no resounding triumph, no parade with Chin Peng dragged behind the conquerors' chariot wheels, and the statistics of suffering perhaps seem paltry beside the carnage and brutality of Vietnam and Cambodia and all the other conflicts before and since that have stained the ground in South East Asia. Military theoreticians describe the Malayan campaign as a low-intensity war, but to the planter on his isolated estate, the Malay peasant in his *kampong*, the Chinese in his *kongsi* threatened by both sides, to the policeman and the worried National Serviceman trying to do his best in a war that was not of his choosing and whose rights and wrongs he could only dimly grasp – to all these it did not seem a low-intensity campaign at the time. In any case, such academic descriptions miss the point: the importance of the Malaya campaign was that it destroyed the presumption that a Communist guerrilla insurgency must always succeed. Malaya was the domino that stood.

CHAPTER TWENTY-TWO

LEARNING
THE LESSONS

There was urgent need to learn lessons from Malaya almost before the Emergency itself was declared officially at an end. In Indonesia, the *ci-devant* insurgent and Communist fellow-traveller, President Sukarno, nursed ambitions of establishing hegemony over a new empire even more sprawling and unwieldy than his ramshackle inheritance from the Dutch, and set out to bring the British possessions in Borneo under his control before extending his sway over Malaya and then the Philippines. He first fostered a bogus independence movement, the *Tentera Nasional Kalimantan Utara* (North Kalimantan National Army), which in 1962 attempted inexpert and shortlived insurrection. When this was pinched out by a handful of British troops acting in support of the local Police together with some Shell employees who formed a small fencible unit, the regular Indonesian Army became involved, but with no greater success. Sukarno's troops proved no match for the British forces, who were able to draw extensively and expertly on their recent experience in Malaya to put a rapid and determined end to Sukarno's dreams. The military lessons of 12 years had been well learnt, at least by the British: sadly, others were to prove less perceptive.

Other lessons were harder to learn, but that has not been for want of trying, either then, or down the years. Not surprisingly, much of the analysis of the 1960s had less to do with trying to dissect a theory of counter-insurgent war from the history of the Emergency than with promoting a prospectus, selling policy and expertise to the Americans in Vietnam. Unfortunately, however, much of that Malayan experience made little sense when transplanted to a different battlefield where soldiers with different attitudes and different expectations were too often to mistake the form for the substance and be disappointed by the results – the attempt to replicate the resettlement programme in the development of Strategic Hamlets is probably the most notorious example of an inappropriate and misunderstood concept being applied inadequately and doing more harm than good. Those who delight in trying to reduce the arts of war to some kind of bogus rule-governed science set about calculating a formula for success from the relative strengths of the Security forces and the MRLA, producing analyses of tie-down ratios, as the jargon went, which revealed little and in any case differed wildly depending on who did the calculations in the first place.

Adding together inaccurate figures for the number of soldiers, policemen, Special Constables and Home Guards involved, and dividing the result by an estimated figure for the number of CTs in the jungle, ratios varying from as high as 49:1 down to 12:1 were produced, and these were then built into the canon of doctrine at staff colleges and military academies around the world as though they were Holy Writ.

Clutterbuck[1] and Cable[2] do a good job of demolishing this kind of shamanism, making the point that the great majority of the Security forces were acting as an administrative tail (to be compared to the role the Min Yuen), and that in bayonet strength – armed troops opposed to armed guerrillas in the jungle – the forces on each side never differed by any significant amount until the insurrection collapsed in 1957/58. And so another attempt to find a simplistic answer failed. The question remains, could the Malayan experience have provided a model for American success in Vietnam, and can it now teach us anything useful about the theory of counter-insurgent war in the guise in which it appears today? In any event, how successful was the campaign, and what was really won? In terms of the very basic British objective set in 1948, the restoration of effective colonial rule, the campaign can be seen as a tactical success but a strategic failure: the MCP was defeated but British rule had to be abandoned. By 1951, however, the overwhelming imperative of British policy had become decolonisation, and in that context the campaign was a British triumph. The handover of power in 1957 was not to a victorious guerrilla force, but to a democratically-elected government broadly representative of popular will, and one that could be relied on, at least for some time, to favour British interests. Beyond that, what appears from the history of the Emergency is a confusing picture of overlapping elements, all of which led to success, but none of which can properly be said to have been the single defining factor.

One can point, first of all, to the deep-seated divisions between the Malay and Chinese communities that ensured that the majority of Malays would support the established administration. (Ironically, it was almost certainly the Emergency that eventually brought these two communities together in common cause, and provided the ground in which the statesmanship of Sir Cheng Lok Tan and Tunku Abdul Rahman could flourish.)

Secondly, there were the unusual (if concealed) strengths of the Government position, which in general were capitalised upon with skill and imagination. History now gives less credit for this to Sir Henry Gurney than was certainly his due, and it is irksome to see so many would-be fathers to his successes decrying him and claiming credit where it is not due. Briggs, too, was so outstandingly competent and successful that it is odd now to see him remembered mainly for the Resettlement programme of which he was not the author, when his record stands so surely on what he did achieve: the structures of command and co-ordination, the systems, the sheer professionalism and the courage to delegate. If it was personalities that won the war, however, then surely the presence that loomed over the campaign was General Sir Gerald Templer, and about him there is little agreement. On the one hand, he has been treated as the

White Knight who came when all seemed lost and transformed the scene to one of glittering success.[3] On the other, there was a smaller band (much smaller) who said that he inherited a defeated enemy, a victorious Army, a booming economy, a sound plan and an efficient administrative machine, so that all he had to do was drive in the right direction. Parallels were drawn between Templer and Montgomery, likening Templer's inheritance to the position that Auchinleck and Dorman-Smith handed over before Alamein, and for these sceptics his reputation was not enhanced by the extremely abrasive way in which he dealt with those for whom he felt no sympathy or by whom he felt threatened.[4] Not all were as antagonistic as Victor Purcell, one time Principal Adviser on Chinese Affairs and Director General of Information, who was one of those old 'Malaya hands' who had come to know, understand and love the Chinese and who crossed swords viciously with the new High Commissioner when retained to advise the MCA about its response to Templer's activities. In February 1954 Purcell published a bitter attack on Templer in the journal *Twentieth Century*, accusing him of being an intellectual bully without respect for his subordinates, a 'ribald plagiarist of the riding school', who used revilements, 'not as a rapier, but as a battleaxe, and a septic one at that'. He talked of Templer's 'thin-lipped tigerish sneer' and his smile 'like a soundless snarl', while condemning his 'wholesale humiliation of Chinese, Malays and Indians', to which he might well have added long-suffering European civilians as well. One gathers that Purcell did not think highly of Templer. He had a much deeper understanding of the consciousness and attitudes of the Chinese than Templer could possibly have garnered in a few short months, and could appreciate the deep offence that was given by the High Commissioner's coarseness and all-too-frequent use of obscenities,[5] but his own intemperate language very largely destroyed his argument, which was not without justification especially when he pinpointed Templer's weakness for surrounding himself with subservient subordinates.

No doubt Templer did himself few favours by indulging his instinct to drive rather than lead, and his term of office left a bitter aftertaste in many mouths. Whether he won the war against the Communists, as his supporters claim, no-one at this remove can say: if the credit does lie with one man, then that man is more probably Gurney. What Templer did do, though, was mobilise the country for war, and however he managed it, he breathed life into a campaign that until then had been at best half asleep and at worst dying. Whether he was responsible for the defeat of the MCP or not, it is quite sure that if the battle had been lost, he would have been the man who lost it.

A third crucial factor was Chin Peng's disastrous strategy. He did not seem to appreciate, until it was far too late, the innate weakness of the Communist position, and relied on a pedantic application of Mao Tse Tung's precepts and tactics in circumstances that were totally different from the conditions in which Mao had formulated them. Fatally, this sentimental reliance led him into one truly vital strategic error, right at the beginning of the campaign. Mao talked about the masses as the water in which the guerrilla insurgents swam like fish: going into the jungle Chin Peng voluntarily stranded his supporters and gave the Security forces the opportunity to sever his links with his base. There was, perhaps, no model at that time for urban guerrilla war to which he might have turned, but a greater leader would have devised his own theory, and in fact the development of the Min Yuen as a military force in 1952 and 1953 came close to providing him with a solution to his problem. As it was, the answer came too late. When we look for reasons why the British won the war, we have to consider the extent to which Chin Peng contributed to his own downfall.

Fourthly, reasons for success can found in the highly successful programme of political and military action, starting with the resettlement programme and culminating with Independence under the 1957 Constitution, which destroyed all vestiges of any claim that the Communists might make to represent the aspirations of the people. Militarily the MCP were defeated because the Security forces never let the MRLA take the initiative, except on a purely local basis and then only for a very short time. Besides that, the Army (and that means, significantly, the British National Serviceman) and in later years the Police, turned out to be much better at fighting in the jungle than the MRLA. Chin Peng's original plan envisaged a small but determined force of insurgents taking on an unwieldy and uncertain army of reluctant conscripts, but instead he found himself confronted by another guerrilla army, one that was perfectly willing to confront him on his own terms. The British have an odd genius for irregular warfare, and nowhere was this better displayed than in Malaya between 1948 and 1960.

The resettlement programme went far from smoothly at first, and there were times when it seemed that Chin Peng might be right, that the Government would never bring it off, that the administrative problems would be insurmountable and the expense unaffordable. Yet to resettle half a million people, to provide local government, security, schooling, medicines and the prospect of prosperity with assured land tenure, all this within three short years, must go down in history as a triumph of determination and effective administration, as well as courage. The programme not only denied the Communists the vital ground of the squatter *kongsis* but was also a vital ingredient in the developing political consciousness that made democratic elections and independence possible. The importance of this political progress cannot be overstressed, for it was an astonishing development that the MCA and UMNO were able in such a short time to turn themselves from being single-issue pressure groups into mature political parties that could be far-sighted enough to sink their differences and form the Alliance. Perhaps even more astonishing is the realisation that the times had brought forward leaders of stature. Abdul Rahman, the new Chief Minister, had it in his hands at Baling to undo the work of seven years and let Chin Peng retrieve his losses, but he never faltered.

Essentially these four main factors added to an unique set of circumstances. It is not possible to single out any one of them as being supremely significant; each was as important as the others with which it interacted, and it is only by looking at them in combination that there can begin to be any understanding of why Britain and the Federation of Malaya achieved victory over a Communist insurgency when many others throughout the world failed. There are individual lessons to be learned, but the unique circumstances that allowed the Colonial power to deal with the terrorist campaign so effectively that it never even got as far as being a truly insurgent war were just that – unique. It seems unlikely that they will ever be replicated at another time or in another place, and those who seek in Malaya a blueprint for counter-insurgency must look elsewhere.

BIBLIOGRAPHY

Allen, Louis, *Singapore, 1941-1942,* Davis Poynter, London (1977).

Barber, Noel, *The War of the Running Dogs,* Collins, London (1971).

Baynes, John, *Urquhart of Arnhem,* Brassey's, London (1993).

Brackman, Arnold C, *Indonesian Communism,* Frederick Praeger, New York (1963).

Cable, Larry, *Conflict of Myths*, Frederick Praeger, New York (1976).

Campbell, Arthur, *Jungle Green,* Allen & Unwin, London (1953).

Carew Hunt, H N, *The Theory and Practice of Communism,* Pelican, London (1963).

Carver, Michael, *War Since 1945,* Weidenfeld & Nicolson, London (1980).

Chapman, F Spencer, *The Jungle is Neutral,* Chatto & Windus, London (1949).

Cloake, J, *Templer - Tiger of Malaya,* Harrap, London (1985).

Clutterbuck, Richard, *The Long Long War - The Emergency in Malaya 1948-1960,* Cassell, London (1966).

Clutterbuck, Richard, *Riot and Revolution in Singapore and Malaya 1945-1963,* Faber & Faber, London (1973).

Crockett, Anthony, *Green Beret, Red Star,* Eyre & Spottiswoode, London (1953).

Geraghty, Tony, *Who Dares Wins,* Arms & Armour Press, London (1980).

Gullick, John, *Malaysia - Economic Expansion and National Unity,* Ernest Benn, London (1981).

Jackson, Robert, *The Malayan Emergency - The Commonwealth's War 1948-1966,* Routledge, London/New York (1991).

James, Harold and Sheil-Small, Danes, *The Undeclared War - The Story of the Indonesian Confrontation 1962-1966,* Leo Cooper, London (1971).

Lau, Albert, *The Malayan Union Controversy 1942-1948,* OUP, Singapore/London (1991).

Lyttleton, Oliver, *The Memoirs of Lord Chandos,* Bodley Head, London (1962).

Miller, Harry, *Menace in Malaya,* Harrap, London (1954).

Miller, Harry, *Jungle War in Malaya - The Campaign against Communism 1948-1960,* Arthur Barker, London (1972).

Miller, Harry, *Prince and Premier: a Biography of Tunku Abdul Rahman Putra,* Eastern University Press, Kuala Lumpur (1982).

Nasution, Abdul Haris, *Fundamentals of Guerrilla Warfare,* Pall Mall Press, London (1965).

O'Ballance, Edger, *Malaya - The Communist Insurgent War 1948-1960,* Faber & Faber, London (1961).

Oldfield, J B, *The Green Howards in Malaya 1949-1952,* Gale & Polden, Aldershot (1953).

Onraet, René, *Singapore - A Police Background,* Dorothy Crisp, London (1946).

Pustay, John S, *Counterinsurgency Warfare,* Collier MacMillan, New York/London (1965).

Purcell, Victor, *Memoirs of a Malayan Official,* Cassell, London (1965).

Pye, Lucian, *Guerrilla Communism in Malaya - Its Social and Political Meaning,* Princeton University Press, NJ (1956).

Short, Anthony, *The Communist Insurrection in Malaya 1948-1960,* Frederick Müller, London (1975).

Slim, William, *Defeat into Victory,* Cassell, London (1956)

Thompson, Robert, *Defeating Communist Insurgency,* Chatto & Windus, London (1966).

Tucker, John, *A Jungle Handbook,* Federal Publications, Kuala Lumpur (1970).

REPORTS AND ARTICLES

Challis, Daniel S, 'Counterinsurgency Success in Malaya', *Selected Readings in Insurgent War,* US Army Command & General Staff College, Fort Leavenworth, Kansas (1973) - RB 31-100, Vol II.

Dowling, J R, 'Helicopters in the Royal Air Force', MOD Air Historical Branch, 1978.

Gregorian, Raffi, '"Jungle Bashing in Malaya" - Towards a Formal Tactical Doctrine', *Small Wars and Insurgencies* 5(3) (1994).

Griffith, Samuel B (trans), 'Mao's Primer on Guerrilla War', *Marine Corps Gazette* (1961).

Mans, Rowland S N, 'Victory in Malaya', *Marine Corps Gazette* (1961).

Purcell, Victor, 'General Templer', *Twentieth Century* (February 1954).

Wilford, D J, 'Some Aspects of Anti-Terrorist Operations - Malaya', MOD Staff College, Camberley (1963).

The Malayan Emergency 1948-1960, RMA Sandhurst Dept. of War Studies.

MINUTES

British Defence Co-ordination Committee, Far East, 9 April 1950.

Cabinet Committee - Malaya Committee (MAL.COM.) 1950-51.

Letter (DO/CIC/65) CMS from GOC-C, FARELF.

War Office File (WO/216/835)

UNPUBLISHED CORRESPONDENCE

Douglas, W D, Lt.Col. 2i/c 1st Bn. Royal Scots Fusiliers, 1954-55.

Neil, J D H, formerly Chinese Affairs Officer, Pahang.

Gent, G N.

Hands, L R.

Mander, D'A J D, Lt.Col., CO, 1st Bn. Green Howards, 1949-52.

Wilmot, Gordon, Major, OC D Coy 1st Bn. Royal Scots Fusilliers, 1955.

Winter, Norman ('Mick'), RSM, 1st Bn. Green Howards.

NOTES

Chapter 2 *The Battlefield Mapped Out*

1   Tin production in 1948 was some 60,000 tons, a third of the world's usage, which meant that a great many people worldwide had a vital interest in the success of the industry.

2   The island colony of Penang had been founded in the late 18th century by Francis Light, as a trading post at the northern end of the Malacca Straits. At the other end of the Straits, by a slightly dubious treaty entered into with the Temmengong of Johore, Stamford Raffles had annexed the island of Singapore in 1819, as an entrepôt to rival the Dutch East Indies trading empire; and in 1824 Malacca was finally ceded to the British in a swap deal that gave the Dutch undisputed sway in Java and Sumatra. These three, Penang, Malacca and Singapore, formed the Crown Colony of the Straits Settlements, administered from India until 1867, and then directly from the Colonial Office in London. The rest of Malaya continued under its feudal and feuding Sultanates, some notionally independent, while the northern States of Kedah, Perlis, Kelantan and Trengganu reluctantly recognised some kind of loose sovereignty exercised by Siam. In 1874 the feuding between the Sultanates became a serious threat to British interests in the Straits Settlements, especially since the Dutch were trying to edge back into the areas they had ceded fifty years before, and were fomenting trouble to excuse their involvement. A brisk war in Pahang in 1875 resulted in four States, Pahang itself, Perak, Selangor and Negri Sembilan being coerced into a treaty under which each accepted a British Resident and were recognised as the Federated Malay States, administered from a Secretariat in Kuala Lumpur, while Johore was already so strongly under British influence that no-one thought it worthwhile to formalise the situation. It was not until 1910 that Kedah, Perlis Kelantan and Trengganu were transferred to British protection, although they were not absorbed into the Federated Malay States and were loosely administered, with Johore, as the Unfederated Malay States. This dispensation continued until the Japanese occupation.

3   Today, antique Selangor pewter is rightly regarded as highly collectable, and there is a thriving modern pewter industry too.

Chapter 3 *The First Steps to Chaos – The Collapse of a Myth*

1   Confronted by the complete collapse of the Empire in South East Asia, the Colonial Office's confidence that it would all come right in the end was not confined to constitutional matters: early in 1943, concerned that the Japanese would withdraw Malaya's coinage to recover the metal content and leave a returning British Military Authority with no means of exchange except Japanese 'banana' money, an order was placed on the Royal Mint for coins of all denominations. 'In the light of the position and prospects of the war' these coins were to be stored until the end of hostilities. Ironically this order caused a major problem as far as the bronze coinage was concerned, and 50 million one cent pieces were minted with only the barest trace of tin in the alloy – the Royal Mint's source of tin, Malaya, being under Japanese occupation.

2   He had been there only once, briefly, when he accompanied his Permanent Under-

Secretary, Sir Samuel Wilson, on a tour in 1932.

3 Much of the advice that he got was conflicting. Men like Winstedt and Swettenham were steeped in the Malay culture, while Victor Purcell, at one time Principal Adviser on Chinese Affairs, saw Malaya as becoming predominantly Chinese, as of right, within the foreseeable future. Purcell, Victor, *Memoirs of a Malayan Official*, p.96f, Cassell, London (1965).

4 Singapore was left out, partly because it was too valuable as an entrepôt to hand over, and partly because its large, predominantly Chinese, population would skew any Malayan franchise based on universal suffrage.

5 Lau, Albert, *The Malayan Union Controversy 1942-1948*, p.101, OUP, Singapore/London (1991).

6 MacMichael's methods became a byword in the Malayan Civil Service. In the dog-Malay jargon that was affected by the junior Civil Servants a favourite phrase of the time was 'jangan MacMichaelise saya' – roughly, 'don't mess me about'.

7 Particularly in matters of land tenure, a point that was to become very important in the months and years to come.

8 The views of Malays, Chinese and Europeans alike seem to have changed dramatically after his death, judging by the appreciative notes published by representatives of all the communities. Even the *Straits Times*, one of his most pungent critics, gave him a most favourable obituary.

Chapter 4   *A History of Subversion*

1 A persistent worry was the growth of Pan-Malay secessionism, a rather half-baked movement that nevertheless troubled the authorities persistently for many years, and was still taking up too much attention in early 1948.

Chapter 5   *'One may smile and smile and be a villain'*

1 He operated under several different aliases: Lai Teck, Lai Teh, Ah Nyock, Chang Hung, and even, improbably, Wright.

2 There are many conflicting rumours about his eventual fate. It seems most likely that he was eventually caught by a murder squad and dealt with, probably in Thailand and probably in the late 1960s.

Chapter 6   *The Impulse to Armed Struggle*

1 A Foochow from Sitiawan, his real name was Ong Boon Hua, but in common with many Chinese, Chin Peng used several aliases (not necessarily for security or political reasons), among them Ch'en P'ing, Wong Ping and Wong Mun-weh, apart from Chin Peng itself.

2 'Wright' was chosen from amongst Loi Tak's pseudonyms presumably because it emphasised his Western links and distanced him from the cultural purity of the new leadership.

NOTES

3 Short, Anthony, *The Communist Insurrection in Malaya, 1948-1960*, pp.42-3, Frederick Müller, London (1975).

4 Pye, Lucian, *Guerrilla Communism in Malaya – Its Social and Political Meaning*, p.60, Princeton University Press, N J (1956).

5 Some drops of arms under the aegis of Force 136 had also mysteriously 'gone astray', to reappear during the early months of the Emergency.

6 Short, *The Communist Insurrection in Malaya*, p.47. Gregorian, Raffi, '"Jungle Bashing in Malaya" – Towards a Formal Tactical Doctrine', *Small Wars and Insurgencies* 5 (3), p. 343 (1994). Short believes that the Calcutta Conference itself was too diffuse and the delegates too inexperienced, for it to have been where the definitive decisions were reached.

7 Short, *The Communist Insurrection in Malaya*, pp.50-1.

8 Barber, Noel, *The War of the Running Dogs*, Collins, London (1971).

9 Short, *The Communist Insurrection in Malaya*, p.86.

10 One member of the British Military Administration who had dealings with him thought that 'he was probably too close to his own men, many of whom became core members of the MCP'. Neill, J D H, letter 17 June 1993.

11 The possibility of sacking Gent had been raised as long ago as the previous September.

Chapter 7   Strengths, Weaknesses, Opportunities and Threats

1 Against an updated establishment of 9,000, Police numbers were not much above 7,000.

2 In 1947, with Indian independence, four Gurkha regiments were transferred to the British Army. Gurkha soldiers were offered the option of staying in the Indian Army, joining the British Army or leaving the service altogether. As a result of the way in which these options were presented and handled, a great number of senior experienced VCOs, NCOs and riflemen were lost, battalion strengths fell to as little as 300 all ranks, and virtually the entire time of those who were left had to be taken up with recruitment and basic training. They were not helped by the fact that an unusually high percentage of the new intakes were unfit, with tuberculosis rife. Gregorian, 'Jungle Bashing in Malaya', p.342.

3 Noel Barber quotes his prophetically over confident comment, 'I can tell you this is by far the easiest problem I have ever tackled'. Barber, *The War of the Running Dogs*, p.29.

4 In the Sungei Siput area, where Walker, Allison and Christian had been murdered, it was said that only one estate smokehouse was left standing. Short, *The Communist Insurrection in Malaya*, p.111.

5 The majority of these 'Blood and Steel' units – usually ten men strong – were found from 5th Regt. MPABA, in Pahang.

6 Spencer Chapman, who met him two or three times, recognised him as an able administrator and convinced Marxist, whose strength lay in the work he did undercover in the towns during the Japanese occupation.

7 Jackson, Robert, *The Malayan Emergency – The Commonwealth's War, 1948-1966*, p.29,

Routledge, London/New York (1991).

Chapter 8 *'All over bar the shouting'*

1. Gullick, John, *Malaysia – Economic Expansion and National Unity*, p.26, Ernest Benn, London (1981).

2. 'The political essence of the problem is . . . the extent and limits of popular support for the Communists. To take the extreme case, if they had the full popular support of both the Malay and the Chinese populations, our position would be untenable.' Secretary of State for War, Minute to Malaya Committee of the Cabinet, [MAL.COM. (50) 21], 17 June 1950. One MRLA Regiment, the 10th, in Pahang, was originally recruited largely from Malays, but suffered so much wastage that it had to be re-formed, and from then on was almost totally Chinese. Some independent Malay bandits were found in the Temerloh District of Pahang, but they were very quickly liquidated. The DO's report stressed that they were NOT Communist and NOT in alliance with the MPABA. 'It was more a case of profitable banditry than Communism'. Short, *The Communist Insurrection in Malaya*, p.208.

3. C C Too, the Head of the Federation's Psychological Warfare Unit later in the Emergency, made the point that very few of the MCP leaders in 1945 or afterwards had been English-educated so that it was almost impossible for them to infiltrate the Government service.

4. In the early days of the Emergency these civilians formed and trained Special Constabulary units, and later were to play an important part as unpaid Registration and Rationing officers, as well as Auxiliary Police Inspectors.

5. Later the numbers rose still further, to 41,000.

6. This progress was continued in 1949 with the addition of a further 3,000, and by the end of 1953 the total strength of the regular Police Force was just under 37,000, all ranks.

7. Jackson, *The Malayan Emergency*, p.27.

8. There was considerable heart-searching at the War Office about this diversion of troops to Malaya, which was seen as weakening the position in Hong Kong, perceived as the most vulnerable area of threat.

9. On 27 July Boucher promised the Legislative Council operations at near divisional strength, 'on battle lines', that would break up enemy formations, drive them into the jungle and keep them on the move so that they could not get food or recruits. Early operations on this basis merely demonstrated that the MPABA moved out of an area that was being 'swept' until the threat was over, and then moved back to resume their previous way of life.

10. In spite of a series of deficit budgets between 1946 and 1948, the public debt stood at only £35 million at the start of the Emergency. Between 1949 and 1953 (despite funding security costs), there was no significant further borrowing requirement, Malaya was a net dollar earner and in 1951 and 1952 there was even a budget surplus. Over the course of the whole Emergency there was a total deficit of $(Straits) 262,000,000 (about £60,000,000), which was mostly incurred through Templer's social welfare programme during the build-up to independence. Loch, J H, 'Malaya – Economic Conditions', *Encyclopaedia Britannica,* Vol.14, p.714. See also Thompson, Robert, *Defeating Communist Insurgency*, p.18, Chatto & Windus, London (1966) and Short, *The Communist Insurrection in Malaya*, pp.346ff.

NOTES

11 Most of the Japanese effort was devoted to eliminating pro-Kuomintang elements among the more prosperous Chinese. The MPAJA engaged in only 340 individual operations against the Japanese, of which 300 were designated 'major' by the MPAJA itself. Challis, Daniel S, 'Counterinsurgency Success in Malaya', *Selected Readings in Insurgent War*, US Army Command and Staff College, Fort Leavenworth, Kansas (1973).

12 In February 1950, the Freedom Press published *Emancipation Series No. 4,* a pamphlet containing articles, written late in 1949, with titles such as 'Let us fight together against the phenomenon of wavering confidence', and 'Maintain a serious attitude to Party resolutions'.

Chapter 9   *Thinking Again*

1 The MCP did have a very limited number of radio transmitters, but they were mostly World War II relics that were almost impossible to keep in service. 'The Conduct of Anti-Communist Operations in Malaya' doubted whether wireless communications had ever been successfully established.

Chapter 11   *The Descent into Terrorism*

1 Tamil estate workers were always keen cattle farmers, an interest which caused endless bad blood with those who lived down-wind, as well as those whose gardens and cash crops went to supplement the cows' diets.

2 On some estates as much as ten per cent of planted acreage had to be cleared each year and replanted with high yielding clones that would not come into bearing for eight years or more.

3 The price on Chin Peng's head was $60,000, which later rose to $250,000.

Chapter 12   *Learning How to Win*

1 There was still justifiable trepidation in Whitehall and at GHQ, FARELF, in Singapore at the way this concentration was denuding Hong Kong.

2 It is true that the number of incidents went down considerably in these areas of intense activity, but at the same time they went up in such places as Gemas in North Johore, as well as in Perak and Selangor.

3 Some training manuals covering limited aspects of such techniques were produced on a localised basis from time to time. Field Marshal Lord Roberts issued detailed instructions about ambush procedures in close country, for instance, during his time as C-in-C, Bengal Army, but such pamphlets were usually set aside when the immediate need for them was over. In 1944, 14th Army issued two instructions, MTP 51, 'Preparation for Warfare in the Far East' and MTP 52, 'Warfare in the Far East', but these were regarded as being of purely local interest. It was not until 1952, when General Sir Gerald Templer became High Commissioner and Director of Operations, that a serious attempt was made to collect and analyse all the knowledge of operations against the MRLA that had been built up over the preceding three and a half years. A questionnaire to all operational units resulted in the definitive manual, *The Conduct of Anti-Terrorist Operations in Malaya*,

(ATOM), issued for the first time in 1952, which, with updates in 1954 and 1958, became the Army's counter-insurgency bible for the rest of the campaign.

4   A critical evaluation of 50 ambushes that were laid during one six-month period showed that 34 had failed, and only six of these failures were due to factors outside the control of the Security forces unit concerned. ATOM, Chap. XI.

5   At no time during the Emergency was any serious attempt made to make any MRLA jungle camp defensible, presumably in part because of the total lack of such equipment as mines and barbed wire.

6   One subaltern (who later himself became an officer of great seniority) was posted with his platoon to a village where the situation had deteriorated so badly that the CTs were virtually able to dominate the local area at will. By sheer hard work and aggressive patrolling based on information that he himself organised, he succeeded in restoring the situation, and was then galled to have his industry and effectiveness questioned from HQ because he had not called for any air supply drops. This was interpreted as meaning that he had not left his base camp!

7   It was known for terrorists to escape an ambush because they heard the noise of a safety catch being released from 50 yards or more.

8   The Bangalore torpedo was a tubular device, developed in the First World War as a means of cutting barbed wire. It was not particularly successful at that, and spent most of its military career looking for a *raison d'être*.

9   An indication of the rather touching, if naïve, faith that many had in the supernatural fighting ability of the Gurkhas is given by the comment of one British soldier that 'the Gurkhas, of course, were superb' when it came to jungle-craft and tracking. In fact, there is a shortage of jungle in Nepal, and the Gurkhas had to learn from scratch in the same way as the Jock from Motherwell. The fact that they did so, and achieved such excellence, is a tribute to their meticulous professionalism and enthusiasm, as well as to the fact that an individual Gurkha soldier might expect to spend far longer in Malaya than his British or Commonwealth counterpart.

10 Tracker dogs were used, too, with mixed results. It is extremely difficult to keep western-bred dogs healthy in Malayan conditions, with tick-borne diseases a particular hazard.

11 Not all senior officers appreciated the irony that this was where the Army Commander had his HQ.

12 The Malayan authorities never went so far as to claim enemy casualties on a statistical probability basis, as later became the totally misleading practice in Vietnam.

13 Field, and later Medium artillery, were both also used in this role, with occasional disconcerting results when prophylactic shoots were targeted on areas selected from maps which could be as much as 30 years out of date.

14 'There is indeed only one test of air-mindedness, and that is not whether you can fly an aeroplane, but whether you regard it as a vehicle. If you do, you are air-minded; if you regard it as anything else – a weapon, a sporting adjunct, or a bag of tricks – you can be an Air Marshal, but you are not air-minded'. Slim, William, Field Marshal, *Defeat into Victory*, p.165, Cassell, London (1956).

15 The most cogent piece of information given in the EY training manual covered the

NOTES

procedure for unloading if it had not been fired. It amounted to, 'go as far away from anyone else as you can, and be very careful'!

16 By the end of the campaign most ration packs were being sourced and filled locally.

17 Helicopters did not become available in any numbers until 1953/54.

18 The 62 set was originally intended for use as Coy HQ set, powered by wet batteries that needed all the paraphernalia of chargers, etc. Later it was modified for use with dry batteries to replace the 68 set, which had been found to be extremely heavy and unreliable in the jungle.

19 The availability of ammunition, and the ability to use it in training in this way without worrying about noise were among the greatest advantages that the Security forces had over the MRLA, for whom the shortage of reliable ammunition was a nightmare.

Chapter 13 *Trying Hard to Lose*

1 A good example of Harding's lack of feeling for constitutional and ethnic sensitivities was given by his proposal to admit Chinese recruits to the Malay Regiment. Leaving aside the question of whether such recruits might actually have come forward, implementation of his proposal would have required virtual renegotiation of the treaties with the rulers, and would have been tantamount to conceding citizenship to all elements of the population by the backdoor – just the rock on which the Malayan Union had foundered a few months earlier! Short, *The Communist Insurrection in Malaya*, p.233.

2 'The senior officials considered all this playing at soldiers to be beneath them or sometimes they were just awkward.' Mander, Lt-Col. D'A (CO, 1st Bn Green Howards, 1949-52). Letter to the author, September 1995.

3 When Lt Nigel Bagnall was posted to Manchis with his platoon of Green Howards, he found upwards of 45 Police barricaded in the Police station and refusing to take any further part in the proceedings. This kind of situation was by no means unusual at this time.

4 Mander, Lt-Col. D'A, letter September 1995.

5 Some Police officers realistically acknowledged that some of their own men were not always entirely trustworthy. As late as 1953 one OCPD was doubtful enough of the reliability of his Chinese Inspectors to call up European Auxiliary Police Inspectors to take part in a sensitive operation.

6 Close ambushes of this kind must have often been a problem in Palestine as well. See St Luke's Gospel, Chapter 10, verses 30-35.

7 Training manuals issued later in the campaign recognised that 'the primary object of the CT in staging an ambush is to gain arms and ammunition'.

8 Twenty-five Lynx scout cars had been ordered when Gray arrived and were delivered in March 1949. No further deliveries were accepted before 1950. Short, *The Communist Insurrection in Malaya*, p.229.

9 The problem of those who were face to face with terrorism being rather less robust in their refusal to withstand threats than those who were never in the slightest danger in the first place was not confined to the Chinese community. Later in the Emergency a European planter, a Mr Jeffrey Watts Carter, was prosecuted for consorting with the CTs but was

acquitted. Most of the evidence against him was circumstantial, consisting of reports that he was able to move around his estate in an unarmoured vehicle and without Police escort, and much of the testimony was so obviously rehearsed as to be nearly as thin as his defence: that he was safe because he treated his workers so well!

10 Later studies of the psychological motives of Surrendered Enemy Personnel (SEPs) by Professor Lucian Pye supported such able officers as Robert Thompson in their advocacy for this course of action. See Pye, *Guerrilla Communism in Malaya*. Spencer Chapman noted the readiness of MPAJA guerrillas to desert, and even to defect to the Japanese, for the most trivial reasons, facing brutal punishment and often death, if they felt that by such betrayals they could get revenge for some grievance or loss of face.

11 'By the spring of 1950, though we had survived two dangerous years, we were undoubtedly losing the war'. Clutterbuck, Richard, *The Long, Long War – The Emergency in Malaya 1948-1960*, p.55, Cassell, London (1966).

12 There is an unconfirmed report that Red Army officers were smuggled into Malaya to attend Chin Peng's conference in Pahang, but were so unimpressed by what they saw that they went back to China with the recommendation that no support should be given. Even if that story is apocryphal, it is a fact that at no time between 1948 and 1960 did the MCP receive significant material help from Communist China.

Chapter 14 *Briggs – The New White Knight*

1 Slim, *Defeat into Victory*, p.145.

2 Baynes, John, *Urquhart of Arnhem*, p.185, Brassey's, London (1993).

3 MAL. COM. Minutes MAL.(C). 50 per cent 19/4/50.

4 In fact, Chinese preoccupations already lay elsewhere.

5 In his initial appreciation, Briggs made the point: 'the essence of the problem is joint HQ and the fullest co-operation'.

6 Within a few weeks of the end of the operation in Johore the number of incidents rose 50% above the previous level.

7 E.g., Operation BRODERICK, mounted in early 1952 against 39 Independent Platoon of 5 Regt MRLA, in the Tapah/Chikus Forest Reserve area of Perak, involved 45 Royal Marine Commando, two troops from 42 RM Commando, 1st Bn Gordon Highlanders, a troop of 25 pounders RA and a squadron of *Lincoln* bombers, RAF, and extended over a period of more than six weeks. During the operation ten CTs were claimed as killed or probably killed (all the bodies were not found), and 1st Gordons lost seven dead in an ambush. Crockett, Anthony, *Green Beret, Red Star*, p.142ff, Eyre & Spottiswoode, London (1954). See also Clutterbuck, *The Long, Long War*, p.51.

8 At the meeting of 1 May 1950 complaints were made about the delay in transmitting transcripts of captured MCP documents to ministers. There was no minute suggesting what on earth they were going to do with them when they got them!

Chapter 15 *The Worst Is Yet to Come*

NOTES

1. Miller, Harry, *Jungle War in Malaya – the Campaign against Communism 1948-1960*, p.71, Arthur Barker, London (1972).
2. MAL.COM (50) 21, 17/6/50.
3. Ironically, although everyone tacitly accepted that the northern People's Republic of Korea was acting as a proxy for the USSR in trying to annex South Korea, the Soviet Union was not able to veto any of the resolutions committing the UN to opposing this aggression since it had been refusing to occupy its seat on the Security Council since January 1950, in protest at the continuing recognition of Chiang Kai Shek's Nationalist regime in Taiwan, after the defeat of the Kuomintang by Mao Tse Tung.
4. The Politburo of the MCP recognised the threat to their campaign of a successful resettlement programme, but assumed that there was no possibility of its being undertaken because it would be too expensive.
5. Short, *The Communist Insurrection in Malaya*, p.507.
6. Kampong Coldstream, in south Perak, takes its name from 2nd Bn, Coldstream Guards, as a token of appreciation from the resettled squatters who were its first occupiers. Its name in Cantonese is Liang Sui Hor Chuen, literally 'Cold Water River Village'.
7. Clutterbuck, Richard, *Riot and Revolution in Singapore and Malaya, 1945-1963*, p.73, Faber & Faber, London (1973).
8. WO 216/835 (DO/CIC/65).

Chapter 16   Dissent, Deceit and Defection

1. Short, *The Communist Insurrection in Malaya*, p.507.
2. 'Contact' was defined as being made when Security forces encountered CTs and opened fire first. All other events where the CTs initiated action, either against the Security forces or against civilians or property, were described as 'incidents'.
3. In his report at the end of October 1951, Briggs talked hopefully in terms of 45 'Jungle Companies', roughly the equivalent of ten battalions
4. Short, *The Communist Insurrection in Malaya*, p.269.
5. Neill, J D H, letter 17 June 1993.
6. His first contribution was a tract, 'My Accusation', which despite its rather Zolaesque name was both a clever piece of self-justification and a subtle appeal to others to give up without abandoning their basic political beliefs.
7. Neill, J D H, letter 17 June 1993.

Chapter 17   The Unkindest Cut of All – Gurney's Death

1. Each hill was called by a comfortingly British name: 'High Pines', 'Richmond', for example, and even 'Methodist Mission'.
2. The signal to open fire was given by waving a red flag, made from a pair of pants.
3. Miller, Harry, *Menace in Malaya*, p.191, Harrap, London (1954).

4   Not so far-fetched an idea – when Oliver Lyttleton stayed at King's House in March 1952, he found that all the staff had been replaced by flustered and untrained Police, following the arrest of the butler who had been unmasked as a member of the Min Yuen.

5   The Security forces never caught up with Siu Mah. It is believed that he survived until early 1959, when he was reported to have been shot by some of his own men before they surrendered.

6   Much later in the Emergency the site was cleared and resettled, some of the original inhabitants being allowed to return when their crime was deemed to have been purged.

Chapter 18 *Two Manifestos of Failure*

1   Once again, there were rumours that Chinese Red Army officers, infiltrated through Thailand, had been present, but these are unsubstantiated, and probably owe more to the fear and wish-fulfilment fantasies of each side than to solid evidence.

2   Under the 'framework' plan, battalions, companies and platoons were spread out in a network of locations, and, in theory, given time to get to know their areas, to build intelligence contacts and develop their own tactical plans to meet local needs, rather than being concentrated in special operations under the directions of Generals.

3   Most officials were entitled to short periods of local leave each year, and home leave every three or four years, this leave lasting six or eight months. In effect, someone on home leave had to be replaced, rather than an assistant 'standing in' for a couple of weeks or so.

4   As resettlement became sufficiently advanced, it had finally become possible to make strict food controls effective on a Federation-wide basis, by means of Directive 14, dated 22 May 1951.

5   British industry was apparently still unable to supply enough barbed wire, and when the Ministry of Supply ordered 1,000 tons in Germany the chosen supplier defaulted on the order. Armoured car deliveries for the Police were months behind schedule. Delivery was also still awaited of 20,000 suits of jungle green promised from Ordnance stocks in the UK out of 80,000 suits which the War Office for some unaccountable reason were reluctant to release.

6   Lyttleton, Oliver, *The Memoirs of Lord Chandos*, p.362, Bodley Head, London (1962).

7   *Ibid.*, pp.66.

8   Gray did not choose to leave in this way; Lyttleton sent him packing to avoid any possible demonstrations of solidarity by his colleagues. An aeroplane was specifically laid on for him, to take off at dawn, and he was seen off by only half-a-dozen friends, including Urquhart and his ADC, Captain Hugh Mackay.

9   Lyttleton, *The Memoirs of Lord Chandos,* p.379.

Chapter 19 *A Very Necessary Purgative*

1   The unofficial history of this incident has it that he was following a three-tonner loaded with a looted piano, and that it was the truck, not his jeep, that was mined; Templer was

NOTES

injured by the flying piano.

2   Miller, *Menace in Malaya*, p.196.

3   If you lived anywhere near the main railway line, fresh foods could be got to you once a week, packed in ice and delivered to the nearest station – provided the train had not been derailed.

4   Miller, *Menace in Malaya*, p.209.

5   'The Conduct of Anti-Terrorist Operations in Malaya'.

6   Including a three-ton armoured Daimler limousine for his own use, to replace the peppered official Rolls.

7   Cloake, J, *Templer – Tiger of Malaya*, p.230, Harrap, London (1985).

8   Clutterbuck, *The Long, Long War*. See also Barber, *The War of the Running Dogs*.

9   The price on Chin Peng's head was increased from $60,000 to $250,000, and smaller amounts were on offer for less important officials, down to $2,500 for ordinary rank-and-file. SEPs received only half the going rate for betraying their friends, and less was paid out for a corpse than for a live prisoner or a surrender.

10 Pye, *Guerrilla Communism in Malaya*.

11 Cloake, *Templer – Tiger of Malaya*, p.237.

12 This did not really work. Forty years later the Police Station was still the *rumah passung* to most villagers.

Chapter 20   Breaking the Circle – The Subalterns' War

1   There is some conflict about this point. Both Barber *The War of the Running Dogs*, p.170, and Jackson, *The Malayan Emergency*, p.46, claim that there was an intelligence report that pinpointed Liew Kon Kim's camp. Hands himself says that 'there was no certain intelligence that he was there at the time' (Letter to the author, 15 June 1995). Possibly such Intelligence as there was was less detailed and specific than journalists were led to believe at the time, and it was also probably sufficiently out of date to justify putting a low degree of reliability on it. Certainly Hands was not given a grid reference to march to, and his account makes it clear that he was carrying out a standard square search on compass bearings when the action took place.

2   It was also typical of Templer that he took the trouble the next day to visit B Coy, 1 Suffolks in its camp at Morib beach, to congratulate Hands in person. When he arrived Hands was asleep, wearing only a sarong, and remembers trying to conduct a suitably deferential conversation with the great man while periodically having to clutch the sarong to prevent a complete loss of dignity.

3   As a macabre ploy in the psychological campaign, Liew Kon Kim's body was paraded in the back of a Landrover round the villages in the Kajang and Ulu Langat district over the next two or three days.

4   It was later reinstated on a larger scale, under the name Fort Iskander. See below.

5   Dowling, J R, *Helicopters in the RAF, 1950-1960*, p.54, MOD Air Historical Branch,

1978.

6   *Ibid.*, p.23.

7   Templer himself thought this bid too conservative, and annotated it saying that at least 50 aircraft were needed. At the same time, profiting from experience in Korea, the Pentagon placed an order on Sikorsky for 2,000 aircraft.

8   There was still a powerful lobby in Washington who baulked at supplying Britain with the material to fight what was seen as a war to maintain colonial rule.

9   Calvert's original ideas had involved using the SAS as an irregular force, operating 'behind enemy lines', missing the point that there were no enemy lines, and that all units operating in an infantry role were in effect acting as irregular forces. When the SAS took hold of the 'hearts and minds' concept and developed it vis-à-vis the aborigines they played an important part in the campaign, literally saving some of the smaller clans from extinction, and building the expertise in working with primitive jungle-dwellers that was such an important factor during 'Confrontasi' in Borneo.

10 Once airstrips had been opened up, Prestwick Pioneer fixed-wing aircraft could be used for communication and supply, freeing valuable helicopter flying-hours.

11 Anyone who has had to deal with an elephant suffering from the effects of sodium arsenite poisoning will know about its 'collateral' effects.

12 This slogan is credited to Templer, and it was one that he used often, but it was current before he arrived in Malaya, and it is probable that Gurney or Briggs was its originator.

13 There was still a lot of blood to be shed, however. On 28 May, two days before he ended his tour, Templer learnt that Neville Godwin, CPO of Kedah and Perlis, had been ambushed and shot dead. Civilians, Police and soldiers continued to be targets for six more years.

Chapter 21   *The Birth Pangs of a New Nation*

1   Templer inherited this perception, and his policy of expanding and arming the Chinese Home Guard compounded the problem.

2   Paradoxically because, having realised that the Malays would have to come to an accommodation with the Chinese and other minorities, he found that he could not persuade UMNO to enlarge its membership to include other races.

3   When Templer tried to cut through this knot in the Army by forming the Federation Regiment that was to be open to all races, it proved very difficult to attract a balanced flow of recruits, and the selection of officers was well nigh impossible.

4. In the early days Dr Ong Chong Kee, who was then acknowledged as a leader of stature and on whom great hopes were placed for the development of the MCA as a political force, was murdered, it is assumed by the MCP. Many believe that if he had survived Malaya might have achieved political maturity very much earlier.

5   On an early visit to one Chinese school, Templer found a picture of Dr Sun Yat Sen in the place of honour on the classroom wall, and flew into one of his famous sub-orbital rages. The picture was removed.

NOTES

6   Baynes, *Urquhart of Arnhem*, p.215. Templer was not always good at choosing his subordinates or associates and cannot be completely exempted from the charge of surrounding himself with sycophants levelled at him by such detractors as Purcell. His tendency to turn for advice on industrial relations to a plausible trade unionist, P P Narayanan, was much regretted by many who knew the Malayan scene well.

7   Deliberately and carefully there was no direct British involvement, apart from the presence of John Davis, who had been a close colleague of Chin Peng in Force 136 days, and who acted as his conducting officer as earnest of his safety.

8   Out of 677 'eliminated', no less than 502 surrendered; Short, *The Communist Insurrection in Malaya*, p.507. Hor Lung, the head of the so-called South Malayan Bureau, surrendered on 5 April 1958, and in the weeks following, at considerable risk to his own life, persuaded 170 terrorists, including District Committee members and commissars, who were operating in the Kluang area, to surrender as well. There was some revulsion at the idea of his going free and anger at his receiving so much bounty money, since he had a most unsavoury record and made no bones about remaining a dyed-in-the-wool Communist, but it was not felt politic to renege on the terms of the amnesty, and he 'retired' a wealthy man.

10 Short, *The Communist Insurrection in Malaya*, p.507. O'Ballance, Edgar, *Malaya – The Communist Insurgent War, 1948-1960*, p.177, Faber & Faber, London (1961), and *The Malayan Emergency 1948-1960*, p.53, RMA Sandhurst Dept. of War Studies.

Chapter 22   Learning the Lessons

1   Clutterbuck, *The Long, Long War,* p.42f(f).

2   Cable, Larry, *Conflict of Myths*, p.83, Frederick Praeger, New York (1976). Cable refers to 'pernicious claptrap'.

3   An appreciation of the situation in Malaya as at the end of September 1952 (CIGS/BM/46/6083), circulated to all senior commanders by the VCIGS, Lt Gen. Sir Nevil Brownjohn, 'upon relinquishing appointment', was typical of the rather uncritical adulation that Templer was accorded by some. It concluded: 'The most important single factor has been the appointment of General Templer as High Commissioner and Director of Operations'.

4   His replacement of General Urquhart, whose military record compared favourably with his own, by Hugh Stockwell, has been cited as an example of this, but can be seen more charitably as a reflection of the practice of senior officers at that time of taking their own staff with them when taking up a new appointment.

5   On one occasion, after Templer had treated a Malayan journalist particularly badly, Lyttleton was forced to offer what amounted to a Ministerial apology in the Commons, explaining that one could not expect 'Parliamentary' language from a man like Templer. In later years Victor Purcell used to tell how (acting as a representative for the MCA) he attended a meeting with Templer at King's House. When he entered the room, Templer bent over his wastepaper basket and pretended to vomit, explaining to the others attending the meeting that the sight of Purcell made him sick. Not everyone regarded this pantomime amusing or edifying.

INDEX

Abdul Rahman, Tunku 142, 145-8, 150, 152.
Alliance Party (*see also* UMNO, MCA and MIC) 145, 146, 152.
Allison, J M 1, 2, 80, 156.
Anti-Bandit Month 91, 92.
Attlee, Clement 13, 15, 118.

Bagnall, Nigel, Lt., (1 Green Howards) 160.
Baling 160.
Barber, Noel 156.
Batang Kali 59, 60.
Batu Arang 7, 22, 38 40, 56, 84, 112.
Batu Caves 24.
Berlin Airlift 29.
BLENHEIM, Operation 71.
Boucher, Lt. Gen. 37, 44, 51, 52, 55-7, 71, 84, 85, 87, 148, 157.
Bourne, Lt. Gen. Sir Geoffrey 145.
Briggs, Lt. Gen. Sir Harold 86-91, 93-6, 99, 101, 102, 104, 116-18, 123, 130, 150, 161, 162, 165.
Briggs Plan 86, 91, 96.
BRODERICK, Operation 161.
Brownjohn, Lt. Gen. Sir Nevil (VCIGS) 104, 167.

Calcutta Conference 28, 29.
Calvert, 'Mad Mike' 135, 136, 165.
Cameronians (Scottish Rifles) (1 Cameronians) 137.
CARP, Operation 101.
Chapman, Major F Spencer 19, 78, 129, 135, 156, 161.
Chiang Kai Shek 16, 22, 30, 84, 162.
Chin Peng 24, 26, 28-30, 37, 40, 45-50, 56, 58, 60, 65, 69, 82, 84, 106-10, 115, 116, 140, 146-8,151, 152, 155, 158, 161, 164, 166.
Christian, I D 1, 2, 80, 156.
Churchill, Sir Winston 3, 118, 120, 123, 124.
CLEAVER, Operation 101.

Clutterbuck, Richard 129, 150.
Codner, Michael 126.
COMMODORE, Operation 138.
Commonwealth Division (in Korea) 96.
Cunningham, General Sir Alan 54, 118.

Dalforce 31.
Dalley, Lt. Col. John 25, 31, 33, 37, 43.
Davis, John 166.
Del Tufo (Chief Secretary) 119, 120, 124.

Devonshire Regt. (1 Devons) 36, 84.
Ducroux, Joseph (alias Lafranc) 18, 23.
Dyak 74.

Federal War Council 89.
Ferret Force 44, 56.
Force 136 20, 44, 67, 146, 156, 166.
Fourniss, W H 126.
Frasers Hill 111, 113, 115.

Gammins, Capt. Lionel, MP 11.
Gavin, Lt. Col. J M E, RE 19.
Gent, Sir Edward 14-17, 30-3, 36, 44, 45, 51, 53-5, 127, 154-6.
Godwin, Neville 165.
Gordon Walker, Rt. Hon. Patrick (Sec. of State, Commonwealth Relations) 87.
Gray, Col. W N (Nicol) 45, 51, 52, 56, 57, 80-2, 85, 86, 92, 99, 102, 117, 119, 131, 160, 164.
Green Howards 73, 160.
Greene, Hugh Carleton (Head of Emergency Information Services) 130.
Griffiths, Rt. Hon. James (Sec. of State for the Colonies) 87, 117, 118.
Gua Musang 39, 40, 56, 74, 84.
Guards (2 Guards Brigade) 40.
Gurkha (26 Gurkha Brigade) 1, 30, 36, 37, 71, 88, 112, 156, 159.

Gurney, Sir Henry 54-6, 62-5, 69, 79, 82-4, 86, 89-1, 93, 95-101, 102, 104-6, 110-15, 117-19, 124, 127, 130, 142, 143, 150, 151, 165.
Hailam Kang 52, 58-60.
Hands, 2/Lt. L R (1 Suffolks) 133, 134, 165.
Harding, Gen. Sir John (GOC-in-C, FARELF) 79, 85, 86, 90, 93, 95, 99, 104, 119, 136, 160.
HAYSTACK, Operation 44.
Helicopter 136-8, 160.
HELSBY, Operation 137.
Ho Chi Minh (Nguyen Ai Quok) 18, 23, 25.
Home Guard 69, 97, 117, 127, 144, 150, 165.
Hor Lung 166.
Hussars (4th Hussars) 44, 67.

Independence of Malaya Party (IMP) 142, 145.
Intelligence (Special Branch) School 129.

JACKAL, Operation 101.
Jelebu 67, 82.
Jenkin, Sir William 99, 102, 117, 119.
Jungle Warfare School *see* Kota Tinggi.

Kachau 52, 53, 60.
Kajang 39, 40, 52, 53, 133-5.
Kamayang Estate 84.
Keightly, Gen. Sir Charles (GOC-in-C, FARELF) 104.
Klian Intan 146, 147.
Korea/Korean War 95-7, 99, 104, 106.
Kota Tinggi Jungle Warfare School 127.
Kings Own Yorkshire Light Infantry (2 KOYLI) 36.
Kuala Krau 83, 91, 106.
Kuomintang 16, 22, 30, 36, 38, 44, 82, 142, 143, 159, 162.
Kumaran, Mr A N (Chief Clerk, Elphil Estate) 1, 2.

Ladang 139
Lafranc, Serge *see* Ducroux.
Lam Swee 108, 109, 130.
Lancers (12th Lancers) 71.
Langworthy (Commissioner of Police) 33, 36, 45.
Lau Yew 40, 47, 133.
Liew Kon Kim 133, 134, 165.

Liberated Areas 35, 39-41.
Listowel, Lord (Minister of State for the Colonies) 36, 127.
Lockhart, Lt. Gen. Sir Robert 116, 119.
Loi Tak 18-20, 23, 24, 26, 29, 31, 155.
Lyttleton, Oliver 118-21, 123, 124, 127, 128, 131, 141, 163, 164.

MacArthur, Gen. Douglas 96.
MacDonald, Malcolm 32, 33, 35, 45, 51, 52, 58, 65, 79, 82, 84, 85, 93, 99, 105, 118, 119, 121, 124, 118, 137.
MacGillivray, Sir Donald 120, 145, 146.
MacMichael, Sir Harold 14, 15, 62, 99, 142, 155.
Malay Regt. 36, 71, 88.
Malaya Committee of the Cabinet 37, 87, 88, 90, 93, 94, 104.
Malayan Chinese Association (MCA) 82, 105, 115, 142, 143, 145, 151, 152, 166, 167.
Malayan Communist Party (MCP) 18-21, 23-8, 29, 30, 31, 40, 43, 47, 48, 50, 51, 65, 83, 91, 95, 108, 109, 116, 139, 140, 144, 146, 147, 148, 150, 151, 152, 161, 162, 166.
Malayan Indian Congress 145.
Malayan Peoples Anti-British Army (MPABA) 29, 33, 35, 37-40, 43-5, 47, 48.
Malayan Peoples Anti-Japanese Army (MPAJA) 19, 20, 23, 24, 28, 29, 36, 39, 46-8, 69, 135, 158, 161.
Malayan Races Liberation Army (MRLA) 48-50, 52, 55, 56, 58, 59, 63-5, 67, 70, 71, 73-5, 82-5, 88-91, 93, 94, 97, 98, 101-3, 106-10, 116, 128-31, 133, 135, 138-40, 143, 147, 149, 152, 159.
Malayan Union 14, 15, 32, 36, 37, 42, 105, 141, 160.
'Mandate of Heaven' 69, 127, 146.
Mao Tse Tung 16, 27, 35, 36, 47, 73, 80, 83, 84, 88, 107, 108, 109, 151, 162.
Maria Hertogh 98, 99, 137.
Marshall, David (Chief Minister of Singapore) 147.
Miller, Harry 94, 112, 124.
Min Yuen 29, 35, 47, 49, 59, 60, 63, 65, 67, 68, 82, 91, 93, 98, 101, 103, 110, 116, 128, 130, 131, 133, 140, 144, 146, 152.

INDEX

Montgomery, F M Viscount 104, 120, 151.
Morton, J (Director of Intelligence) 128.

National Service 94, 133, 140, 148, 152.
Neill, Desmond (Chinese Affairs Officer, Pahang) 108, 109.
Newboult, Sir Alec (Chief Secretary) 36, 37, 52, 58.
Nguyen Ai Quok *see* Ho Chi Minh

October Manifesto 115, 116, 125, 139.
Ong Chong Kee, Dr 166.
Onn bin Jafar, Dato 99, 142, 145.
Onraet, René 18, 19, 23, 25.
Operation Service 132.
Orang Asli 6, 139.

Palestine 44, 45, 51, 54, 55, 81, 122, 124.
Pan-Malayan Federation of Trades Unions (PMFTU) 16, 21, 22, 27, 30, 108.
Party Negara 145.
PEPPER, Operation 44.
Peterson, Alec (Director General, Information Services) 130.
Prince of Wales, HMS 3.
Purcell, Victor (formerly Principal Adviser on Chinese Affairs) 151, 155, 166, 167.
Pye, Lucian 129, 161.
'Python' 93, 94.

RAMILLIES, Operation 71.
Registration 64, 65, 68, 69.
Repulse, HMS 3.
Resettlement 61, 62, 65, 97, 102, 117, 139, 142, 149 150, 152, 162.
Robertson, Gen. Sir Brian (GOC-in-C, MELF) 120, 121.
Royal Artillery 36, 71.
Royal Marines (3 Cornmando Bde.) 73, 88.
Royal West Kents (1 Royal West Kents) 101, 111.

SARONG, Operation 71.
Scots Guards (2nd Bn.) 59.
Seaforth Highlanders (1 Seaforths) 36, 58, 135.
Shinwell, Rt. Hon. Emmanuel (Minister of Defence) 87-9, 117.
Siew Lau 109, 110, 115, 116.
Singapore 3, 4, 8, 18, 19, 21, 23, 24, 28, 31-3, 36, 37, 98, 108, 118, 119, 128, 154, 155.
Siu Mah 38, 112-14, 163.
Slim, FM Sir William (CIGS) 86, 87, 99, 104.
Sloan, A, MP 3, 11.
Special Air Service [22 SAS Regt (Malayan Scouts)] 133, 136, 138, 139, 164.
Special Constables/Constabulary 43, 44, 64, 68, 69, 80, 102, 103, 125, 144, 150, 157.
Special Training Centre 35.
SPITFIRE, Operation 71.
Squatters 50, 52, 53, 57, 61, 69, 98, 102, 152.
Squatters' Committee 58, 60.
Stafford, Superintendent W F 40, 133.
Staples, D J 111, 112.
Stockwell, Lt. Gen. Sir Hugh 145.
Strachey, Rt. Hon. John (Secretary of State for War) 87, 94, 117.
Straits Times 1, 2, 33, 92, 94, 124, 155.
Suffolk Regt. (1 Suffolks) 133, 134.
Sungei Siput 1, 30, 31, 67, 156.
Surrendered Enemy Personnel (SEPs) 129, 130, 140, 161.
Sutro, 2/Lt John (4th Hussars) 67.

Tan Ah Joo (Chief Clerk, Sungei Siput Est.) 1.
Tan Cheng Lok (Sir Cheng Lok Tan) 82, 105 142, 141, 145, 147, 150.
Tanjong Malim 125-7.
Tasek Berak 108, 135, 138.
Templer, Gen. Sir Gerald 121-31, 136, 138-40, 141-3, 145, 150, 151, 158, 164-6.
Thompson, Sir Robert 161.
Thompson, Susan 103.
Tie-down ratios 149.
Too, C C 130, 157.
Tras 114.
Trades Unions (State Federations) 16, 22, 27, 30.
Truman, Harry S 96.

United Malay Nationalist Organisation (UMNO) 99, 142, 145, 152, 166.
Urquhart, Maj. Gen. Roy (GOC Malaya) 87, 102, 119, 126, 145, 167.

Village Councils Ordinance 144.

War Executive Committees 89, 148.
Walker, Arthur 1, 2, 80, 156.

173

Wade, Gen. (GOC Malaya) 33, 37.
White Areas 144, 145, 148.
Wright J *see* Loi Tak.
Wylie, JS 146.

Young, Sir Arthur (Commissioner of Police)
    131, 132.